# SCAN

# 3

# SCANNERS

# 3

## Putting Scanners into Practice

Peter Rouse

Edited by Chris Lorek

**Nexus Special Interests**

Nexus Special Interests Ltd.
Nexus House
Boundary Way
Hemel Hempstead
Herts HP2 7ST
England

First published by Argus Books 1994

ISBN 1-85486-106-9

Phototypesetting by The Studio, Exeter
Printed and bound by Whitstable Litho Printers Ltd.,
Whitstable, Kent.

# Contents

# Foreword

by Chris Lorek BSc. (Hons) C.Eng M.I.E.E. G4HCL
Consultant Technical Editor, *Ham Radio Today*

As many readers may know, the author of this book, Peter Rouse, is regrettably no longer with us. Sadly, Peter died on the 29th June 1993 after suffering from leukaemia for some time. Peter, who was a well-known writer, was remarkably bright and cheerful throughout his illness. I saw him give real inspiration and hope to fellow sufferers, both in hospital and through his job as News Presenter for Channel TV. The happiness he imparted to others around him had to be seen to be believed.

I was fortunate in living relatively close to where Peter received treatment for the last couple of years, and I was glad that we managed to continue our friendship with frequent visits. I fondly remember receiving an extremely cheerful new year's greeting telephone call from him, telling me that his doctor had allowed him to have a limited quantity of lager each day. That January 1st afternoon, the hospital nurses were surprised to see me walking through the wards carrying a large quantity of tins of the said liquid under each arm. Being in hospital certainly didn't stop Peter having an enjoyable time!

He underwent two years of 'in and out of hospital' treatment for recurrent bouts of his illness, yet kept his hobby interest alive even from his hospital bed with his radio gear and portable computer. During one of my visits, he pulled out from his hospital bedside locker a complete weather satellite review for the monthly 'Scanners' section of *Ham Radio Today* magazine, just to surprise me!

I felt very honoured when I heard that Peter had asked the publishers if I would 'finish off' his latest book. I knew that he'd spent a considerable time in putting it together, but was sadly unable to finish it. The vast majority of what you read in these pages is his work – all I have done is update and add to a few sections in line with his requests.

Peter's name will certainly be kept alive, a fitting tribute to someone who helped many get started in the hobby of HF/VHF/UHF listening. The world has lost a great 'helper', and I know that he would wish this book to be dedicated to his wife Val and children James, Abbi, and Arron.

Chris Lorek, 1994

# Introduction 1

When I first pounded out the words for the original issue of this book I never thought we would see so many revisions and reprints but here we are six years later on this issue. This one has seen the biggest number of changes and additions to the point of a virtual re-write and so we have decided to call it Scanners 3 to avoid confusion. The first few chapters have been considerably condensed because it is now clear that most of you buy the updated copies and obviously do not want the same old stuff over and over again.

Vastly more detail has been put into the frequency listings and in particular you will find a lot more information on coastal stations, airfields and the emergency services. This has been largely made possible by a public clarification by the Home Office on the legal position of publications such as this.

For the first time I have also included a small section on the HF (Short Wave) bands because so many scanners now cover this section of the spectrum. However, it is the VHF and UHF frequency listings where the biggest changes have occurred. The explanations and detailed sections on the various users of the VHF/UHF bands has always been popular with readers allowing them to instantly sweep certain bands for activity in their own area. I have avoided padding-out the book with lists of obscure taxi firms, pizza delivery services and frequency listings of television and radio channels as I know of no scanner users who use their expensive and specialized equipment to tune into these services when they can be obtained on ordinary domestic equipment.

## Caution

The aim of this book is to provide a basic understanding of the use of scanning receivers and VHF/UHF communications. Contrary to popular belief this type of equipment is *not* solely purchased by people who have no legitimate right to listen in to certain kinds of radio traffic and who wish to illegally snoop on other people's messages. Many people from amateurs to commercial and professional users buy this type of equipment for perfectly legitimate reasons. However, such people may still not fully understand how to use the scanner to its best ability. This book is aimed at all scanner users who want a better understanding of how their equipment works. In order to achieve that aim it has been necessary to include a wide range of information, some of which might be considered sensitive. I must stress that although certain bands and frequency allocations are shown, the book should *not* be interpreted as an invitation to listen-in — unless the appropriate licence or authority is held.

To sum up: *The responsibility lies with the equipment owner to satisfy himself that he has a legal right to listen-in to any radio transmission.* All information published here has been published before at some time, much of it by the Government. However its publication here must not be interpreted as some kind of right to listen-in. The unlicensed user will find the following information useful.

In the British Isles you are not allowed to listen to anything other than legitimate broadcast stations, CB stations, licenced radio amateurs and, whilst at sea, coastguard broadcasts. The laws covering this are the Wireless Telegraphy Act and the more recent Interception of Communications Act. However, I was interested to see recently a document from the Department of Trade and Industry (who regulate communication licencing) to police forces which provided advice on seizing scanners. The document said that tuning into airband and marine transmissions could not be considered "a serious offence". For the first time the authorities appear to be admitting that they are virtually turning a blind eye to some communications eavesdropping and I have yet to hear of a single case of a prosecution against the thousands of people who openly use airband radios at airports.

The UK government, however, has recently been taking a 'hard line' against users of scanners for illegal purposes, and has been known to distribute leaflets giving police officers guidance on what to do if someone is suspected of operating a scanner illegally. A number of such users have been successfully convicted of listening into police transmissions – in one reported case the user was imprisoned. At the other end of the scale, newspapers have 'got away' with printing details of how they deliberately sent their reporters out to monitor cellular conversations, publishing what they heard.

If you are in *any* doubt as to what you are, and are not, allowed to listen to, you should seek guidance from your national radio regulatory body. In the UK, this is the Radiocommunications Agency (the RA), whose contact details are given in Chapter 8. They publish a free leaflet, entitled *Receive only – Scanners, etc.*, publication ref.

RA 169 which explains the situation in the UK. The RA will be happy to send you a copy of this free of charge if you ask them.

## Today's scene

What else has happened since the last revision? Well there have been some changes and as you look through the lists you will find that part of the VHF high-band has had its Private Mobile Radio allocation removed to make way for the Pan European paging system, ERMES. There are also a number of less dramatic changes scattered through the various allocations.

You will also notice that the list of available scanners has changed dramatically. It is safe to say that since the last revision we have seen more new models introduced than during any comparable period in the past. More manufacturers have put models onto the scanner markets as well and we have seen the arrival of products from such firms such as Yupiteru, Icom and Alinco. One major innovation has been the inclusion of the HF bands and we now have scanners (including hand-helds) that cover from long wave through to 2000MHz with no gaps (something I predicted in earlier editions of this book).

So what of the future? First I think it is likely that even more users of sensitive forms of communication will go digital or scrambled. Bodies such as specialized police and customs units have already started to use such equipment and a scanner will not be able to decipher the transmissions. It appears that at last the authorities have realized that if they squirt "open" transmissions into your home it is unrealistic to order you not to listen to them; they might as well use Semaphore and order everyone not to look.

Equipment will almost certainly get smaller. The Icom IC–R1 set the trend and manufacturers such as Alinco have followed with full coverage scanners packed into tiny cases. Hopefully the performance of RF front ends will improve. Wideband coverage is all very well but front ends with minimum filtering *do* invite problems from powerful transmissions, which you do not want to hear, and many of these new scanners suffer dreadfully from overload and intermodulation effects when attached to an external aerial.

I suspect there will not be as many new models appearing in the next few years. The market must be reaching saturation point by now and it is difficult to see what new features can be added to scanners to get users to abandon existing ones and go out and spend hundreds of pounds on a new one. Where we might see some new products are in accessories and aerials. The popular discone and some active types have their disadvantages and hopefully some improved products may not be far away.

I hope you enjoy this latest edition of the book.

Peter Rouse
Guernsey C.I.
1993

# Understanding radio 2

No mathematics, no theory, no problems. If you are new to the hobby, then have a browse through this chapter, because it answers the queries most frequently raised by scanner owners who are not familiar with VHF and UHF communications.

First of all let us look at what we mean by VHF and UHF. The entire radio spectrum stretches from Long Wave upwards and as we go higher in frequency so different parts of the spectrum are given different names. The best way to imagine it is to think of a very long tuning scale on a radio. At the left side we have long wave, then comes medium. From then on we talk in terms of frequency rather than waves. Note that there is a fixed relationship between wavelength and frequency and it is always possible to determine the wavelength of any given frequency or vice versa. So a look at Table 2.1 will show how things progress beyond medium wave. Next comes Medium Frequency (MF), then High Frequency (HF) which is also still known as Short Wave. From 30 MHz (Megahertz) to 300 MHz we have Very High Frequency (VHF) and between 300 MHz and 3000 MHz we have Ultra High Frequency (UHF). It is these latter two parts of the spectrum that we are mainly interested in as these are the bands covered by most scanners.

Look again at Table 2.1 and you will see reference to both kHz (Kilohertz) and MHz and it is useful to understand the relationship between the two. They are simply measurements and the Kilo and Mega parts are the same as those applied to measuring metric length and weight. Kilo means a thousand times and Mega means a million times. So 1000 kHz is exactly the same as 1 MHz. Understanding this will help you grasp the idea of what is known as tuning or stepping rates on your scanner. Scanners are not tuned like an ordinary radio. If you want to alter a frequency up or down you will have to do it in small jumps. Often the scanner will tune in 5 or 10 kHz increments but those designed specifically for the British market will often have 12.5 kHz increments because this is a common British channel spacing.

5

**Table 2.1 Radio frequency spectrum, each division as a frequency range**

| Frequency division | Frequency range |
| --- | --- |
| Very low frequency (VLF) | 3-30 kHz |
| Low frequency (LF) | 30-300 kHz |
| Medium frequency (MF) | 300-3000 kHz |
| High frequency (HF) | 3-30 MHz |
| Very high frequency (VHF) | 30-300 MHz |
| Ultra high frequency (UHF) | 300-3000 MHz |
| Super high frequency (SHF) | 3-30 GHz |
| Extremely high frequency (EHF) | 30-300 GHz |
| No designation | 300-3000 GHz |

k = kilo = x1,000.
M = mega = x1,000,000.
G = giga = x1,000,000,000

## Channels

Channelizing is something which often confuses newcomers and yet it is quite simple. We can take any part of the radio spectrum and divide it up into small blocks. A look at Figure 2.1 will show how this is done. In most countries, the authorities determine how the channel spacing will work. It is common in Britain on the bands used for emergency services and Private Mobile Radio (PMR) to use channelizing, rather than allocate frequencies to users at random. Typical spacing in Britain is 12.5 kHz but in the USA and other countries the spacing is usually 10 kHz. This can present problems for some scanner owners who have receivers designed for the American market, because they cannot tune exactly onto the right frequency of many British channels.

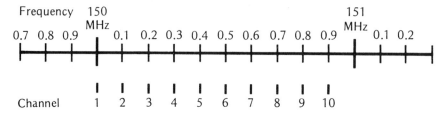

**Figure 2.1** Channelizing. Any section of the radio spectrum can be divided up and each spot frequency given a channel number.

For example it is not possible to enter the frequency 144.7625 on some scanners although dialling-in 144.760 may be close enough to hear the signal: it varies from one model to another. It is a point to watch when buying a scanner.

## Distance

How far will a signal travel? Why can I hear an airport control tower 30 miles away but not my own airport which is just over the hill behind my house? These are typical of the questions from newcomers.

VHF and UHF signals travel nowhere near as far as medium and long wave signals. In fact they only travel over what is known as "line of sight"; typically 20 to 30 miles. In practice the distance can be far less or much greater depending on circumstances. One factor is the power output of the station we are listening to. A base station with between 25 and 50 Watts output power may come in loud and clear over a given distance but a small walkie-talkie with only a fraction of a Watt output might not cover the same distance.

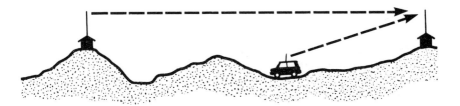

Figure 2.2 Ground wave. Typically 'line of sight' at VHF and UHF.

You should also bear in mind that VHF and UHF signals are easily blocked by obstructions such as high buildings, hills and even trees.

There are also strange weather based conditions that can cause signals to travel massive distances. One of these is known as Sporadic-E. VHF signals do not normally bounce back to earth off the ionosphere (the effect that causes HF signals to travel great distances) but on occasion the E-layer of the Ionosphere thickens up and the signals do bounce back. Another effect is known as Tropospheric Ducting. This happens when cold and warm air streams meet at about 2 kilometres above the earth's surface. A layer is formed that can act as a sort of pipe for signals and send them considerable distances (several thousand kilometres in some cases). This effect is often associated with high barometric pressure and fog and the effect is often seen in the summer when it can cause television interference.

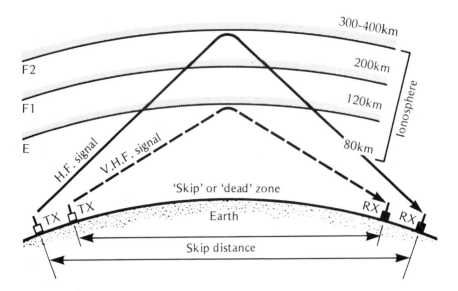

**Figure 2.3** Sky wave. Note that VHF signals will not normally skip as far as HF signals.

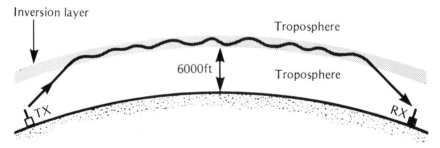

**Figure 2.4** Tropospheric ducting 'Tropo'.

## Modes

There are several ways of imposing speech (and music and television pictures) onto a radio signal. For speech the three common methods are frequency modulation (FM), amplitude modulation (AM) and single sideband (SSB). You do not need to understand the technical difference between the modes but you must appreciate that they are different and your scanner must have different circuits to cope with the different modes. For instance all transmissions in the international VHF aircraft band use AM, and if your scanner is tuned to a station but FM mode is selected, you will hear nothing or at best a very distorted signal.

Britain is one of the few places in the world now that uses AM mode for communications outside the aircraft band. For instance in a given area you are likely to find both AM and FM transmissions being used in a PMR band. Most countries (particularly the U.S.A.) exclusively use FM with its many advantages. If you want to pick up a wide selection of transmissions then you need a scanner that allows you to select FM or AM regardless of the frequency you are tuned to. Many scanners now allow you to store a frequency into memory along with the mode. However, you will find several scanners on the U.K. market which do not allow you to do this. Notably scanners designed for the American market have no FM/AM select button and instead automatically switch to FM on any frequency except the air band when they switch to AM.

Single sideband is a rather specialised mode and is divided into upper and lower sidebands. To resolve SSB your scanner needs special circuitry and this is only found on a handful of models. The mode is used by amateurs on the VHF and UHF bands. However, on some later models such as those from AOR and Yupiteru the inclusion of SSB circuitry can be quite useful because these receivers will also tune the short wave (HF) bands where SSB is used extensively for communications.

## Simplex and duplex

One question often raised by newcomers to VHF/UHF communications is why can they only hear one of two stations who are communicating with each other. This is because they may be using either split frequency simplex or duplex. First though, let us start at the beginning and look at the simplest arrangement which is called simplex.

A typical example of single frequency simplex is the international aircraft band between 118 and 137 MHz. A control tower for example may be operating on 119.950 MHz and the aircraft will also transmit on exactly the same frequency. Assuming that both are within range of your scanner then you will hear both sides of the conversation on the single frequency of 119.95 MHz. However, some transmissions use a pair of frequencies with the base transmitting on one frequency but mobile stations on another, this is split frequency simplex. In this instance the transmitters and receivers will have to be tuned to the appropriate frequencies. The scanner user will need to enter both frequencies into the scanner and switch between them to hear both sides of the conversation. A variation on this is duplex where the transmitters and receivers are fitted with special filters to allow them to transmit simultaneously. A typical example of this is the cellular telephone service where subscribers are able to talk and listen at the same time as if using an ordinary telephone.

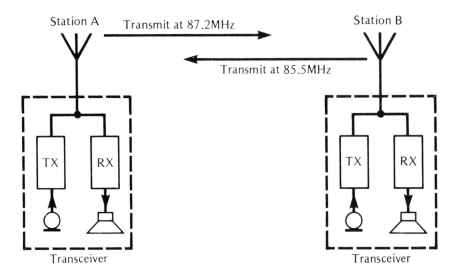

**Figure 2.5** Split frequency simplex.

## Repeaters and trunking

Some users who need to obtain greater range for their communications rely on what are known as repeaters. These transmitters/ receivers are normally situated on high ground and have the added advantage of allowing one mobile unit to talk to another, known as 'Talkthrough''. Repeaters work on split frequencies. In other words the 'input' or receiver frequency is usually several Megahertz away from the transmit or 'output frequency'. The transmitter normally is switched off but when the repeater's receiver picks-up a signal it then activates the transmitter and the audio output of the receiver is fed to the input of the transmitter and so rebroadcasts it. In practice the receiver will not respond to just any signal but also requires a valid tone. On amateur repeaters this is a simple audible tone burst of 1750Hz that is detected by a circuit in the repeater. On commercial systems as well as some UK amateur repeaters sub-audible tones are used (known as CTCSS) and the commercial repeaters may be programmed to respond to several different tones. This is the case where more than one operator is using the repeater. The system is often referred to as a 'Community Repeater' and can be used by

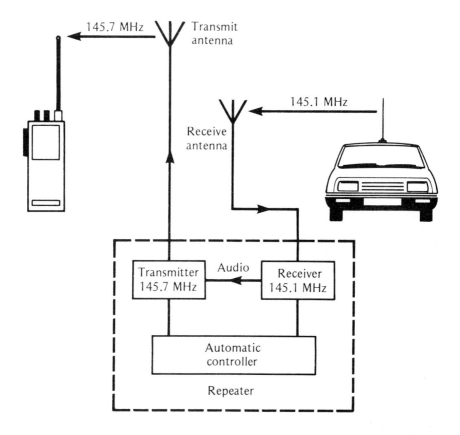

**Figure 2.6** Repeater. Automatic turn-on and turn-off. In the case of 'talkthrough' the switching controller is operated manually.

several companies or organizations. Each has its own CTCSS tone and the access circuits are not only fitted to the repeater but also the individual mobile or handheld transceivers. In that way the various users only hear calls from their own base station or mobiles.

In order to monitor calls on a repeater system you only need to tune to the repeater output frequency.

A variation on this theme is what are known as trunked systems. This is where a network of repeaters is used and controlled by computer. A typical network may cover most of the country and so a base station can call its mobiles as long as they are within range of any of the trunked repeaters. In practice the mobile unit at switch on, or pre-determined intervals, will transmit a short burst of digital code identifying itself. This is picked up by the repeater's receiver and passed to the computer which can then keep track of where each mobile unit is. When a base station calls that unit the computer then routes the signal (this is done through dedicated telephone or radio/microwave links) to the appropriate repeater.

In the UK, national trunking systems are located in the old Band III which became available when 405 line television transmissions were phased out.

# The hardware 3

So what is a scanner? The simple answer is that it is a radio capable of tuning into radio bands that you will not find on your ordinary domestic radio. It will also look automatically through dozens or even hundreds or thousands of channels looking for radio signals. The simplest scanners may only have the capacity to store a few dozen channels and these can be programmed with the frequencies that you want to monitor. Unlike broadcast transmissions those frequencies will only carry occasional conversations and so the scanner constantly sweeps through its memory channels and only stops when it finds an active one. Once the transmission ends the scanner then resumes sweeping its pre-programmed channels looking for another active one.

These days the majority of scanners are what are known as synthesized types. The earliest scanners used quartz crystals to generate each of the frequencies that the owner wished to receive. A typical early scanner may have had around 12 available channels and appropriate crystals had to be plugged into sockets inside the equipment. In order to change a frequency it was necessary to order a replacement crystal which had been specially cut or tuned. Many old crystal controlled types are still in use and occasionally seen on the secondhand market, but these days it is the synthesized type of scanner that dominates the market. These allow much greater flexibility. Not only can the required frequency be entered on a key pad but the ability to store the frequency in a computer style memory has meant that many more channels can be stored even in a small handheld scanner.

The more sophisticated scanners now also allow such things as mode to be stored along with the frequency, so that once the scanner is put to work it automatically switches to the correct mode for the frequency concerned. All of this is made possible by a simple and compact microprocessor within the scanner and in most instances it allows for even greater sophistication. For example it is usually possible to set the scanner searching between a low and upper frequency limit so allowing you to discover new channels that may be in operation in your area.

## Memory backup

One point to note with these scanners is that the memory that stores all the frequencies is often what is known as *volatile* RAM (random access memory), VRAM. In order for the information to be retained whilst the scanner is switched off it is necessary to keep a small amount of power running to the memory chips. This is done either by having a separate battery or batteries to provide memory power or the inclusion of a small lithium cell in the circuit. These cells will not last forever and from time to time will need to be replaced. It is always a good idea to keep a list of all the frequencies and modes you have stored in each memory, providing of course you are allowed to listen to these, because the day may well come when you switch on and find that everything has gone blank. It is worth noting that sometimes the loss of backup power can also cause the scanner to behave in an odd way. If it has lost all memory and fails to operate correctly even when all data has been re-entered then it may still mean that the system needs to be reset by the inclusion of a new backup cell.

## You get what you pay for

Newcomers to the scanning hobby often ask what the difference is between a cheap scanner and another costing a small fortune. The answer is facilities. Tandy's PRO-38 is probably the cheapest and simplest scanner on the market. It has just 10 memory channels, limited frequency coverage and is FM only. I must stress that, despite that, it may well fill the needs of someone who for example only wants to monitor a handful of marine channels. At the other end of the scale are the Icom IC-R-7100, IC-R9000 and AOR 3000A with very wideband coverage and good front-end filtering. This latter facility is often not understood by scanner owners and it is worthwhile looking briefly at what it involves.

In any given area there will be a vast number of radio signals travelling through the airwaves—everything from powerful broadcast transmissions to weak communications signals. The less expensive scanners will simply amplify all these signals in what are known as the Radio Frequency, or RF, stages of its circuitry before passing the signals to those parts of the circuit that at any given moment select the required signal which eventually passes through to the loudspeaker. In practice, the RF amplification is usually divided into at least two separate stages, one for the lower frequency coverage and one for the upper. However, what can happen is that strong signals, that you do not wish to hear, can interfere with the scanner circuitry and block out those signals you are trying to listen to. In severe cases, several undesirable effects may be introduced into the scanner's circuit. Typical examples are blocking, reciprocal mixing and intermodulation distortion. One of the most obvious effects is where you are listening to a transmission and it suddenly seems to stop for no apparent reason. What has probably happened is that a very strong signal has appeared on a slightly different frequency and has desensitised the scanner causing the squelch to close. Another undesirable effect that can occur is when two or more strong signals appear to upset the scanner's mixing circuits. This can often be identified by a signal suddenly breaking through on a frequency which you know is incorrect for that transmission. For example, at my own location which is close to a tower with many aerials, a certain mixture of cellular transmissions and a local radio FM broadcast can cause the latter station to appear on some UHF channels on one of my scanners. Of course the signal is not really there, the internal mixing circuits in my scanner are being overloaded and cause this effect.

The way that the above problems can be overcome is to have more selective circuits in the scanner's RF stage. Tuned filters ensure that only the desired signals are passed to the tuning and mixing stages. As the scanner steps through each frequency in its memory, so the correct filter is seleccted or the RF stages are electronically tuned to peak at that frequency. Naturally all of this makes the scanner more complex and so more expensive. The added components also make the set bulkier and that is why most small handheld scanners do not incorporate much in the way of front-end filtering. Owners of handhelds now know why their equipment often suffers problems when connected to an outside aerial such as a discone. The RF stages are presented with stronger signals than they are designed to cope with.

## Switches, knobs, sockets and things that go click and squeak

The average scanner presents a bewildering array of facilities for anyone not used to communications equipment. However, most of the facilities are fairly straightforward although some handbooks do leave a lot to be desired in the way they explain them. Let us have a look at some of the things you will find on most scanners. I have not included the obvious ones such as volume.

### Squelch or mute
This is an electronic switch that cuts noise to the loudspeaker when no

signal is being received. It also serves the important function on a scanner of telling the set that transmissions have stopped, so please start scanning again. You need to set the squelch by turning it to the point where, with no signal being received, the loudspeaker cuts out. It is important to note that you should never advance the squelch any further than is necessary. The more you turn it, the more you desensitise the scanner to the point where it will only respond to very strong signals—the weak ones will be missed. In practice, do not be surprised if the squelch needs adjusting for different bands. For instance, you may find that having set the squelch correctly for a signal at 80 Megahertz, the squelch suddenly opens when it hops to a frequency at 170 Megahertz. This is quite normal. In any given area there may well be bands where there is a small amount of background noise that will need the squelch to be advanced a bit further to get it to close.

Some scanners offer a variety of types of squelch including one where even if lack of background noise opens the squelch, the scanner will continue to hunt through its memories unless there is sound such as a voice present. In fact this is often known as voice-scan. My personal experience is that this facility rarely works very well.

One further facility is scan 'Delay'. Sometimes you do not want the scanner to resume scanning until you have heard any replies to a transmission. Scan Delay allows for a small lag before scanning commences so that you can catch the reply. Only when the scan delay period is exceeded with no further transmissions does the circuitry recommence scanning.

### Bandwidth and mode

Many modern scanners allow the user to select the bandwidth for the received signal. This is usually stored in the scanner's memory. Typically, you will find a choice of narrow or wide FM. The former is for communications transmissions and the latter for broadcasts. AM is nearly always assumed to be narrow band. On some more advanced scanners a further facility may be single sideband, SSB and depending on the scanner very narrow-band circuits may be employed for this mode. These will usually be automatically selected.

When choosing a scanner, do remember the comments in chapter 2. Some scanners sold in the UK do not allow you to select the mode at all. Equipment designed primarily for the American market always assumes that transmissions outside the aircraft band will be FM mode. In the UK however, both AM and FM are used.

### Search

With this facility, nobody's frequency is safe from you. Let us assume that you have a sneaking suspicion that interesting transmissions are taking place in your area between 160 and 170 Megahertz. Now because of the intermittent nature of communications transmissions it can be like looking for a needle in a haystack to discover which actual frequencies are in use. Get the scanner to do the hard work. On many machines it is possible to select a lower and upper search limit and leave the scanner to sweep between those two frequencies. Naturally, it will stop when it finds something. A further refinement on this appears on scanners such as the R-7100 when the scanner will also store the frequency into a spare memory. This means you can even go off for the day and come back and see which frequencies were active.

## Stepping rates

Searching is always done in conjunction with stepping rates. Unlike a conventional radio, a scanner does not have infinite degrees of tuning. In other words as it goes up or down in frequency, it does it in small 'hops'. The steps available on the scanner are important, because they may prevent you from properly tuning into the correct frequency. In the UK we use 12.5 kHz channel spacing and that can be a problem for scanners that can only tune in 5 or 10 kHz steps. What will usually happen is that you try to enter the correct digits and press the 'enter' key, the scanner's circuit will round the number up or down to suit its available stepping rate. In the worst case this means that you are slightly off-tuned from the frequency you want, and will either not hear the required signal or it will be distorted. At best, the scanner's filters may be fairly broad band and you will still receive the signals with little difficulty.

Again, the above should be noted when choosing a scanner and you should be aware that the previously mentioned units designed for the American market may well not have 12.5 kHz stepping rates.

## Priority channel

Some scanners include what is known as a priority channel and indeed may have more than one. This channel or channels are scanned more frequently than the others and the idea is that the most important frequencies are assigned to the priority positions.

## RF Attenuator

This is a switch (it may be marked Local/DX) that allows you to desensitize the scanner. Remember the earlier comments about strong signals upsetting the tuning stages, this facility will reduce or can even eliminate the problem. Unfortunately the side-effect is that it will also cut down the weaker signals so that you can probably no longer hear them. Even so, in extreme cases it can be useful and at least allow you to hear *some* transmissions, whereas the scanner may otherwise permanently lock-up because of overload.

## Tape control

This is coupled to the squelch circuit and will automatically switch a tape recorder on when transmissions are received. It is only available on the more expensive base models.

## Computer control

Big in America. Dead here. This should have been the biggest thing in scanning but it has never caught on here largely for two reasons. The lack of earlier legislation to ensure minimum hash radiation from computers meant that most machines previously sold in Britain have radiated the most appalling noise, which cause the scanner to lock-up on the spurious signals. The other factor has obviously been the cost difference in computers between Britain and the U.S.A. where many people can afford to have an inexpensive PC sat doing nothing but controlling a scanner. AOR, Yaesu and Icom all offer scanners with the necessary sockets for computer control, but at the time of writing the only one that is supported by commercially available external hardware and software is the AOR 3000A although others are now becoming available. Lowe Electronics can also supply software but the interfacing is up to you. AOR(UK) can provide the superb AcePac 3A software for controlling the AR–3000A from a PC, and TMP Communications can supply software for the Amiga range of computers.

# Throw away the 4 telescopic

Nearly all scanners are supplied with some sort of aerial to get you going. With the exception of handheld types that is about all the telescopic ones are good for. To get the best out of your base or mobile scanner you will need to invest in a proper aerial ('Antenna' is essentially the same for non-UK English language readers). You will also need to connect between aerial and scanner using the proper type of cable.

It can never be stressed enough that an outside aerial mounted as high as possible is an essential part of the receiving system. We are dealing with low-level communications signals and so we need to gather every bit of them that we can. A proper aerial system will pull in signals that you will never hear just using a telescopic whip attached to the scanner.

If you use an external aerial then note that you must disconnect the telescopic as leaving it in circuit will upset the input impedance to the equipment.

## VHF/UHF aerials

The aerial needed for a scanner must not be confused with the long wire types used for other types of radio reception. This is a very specialized area and the aerial and cable must be well sited and in good condition. Signals are subject to the high losses at these frequencies and even minor defects in the system will almost certainly degrade performance.

VHF/UHF aerials fall into two broad categories; broadband and narrowband. The former performs well across a wide range of frequencies and the latter is suited to one particular band. The narrow

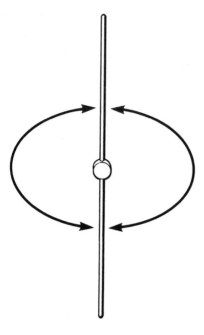

**Figure 4.1** Vertical polarisation.
Pick up pattern is in all directions.

band type should not be ignored as it has its uses, for instance where the air and marine bands are concerned it may well perform much better than a broadband type. The broadband aerial is in fact something of a compromise.

It is also advisable that you understand about polarization. This simply means that transmission or reception takes place via elements that are either vertical to the ground or horizontal. Most communica-

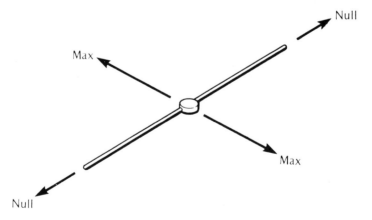

**Figure 4.2** Horizontal polarisation. The aerial is sensitive in two directions on and picks up very little end-on.

tions take place using vertically polarized aerials and for optimum reception the scanner aerial should also be polarized the same way. The occasional exception to the rule is with some amateur transmissions and commercial communications between two fixed points. The disadvantage of using horizontally polarized transmission for most communications is that horizontal aerials are usually directional to one degree or another. This is hardly desirable where mobile communications are concerned because the signals can come from any direction.

## Narrowband aerials

The simplest narrowband aerial is the quarter wave element or whip. Remember how we described earlier the relationship between frequency and wavelength? It is possible to cut a whip to match the frequency in use. We must note that the input impedance (or resistance) to the scanner will be the standard 50 ohms. Using a standard formula we can work out what the length of the whip should be but note that we must reduce it by 5 percent to produce the 50 ohm match. If we mismatch then some signal will be lost. You do not have to worry about the formula or match because these have already been worked out for you and supplied as a cutting chart.

Note that the aerial will work at its best and be 50 ohm matched only when it is mounted above a ground plane such as a vehicle body or rod radials. Although this is technically a narrowband aerial it will provide good receive performance over several Megahertz and is ideal for marine or air bands. This type of aerial can easily be made from the parts of old TV or broadcast FM radio aerials. A further simple aerial is the dipole (Fig 4.4) with each 'leg' being a quarter wave whip.

A refinement is the ⅝th whip which is in fact a three quarter wave element with the bottom ⅛th wound into a coil. This aerial can provide a few decibels of gain and so give even better performance. You may have seen this type of aerial mounted on emergency vehicles where a long whip terminates in a small black coil close to the mounting unit. Again details are given in the cutting chart (see Table 4.1 page 33) if you want to build an aerial of this type.

## Broadband aerials

These are by far the most popular aerials for scanner use and they can be subdivided into active and passive types. The most popular is an aerial known as a discone, and despite what some advertisements claim by suppliers this is a vertically polarized aerial even though the

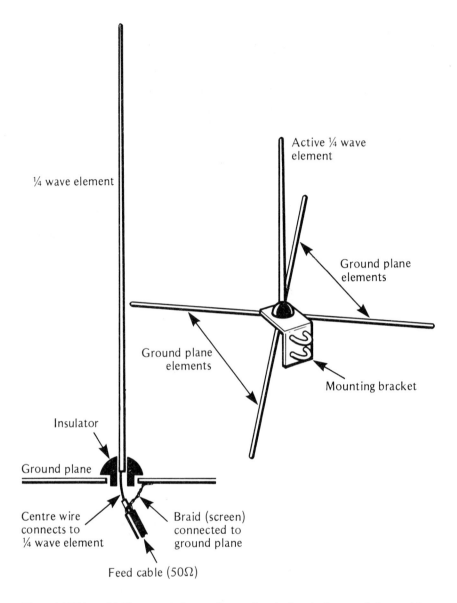

**Figure 4.3** Whip aerial. The ground plane can be a steel car body or in the case of a base aerial can be ¼ wave long rods.

top elements are mounted horizontally. It is what happens between the top and bottom elements that determines the polarization.

The discone is a reasonable compromise for broadband use although it must be noted that at any given frequency it will not be as good as a quarter wave despite some of the exaggerated claims made for its

Typical ground plane aerial. This one is designed for airband and the 'drooping' radials give a better 50 Ohm match.

performance. A variation on the discone incorporates an additional top element which is often a ⅝th wave whip for a specific band such as the amateur 2 Metre one.

Another broadband type for scanner use is what is known as the nest of dipoles. Strictly speaking this is a multiband aerial rather than broadband one, as its peak performance occurs when the dimensions of the elements act as half wave dipoles. I have used a Revco Radac type for a number of years and find that on some bands its performance is noticeably better than a discone. This aerial should not be confused with discones that are offered with multiple elements on top. These latter aerials are known in the trade as 'Gimmick Discones'; in other words they look elaborate but rarely perform very well. Quite simply, unless the upper elements are properly offset they will suffer from mutual inductance. One firm that has advertised this type of aerial for several years still makes the absurd claim that it turns a

This discone uses staggered length elements to achieve wider coverage.

normally horizontally polarized discone into a vertically polarized one. A discone is vertically polarized despite the fact that the top elements are horizontal.

Still with multiband aerials are what are known as the sleeved types. These will not usually perform as well as the two aerials mentioned above but are less obtrusive. A good example of this type is the Scanmaster from Nevada.

Finally comes the log periodic. This is a multi-element dipole and for correct use must be operated with an aerial rotator, because it is directional. Commercial ones usually cover about an octave (typically 50–500MHz) and offer several dB gain over a discone. The problem of course is that they are directional, but in some cases this can be an advantage if the majority of required signals are being received from approximately the same direction.

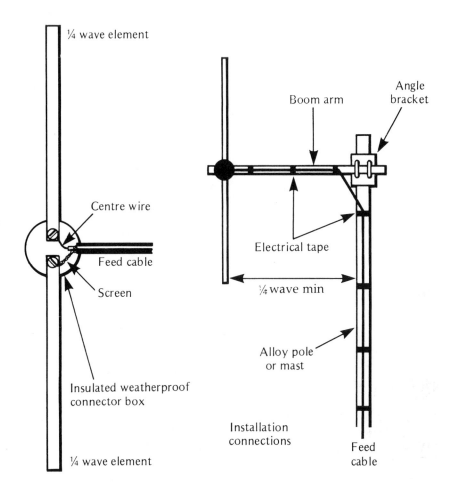

¼ wave element

Centre wire

Feed cable

Screen

Insulated weatherproof
connector box

¼ wave element

Boom arm

Angle
bracket

Electrical tape

¼ wave min

Alloy pole
or mast

Installation
connections

Feed
cable

**Figure 4.4** The dipole. Vertically polarised it provides good all round reception.

## Mobile aerials

The true broadband vehicle aerial has yet to be invented. However, compromises are obtained in a number of ways. The first is to use a series of coils along a whip aerial and depending on frequency these can act as resonators or chokes, appearing either high impedance or 'electrically transparent'. The result is a complex multi-band aerial. The second alternative is to use a nominal 100MHz whip and provide broadband amplification at the base.

Finally an interesting solution comes from Tandy who offer an adaptor that allows your car radio aerial to feed you scanner as well.

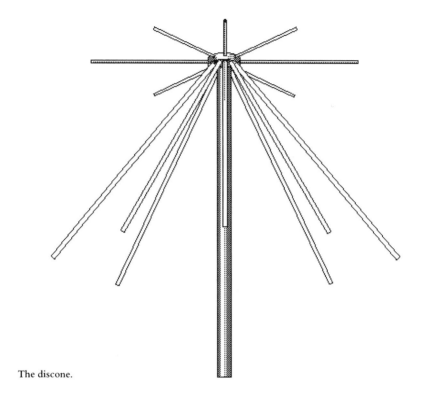

The discone.

Tandy claim the adaptor (which is inexpensive and requires no power) has no effect on the car radio but in tests I could not establish this. A number of scanner/car radios were tested with varying results. Older scanners such as the SX-200 and Bearcat 220FB caused scanning noise back through the car radio particularly on VHF. Newer handheld scanners did not cause the same problem and indeed newer and better quality car radios also improved matters. In my own view the matter is quite academic anyway—either you are going to listen to Radio Thingy or you're going to listen to the scanner—surely not both. The final point concerns the scanner aerial plug. It is a Motorola type and so if you are using one of the new generation of handhelds you will need to change it to a BNC, etc.

## Aerials for portables

A hand-portable scanner can be used with virtually any type of mobile or base aerial and the consequent performance will be better than any small aerial that is normally attached directly to the scanner. However, use of such aerials defeats the portability feature of the scanner.

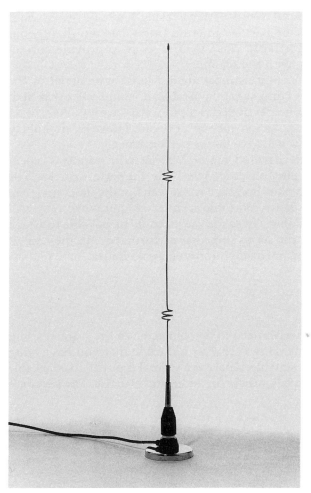

A multi-band mobile aerial.

Some portable scanners are supplied with only a small length of wire to act as an aerial. These are probably the poorest aerials as they can rarely be kept in an upright position. A far better choice is the use of a telescopic or helical, and to this end most portable scanners have a socket, frequently either a BNC type or miniature jack plug, for an external aerial. By far the most common aerial used on portable scanners is the helical whip.

### Helicals (rubber ducks)
A helical aerial comprises a metal spring, shrouded in rubber or plastic. They are often seen on walkie-talkies and offer the advantage that unlike a telescopic they are flexible and not easily broken. In practice, the spring

usually consists of a metal wire of ⅝th wavelength wound over a width of about 10mm. The top part is sometimes stretched out slightly but often the lower end is fairly close wound so as to provide correct impedance matching with the scanner.

Helicals offer better performance than a loose wire aerial of the same length, are very compact and portable, do not easily break and, being far shorter than respective telescopic aerials, are less likely to do personal damage like poking someone's eye out. However, it is likely that a telescopic aerial will give better performance.

Whatever kind of aerial is used, remember that if the scanner is kept in a pocket or any other position close to the body, the performance will be reduced. Not only does the body act as a screen but the sheer mass can upset the aerial impedance. Portable scanners do not work very well inside vehicles or buildings. In each case it should be possible to attach an external aerial to the set to improve performance. In the case of mobile operation a magnetically mounted aerial is ideal.

## Cable

All base and mobile aerials need to be connected to the scanner using screened coaxial cable. However, any old cable that you have lying around might not be suitable. There are several types of coaxial cable available, some for aerials, others for audio and hi-fi use. The latter are

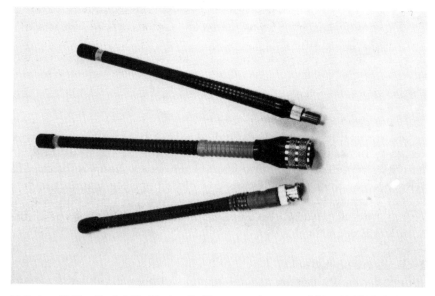

Helicals or 'Rubber Ducks'. Ideal for hand held scanners, they are available with BNC, PL259 and screw-in connectors.

unsuitable as are cables designed for use with a normal car radio.

The remaining aerial cables fall into two sections, 50 ohm and 75 ohm impedance types. Cable impedance is most critical. The 50 ohm variety is normally used to connect professional, commercial, amateur and CB aerials while 75 ohm cable is used for domestic VHF radio and television. You must use the right one for your scanner. The scanner instruction manual should tell you which cable impedance to use. Failing that the aerial socket on the set may be labelled with the impedance. If it is not shown then it is reasonably safe to assume that the correct cable is the 50 ohm type.

50 ohm cable is available from amateur and CB radio dealers, but like the 75 ohm types two main kinds are available; normal or low-loss. If the scanner is only being used for VHF reception and only about 8 or 10 metres of cable is to be used then normal cable can be used. However, if UHF reception or long cable lengths are required then low loss cable is needed.

### Cable construction

Whatever kind of coaxial cable you use, it will have roughly the construction shown in Figure 4.5. Starting at the middle is the core wire which carries the signal, shrouded in a plastic insulator. The insulator prevents the core from touching the outer braid, which is wound in such a way as to provide an earthed screen for the core. This screen serves two purposes: it ensures that the correct impedence is maintained along the entire length of the cable, and it stops any interference from reaching the inner core. Finally, the entire cable is covered in plastic insulation. It is important when installing an aerial that this outer insulation is intact, and not torn or gouged so that the braid is exposed. Rainwater getting into the cable in such circumstances will almost certainly ruin the cable.

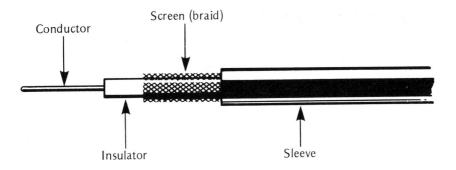

Conductor

Screen (braid)

Insulator

Sleeve

**Figure 4.5** Coaxial cable.

As the screen of the cable is earthed, it is important when connecting the cable to either the aerial or the connector plug that the inner wire and the braid wire *never touch*. If they do, the incoming signal is earthed, and so lost.

**Connectors**
In order to plug the aerial cable into the scanner you will need appropriate connectors. If you intend to fit your own then note that you usually will need a soldering iron: twisted wires or wires poked into sockets will almost certainly lead to signal losses. Several types of plug are in common use and are shown in Figure 4.6. Some 'solderless' connectors are also available, and it is also possible to purchase adaptors so that an aerial which has one type of plug can be connected to a scanner which takes another type.

*PL259*
Commonly found on CB sets and amateur HF and VHF equipment, PL259 connectors are only occasionally encountered on scanners, usually of the older variety. However, they are used extensively to connect to aerials. For instance a socket for a PL259 plug will be found on the base of many discones.

The plug comes in several varieties, some of which are easier to fit than others. The simplest are designed for use with the thinner, standard (non low-loss), cable. The cable is trimmed, about a quarter inch of braid is left and folded back over the outer insulator. The cable is then pushed into the plug and the braiding and insulator screwed into the plug's shell. Once fully home, the centre conductor is then soldered or crimped depending on the plug type.

Other types of PL259 have a separate inner sleeve which is either a wide or narrow type depending on the coaxial cable used. This type of plug can be fitted to thicker, low-loss, cables and the appropriate sleeve is purchased separately. When fitting, the braid must be worked back over the sleeve. The inner conductor is then soldered in the normal way. It is a good idea with both types of plug to expose more centre conductor than is needed. The surplus can be snipped off after fitting.

PL259 plugs have an outer shell that is internally threaded and when mated with the socket, this shell is screwed up tight to ensure firm contact.

*BNC*
This connector is often found on professional communication and test equipment and is much smaller than the PL259. However, it has a simple twist and pull bayonet action for release, which makes it a lot quicker to change over than the PL259. This type of plug is used for connecting to most scanners nowadays. Unfortunately, its smaller dimensions make

it more fiddly to attach to the cable. It is difficult to give specific instructions on fitting as construction differs greatly between makes of plugs.

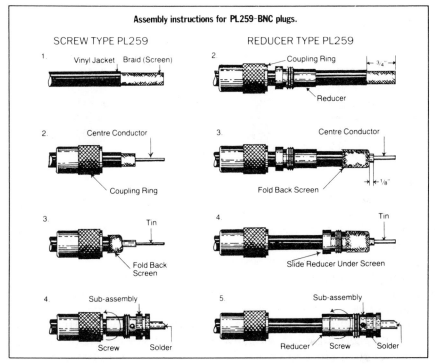

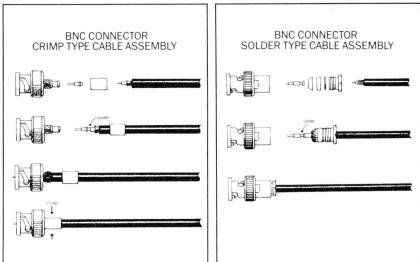

**Figure 4.6** Various plugs and connectors (*courtesy of S.S.E. (UK)*).

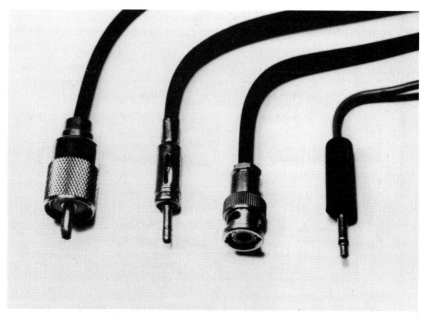

Typical aerial plugs found on scanners. From left to right: PL259, Motorola, BNC and miniature jack. The latter is usually confined to hand held sets.

### Motorola type

This is the car radio aerial type of plug that will be familiar to many people. Surprisingly in a way, this low quality type of plug (low quality in terms of performance at VHF and UHF) was found on several scanners including the SX200N and some early Bearcats. Types vary with manufacturer, but a look at the plug will usually make it clear how it is attached to the cable.

### Miniature jack

A plug that is far from suited to VHF/UHF but it is occasionally found on some of the smaller portable crystal controlled scanners: probably chosen because it is small and very cheap. A look inside will make it obvious as to what is soldered to where, but a difficulty arises in that most miniature jack plugs do not have a big enough opening in the barrel to take 50 ohm coaxial cable. One way round this problem is to cut off the back end of the barrel with say, a hacksaw, so leaving a bigger opening.

## Table 4.1 Cutting chart for aerials

| MHz | ¼ Wave | Corr | ¾ Wave | MHz | ¼ Wave | Corr | ¾ Wave |
|-----|--------|------|--------|-----|--------|------|--------|
| 30 | 2483 | 2359 | 7450 | 225 | 331 | 314 | 993 |
| 35 | 2128 | 2022 | 6385 | 230 | 323 | 307 | 971 |
| 40 | 1862 | 1769 | 5587 | 235 | 317 | 301 | 951 |
| 45 | 1655 | 1572 | 4966 | 240 | 310 | 294 | 931 |
| 50 | 1490 | 1415 | 4470 | 245 | 304 | 288 | 912 |
| 55 | 1354 | 1286 | 4063 | 250 | 298 | 283 | 894 |
| 60 | 1241 | 1179 | 3725 | 255 | 292 | 277 | 876 |
| 65 | 1146 | 1088 | 3438 | 260 | 286 | 272 | 859 |
| 70 | 1064 | 1011 | 3192 | 265 | 281 | 267 | 843 |
| 75 | 993 | 943 | 2980 | 270 | 275 | 262 | 827 |
| 80 | 931 | 884 | 2793 | 275 | 270 | 257 | 812 |
| 85 | 876 | 832 | 2629 | 280 | 266 | 252 | 798 |
| 90 | 827 | 786 | 2483 | 285 | 261 | 248 | 784 |
| 95 | 784 | 745 | 2352 | 290 | 256 | 244 | 770 |
| 100 | 745 | 707 | 2235 | 295 | 252 | 239 | 757 |
| 105 | 709 | 674 | 2128 | 300 | 248 | 235 | 745 |
| 110 | 677 | 643 | 2031 | 305 | 244 | 232 | 732 |
| 115 | 647 | 615 | 1943 | 310 | 240 | 228 | 720 |
| 120 | 620 | 589 | 1862 | 315 | 236 | 224 | 709 |
| 125 | 596 | 566 | 1788 | 320 | 232 | 221 | 698 |
| 130 | 573 | 544 | 1719 | 325 | 229 | 217 | 687 |
| 135 | 551 | 524 | 1655 | 330 | 225 | 214 | 677 |
| 140 | 532 | 505 | 1596 | 335 | 222 | 211 | 667 |
| 145 | 513 | 488 | 1541 | 340 | 219 | 208 | 657 |
| 150 | 496 | 471 | 1490 | 345 | 215 | 205 | 647 |
| 155 | 480 | 456 | 1441 | 350 | 212 | 202 | 638 |
| 160 | 465 | 442 | 1396 | 355 | 209 | 199 | 629 |
| 165 | 451 | 428 | 1354 | 360 | 206 | 196 | 620 |
| 170 | 438 | 416 | 1314 | 365 | 204 | 193 | 612 |
| 175 | 425 | 404 | 1277 | 370 | 201 | 191 | 604 |
| 180 | 413 | 393 | 1241 | 375 | 198 | 188 | 596 |
| 185 | 402 | 382 | 1208 | 380 | 196 | 186 | 588 |
| 190 | 392 | 372 | 1176 | 385 | 193 | 183 | 580 |
| 195 | 382 | 362 | 1146 | 390 | 191 | 181 | 573 |
| 200 | 372 | 353 | 1117 | 395 | 188 | 179 | 565 |
| 205 | 363 | 345 | 1090 | 400 | 186 | 176 | 558 |
| 210 | 354 | 337 | 1064 | 405 | 183 | 174 | 551 |
| 215 | 346 | 329 | 1039 | 410 | 181 | 172 | 545 |
| 220 | 338 | 321 | 1015 | 415 | 179 | 170 | 538 |

All dimensions given in mm.

**Table 4.1** *continued*

| MHz | ¼ Wave | Corr | ¾ Wave | MHz | ¼ Wave | Corr | ¾ Wave |
|-----|--------|------|--------|-----|--------|------|--------|
| 420 | 177 | 168 | 532 | 620 | 120 | 114 | 360 |
| 425 | 175 | 166 | 525 | 630 | 118 | 112 | 354 |
| 430 | 173 | 164 | 519 | 640 | 116 | 110 | 349 |
| 435 | 171 | 162 | 513 | 650 | 114 | 108 | 343 |
| 440 | 169 | 160 | 507 | 660 | 112 | 107 | 338 |
| 445 | 167 | 159 | 502 | 670 | 111 | 105 | 333 |
| 450 | 165 | 157 | 496 | 680 | 109 | 104 | 328 |
| 455 | 163 | 155 | 491 | 690 | 107 | 102 | 323 |
| 460 | 161 | 153 | 485 | 700 | 106 | 101 | 319 |
| 465 | 160 | 152 | 480 | 710 | 104 | 99 | 314 |
| 470 | 158 | 150 | 475 | 720 | 103 | 98 | 310 |
| 475 | 156 | 149 | 470 | 730 | 102 | 96 | 306 |
| 480 | 155 | 147 | 465 | 740 | 100 | 95 | 302 |
| 485 | 153 | 145 | 460 | 750 | 99 | 94 | 298 |
| 490 | 152 | 144 | 456 | 760 | 98 | 93 | 294 |
| 495 | 150 | 142 | 451 | 770 | 96 | 91 | 290 |
| 500 | 149 | 141 | 447 | 780 | 95 | 90 | 286 |
| 505 | 147 | 140 | 442 | 790 | 94 | 89 | 282 |
| 510 | 146 | 138 | 438 | 800 | 93 | 88 | 279 |
| 515 | 144 | 137 | 433 | 810 | 91 | 87 | 275 |
| 520 | 143 | 136 | 429 | 820 | 90 | 86 | 272 |
| 525 | 141 | 134 | 425 | 830 | 89 | 85 | 269 |
| 530 | 140 | 133 | 421 | 840 | 88 | 84 | 266 |
| 535 | 139 | 132 | 417 | 850 | 87 | 83 | 262 |
| 540 | 137 | 131 | 413 | 860 | 86 | 82 | 259 |
| 545 | 136 | 129 | 410 | 870 | 85 | 81 | 256 |
| 550 | 135 | 128 | 406 | 880 | 84 | 80 | 253 |
| 555 | 134 | 127 | 402 | 890 | 83 | 79 | 251 |
| 560 | 133 | 126 | 399 | 900 | 82 | 78 | 248 |
| 565 | 131 | 125 | 395 | 910 | 81 | 77 | 245 |
| 570 | 130 | 124 | 392 | 920 | 80 | 76 | 242 |
| 575 | 129 | 123 | 388 | 930 | 80 | 76 | 240 |
| 580 | 128 | 122 | 385 | 940 | 79 | 75 | 237 |
| 585 | 127 | 120 | 382 | 950 | 78 | 74 | 235 |
| 590 | 126 | 119 | 378 | 960 | 77 | 73 | 232 |
| 595 | 125 | 118 | 375 | 970 | 76 | 72 | 230 |
| 600 | 124 | 117 | 372 | 980 | 76 | 72 | 228 |
| 610 | 122 | 116 | 366 | 990 | 75 | 71 | 225 |

All dimensions given in mm.

# Mounting external aerials

A whole range of fittings and mounting kits is available for installing aerials and your local TV aerial erection firm should be only too happy to sell you poles, fixing kits, etc.

There are four basic ways of mounting an aerial outside and the corresponding kits are:

1 Wall mounting. This consists of a plate with brackets to hold a mounting pole. A drill capable of drilling into brick or masonry will be needed and expanding bolts should be used to retain the plate.

2 Eaves mounting. A smaller version of the wall mounting version, it is used with wood screws to fix onto the eaves. Note, though, that this method is only suitable for small lightweight aerials: even a small aerial can put considerable strain on its mountings during high winds.

3 Chimney lashing. The method often used for TV aerials, comprising one or two brackets held to a chimney by wire cable. Although easy to fit, it places the aerial in close proximity to the heat and smoke from the chimney which may accelerate the inevitable corrosion of the aerial.

4 Free standing mast. This is the most expensive solution but usually the best if you can afford it. An aluminium mast of 6 metres or more in length is partially sunk into the ground and held upright with wire guys. This mounting method can improve performance remarkably at some locations as it allows the aerial to be sited away from obstructions and above the level of trees and buildings that block signals. Planning permission may be required for this kind of installation.

# Aerial amplifiers

Also known as RF or wideband preamps, signal boosters, etc. These devices fall into two categories:

### Masthead amplifiers
These units consist of a small-signal amplifier housed in a weatherproof box, close to the aerial. They are useful for making-up for the signal losses that occur when long cables are used between the aerial and the scanner. DC voltage to power the unit is fed up the centre core of the coaxial cable—as the signal comes down, the DC goes up, without interference. One variant on this theme is a broadband aerial that actually has an aerial amplifier built into its base.

### Cable-end amplifiers
These connect between the end of the cable and the scanner. They are often powered by a small battery, although some do plug into the

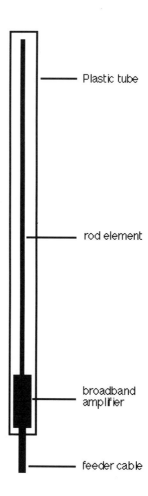

Figure 4.7 The active whip for base use.

domestic AC supply. Cable-end amplifiers have limitations as, unlike masthead amplifiers, they cannot improve a poor signal-to-noise ratio of an aerial system.

### When to use an amplifier

In the ideal circumstances, that is, with an aerial of sufficient quality and short enough cable, an aerial amplifier is not needed. While capable of boosting weaker signals an aerial amplifier can also cause problems. For instance, strong signals received on other frequencies are also boosted and may overload the scanner.

However, some scanner users may live in areas where they are screened by high buildings or land, or may not be able to fit an aerial of sufficiently high quality. In such circumstances an amplifier *may* help. It may also be of use where long cable runs are necessary between the scanner and the aerial.

As a caution, users are advised to seek expert advice *before* installing an aerial amplifier, as wrongly doing so will cause more problems than it solves.

A typical wideband amplified aerial.

# 5 UK frequency allocations

The decision on who transmits what, on which frequency, is made by international agreement. Clearly, governments must agree on allocations if they are to avoid causing interference. There would be chaos if, say, one country allocated a band to low powered radio telephones while a neighbouring country allocated the same band for high powered broadcasting. The body which co-ordinates radio frequency allocations on behalf of world governments is the International Telecommunications Union, known simply as the ITU.

For the purpose of agreed allocations the ITU splits the world into three regions. The United Kingdom falls in Region 1, which includes most of Europe and a small section of North Africa. However, it does not necessarily follow that each country conforms strictly with the allocations drawn up for that region. Where there is little likelihood of interference, countries may opt for local variations and, obviously, many such variations exist. For this reason, listings given in this book strictly apply only to the United Kingdom, although most allocations do match the standard format for Region 1.

We shall look first at general VHF/UHF frequency allocations, then consider in detail some of the services on those allocations. Table 5.1/2 is a listing of UK frequency allocations.

**Table 5.1/2 United Kingdom frequency allocations**

| From-to | Pairing | Allocation |
|---|---|---|
| 25.0050–25.0100 | | Standard Frequency, time signals, space research |
| 25.0100–25.0700 | | Fixed (PTO & Government), Maritime & Land Mobile (Government) |

**Table 5.1/2**  *continued*

| From-to | Pairing | Allocation |
|---|---|---|
| **25.0700–25.2100** | | Maritime Mobile (mostly USB and RTTY) |
| 25.0539 | 26.1444 | Ship-to-shore (SSB) |
| 25.0601 | 26.1506 | Ship-to-shore (SSB) |
| 25.0710 | | Marine Calling channel 'A' |
| 25.0730 | | Marine Calling channel 'B' |
| 25.0750 | | Marine Calling channel 'C' |
| 25.0763 to 25.0898 | | Marine channels spaced 0.5kHz |
| **25.2100–25.6000** | | Fixed (PTO & Government), Maritime & Land Mobile (government) |
| 25.2100 to 25.5350 | | World-wide coastal stations |
| 25.5500 to 25.6000 | | Radio Astronomy |
| **25.6000–26.1000** | | Broadcasting (AM) plus Radio Astronomy |
| **26.1000–27.5000** | | Fixed (PTO & Government), Land Mobile (including CEPT CB system), pagers, ISM, Maritime Mobile, model control |
| 26.1000 | 26.1750 | MOD tactical land mobile |
| 26.1444 | 25.0539 | Shore-to-ship (SSB) |
| 26.1506 | 25.0601 | Shore-to-ship (SSB) |
| 26.2375 to 26.8655 | | One-way paging systems (new band) |
| 26.9780 to 27.2620 | | One-way paging systems (old band) |

**Table 5.1/2**  *continued*

| From-to | Pairing | Allocation |
|---|---|---|
| 26.9570 to 27.2830 | | Industrial, scientific and medical |
| 26.9600 to 27.2800 | | Model control (AM & FM & 1.5Watt maximum power) & Data Buoys |
| 26.9650 to 27.4050 | | CEPT Citizens Band radio (mostly NFM but some illegal AM & SSB) |
| 27.4500 | | Emergency alarm systems for the elderly or infirmed |
| 27.5000–27.6000 | | Land Mobile (government) Meteorological aids (Sondes, etc) |
| 27.6000–28.0000 | | Land Mobile (UK CB system) & Meteorological Aids |
| 27.60125 to 27.99125 | | UK Citizens Band radio system (NFM) |
| 28.0000–29.7000 | | Amateur Radio (10 Metre Band) including Russian RS-series satellites |
| 29.7000–30.7000 | | Space (satellite identification), Mobile (Government) & Fixed |
| 29.7000 to 29.9700 | | Military 25kHz channel spacing simplex communications |
| 29.7000 to 30.0100 | | Satellite identification |

**Table 5.1/2** *continued*

| From-to | Pairing | Allocation |
|---|---|---|
| 30.0250<br>to<br>30.7000 | | USAF (Europe) mobile communications 25kHz channels |
| 30.4500 | | US Military 'MARS' radio integration network |
| **30.700–34.5000** | | Fixed, Mobile & Paging systems (at the peak of 11 year sunspot cycles many US services operating in this band can be heard) |
| 30.7000<br>to<br>34.5000 | | Use by USAF in UK/Europe and MOD. Mostly NFM at 25kHz channel spacing |
| 31.7250<br>31.7500<br>31.7750 | | Hospital paging systems<br>Hospital paging systems<br>Hospital paging systems |
| 31.8000<br>to<br>34.9000 | | Military Fixed/Mobile 50kHz channel spacing |
| **34.5000–37.5000** | | Mobile (mostly government & military), Model Control, Alarms |
| 34.9250 | | Emergency alarm systems for the elderly or infirmed |
| 34.9500 | | Emergency alarm systems for the elderly or infirmed |
| 34.9750 | | Emergency alarm systems for the elderly or infirmed |
| 35.0050<br>to<br>35.2050 | | Model Control (aircraft only) 1.5Watt maximum power |
| 35.2500<br>to<br>37.7500 | | Military (mostly army) Fixed/Mobile 50kHz channel spacing |

**Table 5.1/2**   *continued*

| From-to | Pairing | Allocation |
|---|---|---|
| **37.5000–47.0000** | | Mobile (extensively military vehicles and manpacks), Radio Astronomy, ISM, cordless telephones, Television broadcasting & model control |
| 37.7500 to 38.2500 | | Cambridge Observatory (astronomy) |
| 37.7500 to 40.0000 | | Military mobile 50kHz channel spacing |
| 39.9150 to 40.1200 | | Some beacons on space satellites have used this sub-band |
| 40.0500 | | ★★★Military Distress Frequency★★★ |
| 40.6650 to 40.9550 | | Model control (100mW maximum) |
| 40.6800 | | Industrial, Scientific & Medical |
| 41.0000 to 47.4500 | | Military tactical mobile (vehicles/manpacks/data)50kHz channel spacing |
| 41.0000 to 68.0000 | | Television Broadcasting (not UK) Band I |
| 46.6100 to 46.9700 | | Unapproved cordless telephone handsets (US system B - NFM) |
| 47.41875 | 77.5500 | Extended range approved |
| 47.43125 | 77.5125 | Cordless phones |

**Table 5.1/2**   *continued*

| From-to | Pairing | Allocation |
|---------|---------|------------|
| 47.45625<br>to<br>47.54375 | 1.6240<br>to<br>1.7829 | Cordless telephone handsets (approved - 8 channels NFM) |
| **47.6800-50.000** | | Land Mobile, Broadcasting, Amateur & unapproved baby listeners, walkie-talkies, wireless microphones & cordless phones (all NFM) |
| 48.9900<br>to<br>49.6800 | 69.7200<br>to<br>70.2750 | Unapproved long range cordless phone bases (22 channels NFM) |
| 49.0000<br>to<br>49.8750 | | Private paging systems |
| 49.0000<br>to<br>50.0000 | | Unapproved devices mostly intended for use in USA |
| 49.4250<br>to<br>49.4750 | | Hospital paging systems |
| 49.6700<br>to<br>49.9700 | | Unapproved cordless telephone bases (US system B NFM) |
| 49.8200<br>to<br>49.9000 | | Low powered radio control toys, baby alarms, walkie talkies etc (100mW max power) |
| 49.8300<br>to<br>49.8900 | | Unapproved cordless telephones |
| **50.0000-54.0000** | | 6 Metre Amateur band (US allocation - NFM, CW & SSB) |
| 50.0000<br>to<br>52.0000 | | 6 Metre Amateur band (UK allocation - NFM, CW & SSB) |
| 54.0000 | | Frequency has been used by space satellite beacons (Anna-1B) |

**Table 5.1/2**  *continued*

| From-to | Pairing | Allocation |
|---|---|---|
| **52.0000–60.0000** | | Land Mobile and radio microphones. |
| 53.8000 to 55.6000 | | BBC high powered (4 Watt) radio microphones |
| **60.0000–64.0000** | | Radio Microphones |
| 60.8000 to 62.6000 | | BBC radio microphones. 100 kHz channel spacing |
| **64.0000–68.0000** | | Fixed & Land Mobile including Military |
| 64.0000 to 68.0000 | | MOD Pegasus-MOULD system. 12.5 kHz channel spacing |
| **68.0000–70.0250** | | Land Mobile & Repeaters (military) |
| 69.3000 | | Spot frequency for Sea Cadets (AM) |
| 69.6000 to 69.8000 | 84.6000 to 84.8000 | Military repeater outputs |
| 69.8250 to 69.9750 | | Outside Broadcast camera links (talkback) |
| 70.0000 to 70.0500 | | Unapproved cordless 'phones |
| **70.0250–70.5000** | | 4 Metre Amateur Band. CW, NFM and SSB in use. |
| **70.5000–71.5000** | | Land Mobile (emergency services) |

**Table 5.1/2**   *continued*

| From-to | Pairing | Allocation |
|---------|---------|------------|
| 70.5125<br>to<br>71.5000 | 80.0000<br>to<br>84.0000 | Fire service bases |
| **71.5000-72.8000** | | **LOW BAND PMR mobiles (bases + 13.5MHz)** |
| 71.5125<br>to<br>72.7875 | 85.0125<br>to<br>86.2875 | Extensively used by Water Boards, Telecoms & Local Authorities using both AM and NFM. |
| 71.9875 | | Automobile Association ('Fanum') Ch 6 (London) |
| 72.0000 | | Automobile Association ('Fanum') Ch 7 |
| 72.0125 | | Automobile Association ('Fanum') Ch 4 |
| 72.0205 | | Automobile Association ('Fanum') Ch 1 |
| 72.0500 | | Automobile Association ('Fanum') Ch 3 |
| 72.0625 | | Automobile Association ('Fanum') Ch 2 |
| 72.0875 | | Automobile Association ('Fanum') Ch 5 |
| 72.3750 | 85.8750 | Short-term hire mobile |
| 72.5250<br>to<br>72.7000 | 86.0250<br>to<br>86.2000 | Ambulance bases in some areas |
| 72.5375 | 86.0375 | Private Ambulances National Network (Mobiles) |
| **72.8000-74.8000** | | Land mobile (Government) |
| 72.8000<br>to<br>73.7000 | | Military simplex channels using 25kHz spacing |
| 73.7000<br>to<br>74.7875 | | Military (RAF ground services) & MOULD repeater inputs |
| **74.8000-75.2000** | | Aeronavigation guard band |

**Table 5.1/2**   *continued*

| From-to | Pairing | Allocation |
|---------|---------|------------|
| 75.0000 | | Approach fan beams, inner, middle & outer markers (AM) |
| **75.2000–76.7000** | | Outside broadcast links and military - mostly allocated to USAF British bases (NFM) and MOULD repeater outputs |
| 75.20000 to 75.30000 | | BBC outside broadcast links |
| 75.30000 to 76.50000 | | Military MOULD repeater outputs |
| **76.7000–78.0000** | | Fixed and Land mobile (PMR and government) |
| 76.9625 to 77.5000 | 86.9625 to 87.5000 | Fixed and Mobile. Government, Customs, British Telecom, RAC and PMR mobiles |
| 77.0000 | 87.0000 | RAC services Ch 2 |
| 77.0125 | 87.0125 | RAC services Ch 4 |
| 77.0250 | 87.0250 | RAC services Ch 1 |
| 77.0375 | 87.0375 | RAC services Ch 5 |
| 77.0500 | 87.0500 | RAC services Ch 3 |
| **78.0000–80.0000** | | Land Mobile. Government and private users. |
| 78.1000 | | Air Training Corps (nationwide) |
| 78.1875 | | BBC OB and engineering |
| 78.2000 | | BBC OB and engineering |
| 78.2125 | | Microwave link setting-up channel (nationwide) and BBC OB crews |
| 78.2225 | | BBC OB and engineering |
| 78.2375 | | BBC OB and engineering |
| 78.2500 | | BBC OB and engineering |

**Table 5.1/2**   *continued*

| From-to | Pairing | Allocation |
|---|---|---|
| 79.0000 to 80.0000 | | MOULD repeater inputs and RAF ground services/police |
| **80.0000–84.0000** | | Land Mobile & Fixed (extensive emergency service use). Allocations which couple with Band II (97.6–102.1) will move from here by 1995. |
| 80.5000 to 82.5000 | | Radio Astronomy (Cambridge University) |
| 80.0000 to 84.0000 | 70.5000 to 71.5000 | Fire Mobiles |
| 80.0125 | | Fire tender intercommunication (Channel 21) |
| 80.0750 | | Fire tender intercommunication (Channel 22) |
| 81.9500 | | Fire operations London |
| 83.9960 to 84.0040 | | ISM |
| **84.0000–85.0000** | | Fixed & Land Mobile (mostly military) |
| 84.1250 to 84.3500 | 73.7000 to 73.9250 | RAF ground service bases |
| 84.3000 | | RAF Mountain rescue teams (single frequency simplex) |
| 84.0000 to 85.0000 | | Military repeater inputs |
| **85.0000–88.0000** | | LOW BAND PMR Bases. |

**Table 5.1/2**  *continued*

| From-to | Pairing | Allocation |
|---------|---------|------------|
| 85.0125 to 86.2875 | 71.5125 to 72.7825 | Extensively used by Water Boards, Telecoms, Local Authorities & Community Repeaters using both AM and NFM |
| 85.1375 to 85.2000 | | Numerous British Telecom engineering channels |
| 85.4875 | | Automobile Association bases ('Fanum') Ch 6 |
| 85.5000 | | Automobile Association bases ('Fanum') Ch 7 |
| 85.5125 | | Automobile Association bases ('Fanum') Ch 4 |
| 85.5250 | | Automobile Association bases ('Fanum') Ch 1 |
| 85.5500 | | Automobile Association bases ('Fanum') Ch 3 |
| 85.5625 | | Automobile Association bases ('Fanum') Ch 2 |
| 85.5875 | | Automobile Association bases ('Fanum') Ch 5 |
| 85.8500 | 72.2500 | Philips Telecom National engineering channel |
| 85.8750 | 72.3750 | Low Band demonstration and short term hire channel bases |
| 86.0375 | 72.5375 | Private Ambulance bases National Network |
| 86.1375 | 72.6375 | Storno Motorola national engineering channel |
| 86.2000 | 72.7000 | Automobile Association 'Fanum' |
| 86.3000 to 86.7000 | | Single Frequency Simplex channels (channels listed below are in use in many parts of Britain but may vary in some areas) |
| 86.3125 | | National Mountain Rescue channel 1 |
| 86.3250 | | St John Ambulance/Red Cross Channel 1 |
| 86.3500 | | National Mountain Rescue channel 2 (in some areas, Red Cross, St John Ambulance, REACT and lifeguards) |
| 86.3625 | | Scouts national channel 1 |
| 86.3750 | | REACT CB emergency teams (nationwide) |
| 86.4125 | | St John Ambulance/Red Cross/mountain rescue channel 2 |
| 86.4250 | | Forestry Commission channel 3 |
| 86.4375 | | Motor Rally Safety channel |
| 86.4500 | | Forestry Commision channel 2 |

**Table 5.1/2**   *continued*

| From-to | Pairing | Allocation |
|---------|---------|------------|
| 86.4625 | | County Councils |
| 86.4750 | | British Rail National Incident Channel |
| 86.5000 | | Nuclear Spills Teams channel 1 |
| 86.5250 | | Nuclear Spills Teams channel 2 |
| 86.5500 | | Nuclear Spills Teams channel 3 |
| 86.5750 | | NCB mine rescue teams |
| 86.6250 | | Scouts national channel 2 |
| 86.6750 | | Nuclear fire and radiation check teams |
| 86.7000 | | BNF nuclear hazard check teams |
| | | |
| 86.9625 to 87.5000 | 76.9625 to 77.5000 | Split Frequency Simplex bases including some custom channels and local authorities. |
| | | |
| 87.0000 | 77.0000 | RAC services Ch 2 |
| 87.0125 | 77.0125 | RAC services Ch 4 |
| 87.0250 | 77.0250 | RAC services Ch 1 |
| 87.0375 | 77.0375 | RAC services Ch 5 |
| 87.0500 | 77.0500 | RAC services Ch 3 |
| | | |
| 87.1625 to 87.6250 | | Numerous County Council Highways Departments |
| | | |
| 87.7625 | 77.7625 | Forestry Commission National channel 2 |
| 87.8250 | 77.8250 | Forestry Commission National channel 1 |
| 87.9625 | 77.9625 | Forestry Commission National channel 3 |
| **88.0000–108.0000** | | Broadcasting & Land Mobile (until 1994). This allocation includes the UK FM Broadcast Band (Band II). |
| | | |
| 99.0230 | | Frequency has been used by Russian Satellites (Cosmos 44) |
| | | |
| 105.0000 to 108.0000 | 138.0000 to 141.0000 | PMR Mobiles (transport services) most now moved |
| | | |
| 105.35625 | 138.35625 | British Rail |

**Table 5.1/2** *continued*

| From-to | Pairing | Allocation |
|---------|---------|------------|
| **108.0000–117.9750** | | Aeronautical Radionavigation beacons including VHF Omnirange (VOR) and Doppler VOR (DVOR). Beacons identified by a three letter code in CW. Some of those located at or near airfields carry AM voice information on weather/runway/warnings etc. This service is known as Aerodrome Terminal Information Service (ATIS). |
| **118.0500–136.9750** | | International Aeronautical Mobile Band. This is the VHF band used by all civilian and some military airfields. It is subdivided into 760 channels (25 kHz spacing) and mode is AM |
| 118.0000 to 123.0000 | | Mostly control tower frequencies |
| 121.5000 121.7500 | | ★★★International Distress Frequency★★★ Soyuz manned T-flights to MIR Space Station (non-standard use of this allocation using NFM) |
| 123.0000 to 130.0000 | | Mostly airways frequencies (some ground & approach control) |
| 123.1000 | | Search & Rescue (SAR) |
| 130.0000 to 132.0000 | | Mostly company frequencies (airline crews to ground staff) |
| 132.0000 to 136.0000 | | Mostly airways |
| 135.5500 to 135.6450 | | Sub-band was once used for the American ATS series satellites |

**Table 5.1/2**  *continued*

| From-to | Pairing | Allocation |
|---------|---------|------------|
| **137.0000–138.0000** | | Space to Earth Communications & Weather Imaging Satellites (see satellite sub-section for full details). |
| **138.0000–141.0000** | | Land Mobile PMR (extensive use by Gas and Electricity Boards). Paired with bases at – 33MHz in Band II due to end in 1995 |
| 138.00625 to 140.89375 | 105.00625 to 107.89375 | PMR bases (extensive use by Department of Trade and Industry, Gas Boards and British Rail) |
| 138.0750 to 138.1750 | | Mercury/Racal Paging Systems. |
| 138.0000 to 138.2000 | | USAF bases in some areas |
| 138.35625 | 105.35625 | British Rail |
| 138.5000 to 139.5000 | | Mostly Gas Boards |
| 139.5000 to 140.5000 | 148.0000 149.0000 | Mostly Electricity Boards (new allocation) |
| 140.1825 | | Electricity line fault teams |
| 140.1875 | | Electricity line fault teams |
| 140.2000 | | Electricity line fault teams |
| 140.5000 to 141.0000 | | Bus companies |
| 140.96875 | | Short-term hire channel (single frequency simplex) |

**Table 5.1/2**  *continued*

| From-to | Pairing | Allocation |
|---|---|---|
| **141.0000–141.9000** | | Land Mobile mostly used by BBC, Independent Television and Radio for outside broadcast links, radio cars, etc. All Single Frequency Simplex using NFM |
| 141.0000 to 141.2000 | | Mostly ITV |
| 141.2000 to 141.9000 | | Mostly BBC |
| **141.9000–143.0000** | | Mobile (Government) including, land, air & space satellite communications & Military MOULD repeater links (NFM) |
| 142.0000 to 143.0000 | | Air-to-Air and Air-to-Ground. Sub-band used fairly extensively by military in continental Europe but rarely in UK |
| 142.4000 to 142.6000 | | Extensively used for Soyuz/Mir (Russian) satellite links (NFM) |
| 142.7200 | | USAF Air-to-Air |
| 142.8200 | | USAF Air-to-Air |
| **143.0000–144.0000** | | Mobile (government) mobiles (largely AM) coupled with bases at + 9MHz. Some Russian space satellite traffic all using NFM |
| 143.0000 to 144.0000 | 152.0000 to 153.0000 | Police bases |
| 143.1450 to 143.6250 | | Soyuz/Mir communications |

**Table 5.1/2** *continued*

| From-to | Pairing | Allocation |
|---|---|---|
| 143.6250 | | Mir main downlink over Europe (very strong when overhead) |
| 144.0000–146.0000 | | Amateur 2 Metre Band including satellite allocation. CW, SSB & NFM used |
| 146.0000–148.0000 | | Land Mobile & Fixed. Police mobile channels paired with bases on 154–156MHz and uplinks to hill top repeaters |
| 146.0000 to 148.0000 | | Police Fixed links (base to hilltop) |
| 146.0000 to 148.0000 | 154.0000 to 156.0000 | Police mobiles |
| 147.8000 | | Used in many areas for Fire Brigade alert pagers |
| 148.0000–149.0000 | | Fixed and Land Mobile. Gas and Electricity Boards paired with mobiles on 138.5–140.5MHz. Satellite uplinks |
| 148.56000 | | NOAA-series satellite telecommand uplink |
| 149.0000–149.9000 | | Mobile (Military). Used particularly by USAF and RAF and MOULD repeaters |
| 149.8500 | | Common channel at many military bases |
| 149.9000 | | Air Training Corps nationwide (channel 2) |
| 149.9000–150.0500 | | Radionavigation by satellite. Doppler shift position fixing using US satellites (TRANSIT) and Russian (COSNAV) paired with 399.9–400.05MHz |
| 150.0500–152.0000 | | Radio Astronomy and Oil Slick Markers |

**Table 5.1/2**  *continued*

| From-to | Pairing | Allocation |
|---|---|---|
| 150.1100<br>to<br>150.1850 | | Slick Markers |
| **152.0000-153.0000** | | Land Mobile police bases paired with mobiles at 143–144MHz |
| 152.0000<br>to<br>152.5500 | | Metropolitan police M2PM talkthrough |
| **153.0000-153.5000** | | National and local area radio paging systems |
| **153.5000-154.0000** | | Land Mobile (military) and meterological aids |
| **154.0000-156.0000** | | Fixed and Mobile (Emergency services). This band is used extensively for downlinks from hill-top repeaters to base stations |
| 154.0000<br>to<br>156.0000 | 146.0000<br>to<br>148.0000 | Police Bases |
| **156.0000-174.0000** | | Fixed & Mobile (land and Marine). The Marine VHF service falls within this band which also includes message handling services and mobile telephone systems. All NFM |
| 156.0000 | | Marine channel '0'. Lifeboats and Coastguard |
| 156.0000<br>to<br>157.4250 | | Marine channels single and split frequency Simplex |
| 156.8000 | | ★★★Marine Distress & Calling channel 16★★★ |
| 157.4500<br>to<br>158.4000 | | Private Marine channels & message handling services |

**Table 5.1/2** *continued*

| From-to | Pairing | Allocation |
|---------|---------|------------|
| 158.4000<br>to<br>158.5250 | | Private and Dockside using Simplex |
| 158.5375<br>to<br>159.9125 | | Digital Pacnets |
| 159.2500<br>to<br>160.5500 | | Private channels and message handling services and a few PMR channels |
| 160.5500<br>to<br>161.0000 | | Marine Channels |
| 161.0000<br>to<br>161.1000 | 459.1000<br>to<br>459.5000 | Paging systems acknowledge |
| 161.1250<br>to<br>161.5000 | | Private Marine channels |
| 161.5000<br>to<br>162.0500 | | Marine channels |
| 162.0500<br>to<br>163.0000 | | Private channels and message handling services |
| 163.0375<br>to<br>164.4125 | | Digital Pacnets |
| 163.9000 | 159.4000 | PMR (not always split) |
| 163.9250 | 159.4250 | PMR (not always split) |
| 163.9875 | | PMR |
| 164.0000 | | PMR |

**Table 5.1/2**   *continued*

| From-to | Pairing | Allocation |
|---------|---------|------------|
| 164.0875 | | PMR |
| 164.1250 | | PMR |
| 164.1875 | | PMR |
| 164.4375 to 165.0375 | | Private message handling services including paging and telephone patching |
| 165.0625 to 168.2500 | 169.8625 to 173.0500 | HIGH BAND PMR bases. Also extensive use by security/message handling services including nationwide links |
| 166.0000 | | Soyuz/Mir (Russian) satellite downlinks |
| 166.1000 to 166.6125 | | Extensively used by ambulances |
| 167.2000 | 172.2000 | HIGH BAND demonstration & short term hire channel bases |
| 167.9920 to 168.0080 | | Industrial, scientific & Medical |
| 168.31215 to 168.8375 | | Emergency service Fixed Links |
| 168.9500 to 169.8500 | | HIGH BAND PMR Simplex channels |
| 168.9750 | | BBC Engineering |
| 169.0125 to 169.7625 | | Short term hire channels (single frequency simplex) all NFM (used extensively during the RAC Rally) |

**Table 5.1/2** *continued*

| From-to | Pairing | Allocation |
|---------|---------|------------|
| 169.4375 to 169.7625 | | Pan-European paging system (ERMES) |
| 169.8625 to 173.0500 | 165.0625 to 168.2500 | PMR mobiles. Extensively used by security/ message handling services including nationwide links |
| 172.000 | 167.2000 | Short term hire mobiles |
| 170.4500 to 170.8000 | 165.8500 to 166.0000 | Private Security Firms mobiles |
| 170.9000 to 171.4250 | | Ambulance mobiles |
| 173.0500 to 173.2000 | | Low powered devices |
| 173.2000 to 173.3500 | | Low Powered telemetry and telecontrol |
| 173.3500 to 173.8000 | | Radio deaf aids, Medical and biological telemetry |
| 173.8000 to 175.0000 | | Radiomicrophones (de-regulated) |

**174.5000-225.0000**   Land Mobile, Fixed, Radiolocation & Radiomicrophones, Television Broadcasting (not UK) Band III upwards from 174MHz falls within the old Band III TV allocation and these frequencies have been released in the UK for Land Mobile. Most services

**Table 5.1/2**  *continued*

| From-to | Pairing | Allocation |
|---|---|---|
| | | operate on a 'Trunked' system where the mobile is automatically switched from one base station to another as in Cellular Radio |
| 174.0000 to 174.5000 | | Emergency service fixed links |
| 174.5000 to 176.5000 | | PMR Simplex channels & Radiomicrophones |
| 176.5000 to 183.5000 | 184.5000 to 191.5000 | PMR bases |
| 183.5000 to 184.5000 | | PMR Simplex channels |
| 184.5000 to 191.5000 | 176.5000 to 183.5000 | PMR mobiles |
| 191.5000 to 192.5000 | | PMR Simplex channels |
| 192.5000 to 199.5000 | 200.5000 to 207.5000 | PMR (Transport Industries)mobiles and trunked networks |
| 196.0000 to 198.0000 | 204.0000 to 206.000 | British Rail |
| 199.5000 to 200.5000 | | PMR Simplex channels |

**Table 5.1/2** *continued*

| From-to | Pairing | Allocation |
|---|---|---|
| 200.5000<br>to<br>207.5000 | 192.5000<br>to<br>199.5000 | PMR (Transport Industries) bases and trunked networks |
| 201.4625<br>to<br>203.7125 | 193.4625<br>to<br>195.7125 | London Transport |
| 207.5000<br>to<br>208.5000 | | PMR Simplex channels |
| 208.5000<br>to<br>215.5000 | 216.5000<br>to<br>223.5000 | PMR bases |
| 215.5000<br>to<br>216.5000 | | PMR Simplex channels |
| 216.5000<br>to<br>223.5000 | 208.5000<br>to<br>215.5000 | PMR mobiles |
| 223.5000<br>to<br>225.0000 | | PMR Simplex channels |
| **225.0000–328.6000** | | Aeronautical mobile (military) using AM simplex, ground-to-air, air-to-air, tactical, etc. Some satellite allocations |
| 235.0000<br>to<br>273.0000 | | Extensively used for military satellite downlinks (FleetSatcom West etc) |
| 243.0000 | | ***Military distress frequency*** Life-raft beacons, SARBE's, PIRBs, etc. Frequency monitored by COSPAS/SARSAT satellites |

**Table 5.1/2**  *continued*

| From-to | Pairing | Allocation |
|---|---|---|
| 257.8000 | | Common airfield frequency |
| 259.7000 | | NASA Shuttles (AM voice) |
| 296.8000 | | NASA Shuttles (AM voice particularly used on 'spacewalks') |
| 326.5000 to 328.5000 | | Radio astronomy (Jodrell Bank) |
| 344.0000 | | Common airfield frequency |
| 362.3000 | | Common airfield frequency |
| | 328.6000-335.4000 | Aeronautical radionavigation - ILS glideslope beams paired with VORs in the 108-118MHz band |
| | 335.4000-399.9000 | Aeronautical mobile (military) using AM simplex, ground-to-air, air-to-air, tactical, etc |
| 360.0440 to 361.4400 | | Band has been used by US ATS-series satellites |
| | 399.9000-400.0500 | Radionavigation by satellite. Doppler shift position fixing using US satellites (TRANSIT) and USSR (COSNAV) paired with 149.9-150.05MHz band |
| | 400.0000-400.1500 | Standard frequency and time signal satellites |
| | 401.0000-406.0000 | Fixed and mobile, meteorological satellites, space-earth communications |
| 401.0000 to 402.0000 | | Space-Earth communications |
| 401.0000 to 403.0000 | | Meteorological sondes & satellites |

**Table 5.1/2**  *continued*

| From-to | Pairing | Allocation |
|---|---|---|
| 401.0000 to 405.0000 | | Military telemetry links |
| **406.0000–406.1000** | | Mobile satellite space-earth communications |
| 406.05000 | | Emergency locator beacons (identification and location by satellite) |
| **406.1000–410.0000** | | Fixed and mobile (Government), radio astronomy & radio positioning aids |
| 406.5000 to 409.0000 | | North Sea oil rig positioning aids |
| **410.0000–420.0000** | | Fixed & mobile (Government). Extensively used by USAF using 25kHz channelling, Simplex |
| 412.0500 | | Frequency has been used by US ATS-series satellites |
| **420.0000–450.0000** | | Fixed, Mobile, Amateur & radiolocation |
| 420.0000 to 422.0000 | | Military MOULD links |
| 422.0000 to 425.0000 | | Military & Radio altimeters |
| 425.0250 to 425.4750 | 445.5250 to 445.9750 | PMR mobiles |
| 425.5250 to 428.9750 | 440.0250 to 443.4750 | PMR bases |

**Table 5.1/2**  *continued*

| From-to | Pairing | Allocation |
|---|---|---|
| 429.0000 to 431.0000 | | Military & Radiolocation |
| 431.00625 to 431.99375 | 448.00625 to 448.99375 | PMR mobiles (London only) |
| 430.0000 to 440.0000 | | 70cm Amateur Band & Military (Syledis radiolocation system and MOULD links). SSB, NFM, CW, slow and fast scan TV, RTTY, Amtor, Packet, etc |
| 440.0250 to 443.4750 | 425.5250 to 428.9750 | PMR bases. Many transport system users (taxis, buses, etc.) |
| 443.5000 to 445.5000 | | Military & radiolocation |
| 445.5250 to 445.9750 | 425.0250 to 425.4750 | PMR bases |
| 446.0250 to 446.4750 | | PMR simplex (extensively used for Outside Broadcast links) |
| 446.4750 | 452.250 | Fire channel 02 F |
| 448.00625 to 448.99375 | 431.00625 to 431.99375 | PMR Bases (London area only) |
| 449.7500 to 450.0000 | | Earth-Space Telecommand |

**Table 5.1/2**  *continued*

| From-to | Pairing | Allocation |
|---------|---------|------------|
| **450.0000–470.0000** | | Fixed & Mobile (including marine). Mostly PMR with some emergency services, Paging, telemetry, etc |
| 450.0000<br>to<br>451.0000 | 464.0000<br>to<br>465.0000 | B.T. Fixed links some police use |
| 451.0000<br>to<br>453.0000 | 464.9000<br>to<br>467.0000 | Extensively used for police bases and fixed links |
| 451.4000<br>451.4500 | | Fire brigade on-site hand-helds Ch1F<br>Fire brigade on-site hand-helds Ch 2F |
| 453.0250<br>to<br>453.9750 | 459.5250<br>to<br>460.4750 | PMR Bases |
| 454.0125<br>to<br>454.8250 | | Wide area paging systems |
| 455.0000<br>to<br>455.5000 | | BBC, ITV, ILR Base units for O.B.'s (some units paired with mobiles at +5.5MHz)<br>Airport ground services including tower relays (typically 455.4750 455.9750 etc) |
| 455.5000<br>to<br>456.0000 | | Some PMR (Scotland) & airport ground services |
| 456.0000<br>to<br>456.9750 | 461.50000<br>to<br>462.4750 | PMR Bases (extensively used at airports) |
| 456.9250 | 462.4250 | Short-term hire bases |

**Table 5.1/2**   *continued*

| From-to | Pairing | Allocation |
|---|---|---|
| 457.0000 to 457.5000 | 462.5000 to 463.0000 | Point-to-point links (fixed) |
| 457.50625 to 458.49375 | 463.00625 to 463.99375 | Scanning telemetry |
| 457.5250 | 467.5250 | On-board-ship communications (international) |
| 457.5500 | 467.5500 | On-board-ship communications (international) |
| 457.5750 | 467.5750 | On-board-ship communications (international) |
| 457.5250 | 467.7500 | On-board-ship communications (US/Canada system) |
| 457.5500 | 467.7750 | On-board-ship communications (US/Canada system) |
| 457.5750 | 467.8000 | On-board-ship communications (US/Canada system) |
| 457.6000 | 467.8250 | On-board-ship communications (US/Canada system) |
| 458.5000 to 459.5000 | | Model control, paging, telemetry & local communications |
| 458.5000 to 458.8000 | | Low power (1/2 Watt) telemetry |
| 459.1000 to 459.5000 | 161.0000 161.0000 | On-site paging systems (VHF channels are return 'acknowledge' signal) |
| 459.5250 to 460.4750 | 453.0250 to 453.9750 | PMR Mobiles |
| 460.5000 to 461.5000 | 467.0000 to 468.0000 | Point-to-point links & some airport ground services, Broadcast engineering, etc |

**Table 5.1/2**  *continued*

| From-to | Pairing | Allocation |
|---|---|---|
| 461.5000 to 462.4750 | 456.0000 to 456.9750 | PMR Mobiles |
| 462.4250 462.4750 | 456.9250 | Short-term hire channel mobiles Long-term hire (single frequency simplex) |
| 462.5000 to 463.0000 | 457.5000 to 458.5000 | Point-to-Point links (fixed) |
| 463.0000 to 464.0000 | 457.5000 to 458.5000 | Telemetry links (fixed) |
| 464.0000 | | Spot frequency has been used by some US & French satellites |
| 464.0000 to 465.0000 | 450.0000 to 457.0000 | B.T. Fixed links |
| 465.0000 to 467.0000 | 451.0000 to 453.0000 | Emergency service mobiles and fixed links (used by some car racing teams) |
| 466.0000 | | Spot frequency has been used by some Soviet 0cean reconnaisance satellites |
| 467.0000 to 467.8250 | | Point-to-point links & ILR brodacast links using simplex & On-board-ship communications |
| 467.5250 467.5500 467.5750 | 457.5250 457.5500 457.5750 | On-board-ship communications (international) On-board-ship communications (international) On-board-ship communications (international) |
| 467.7500 | 457.5250 | On-board-ship communications (US/Canada system) |

**Table 5.1/2**  *continued*

| From-to | Pairing | Allocation |
|---------|---------|------------|
| 467.7750 | 457.5500 | On-board-ship communications (US/Canada system) |
| 467.8000 | 457.5750 | On-board-ship communications (US/Canada system) |
| 467.8250 | 457.6000 | On-board-ship communications (US/Canada system) |
| 467.8250 to 468.0000 | 455.0000 to 462.0000 | Point-to-point links |
| 468.5000 to 469.0000 | | Some Outside broadcast links, model control and reserved for future PMR expansion |
| 469.0000 to 470.0000 | | Some Outside Broadcast link talkback and mobiles |
| 470.0000–854.0000 | | U.K. Band IV Television broadcasting, Studio talkback systems, Radio Astronomy & Aeronautical radionavigation, Russian/CIS communication satellites |
| 471.0000 to 585.0000 | | Television broadcasting Band IV |
| 537.0000 to 544.0000 | 716.000 to 725.000 | Studio talkback mobiles on unused broadcast channels |
| 582.0000 to 590.0000 | | Aeronavigation ground radar (due to be phased-out in 1995) |
| 590.0000 to 598.0000 | | Aeronavigation ground radar |

**Table 5.1/2**   *continued*

| From-to | Pairing | Allocation |
|---|---|---|
| 598.0000 to 606.0000 | | Aeronavigation ground radar (due to be phased-out in 1995) |
| 614.0000 | | Radio Astronomy (Cambridge & Jodrell Bank) |
| 610.0000 to 890.0000 | | Television Broadcasting Band V |
| 702.0000 to 726.0000 | | Soviet direct TV broadcast satellites |
| 716.0000 to 725.0000 | 537.0000 to 544.0000 | Studio talkback bases on unused broadcast channels |
| 800.0000 to 1000.0000 | | Molniya communication satellites (data & NFM) |
| **854.0000-862.0000** | | Fixed & land mobile |
| 854.0000 to 862.0000 | | Outside broadcast links |
| **862.0000-864.0000** | | Land mobile (emergency services) |
| **864.0000-870.0000** | | Mobile (not aeronautical) |
| 864.0000 to 868.0000 | | Digital portable telephones |
| **870.0000-889.0000** | | Fixed & Mobile(mostly military), Industrial, scientific & medical & Anti-theft devices. ETACS (cellular telephone) |

**Table 5.1/2** *continued*

| From-to | Pairing | Allocation |
|---|---|---|
| 872.0000 to 888.0000 | 917.0000 to 933.0000 | ETACS (cellular telephones) 25kHz steps with 12.5kHz offset |
| 886.0000 to 890.0000 | | Industrial, scientific & medical |
| 888.0000 to 889.0000 | | Anti-theft devices (1/2 Watt maximum) |
| **890.0000-915.0000** | | Mobile (TACS Cellular telephone & Government) |
| 890.0125 to 904.9875 | 935.0125 to 949.9875 | Cellular telephone mobiles (Full Duplex NFM) 25kHz steps with 12.5kHz offset |
| 905.0000 to 915.0000 | 950.0000 to 960.0000 | Pan-European Cellular system GSM using digital speech transmission |
| **915.0000-935.0000** | | Fixed & Mobile (Government) & Space communications, E-TACS Cellular telephones and new UK personal radio system |
| 917.0000 to 933.000 | 872.0000 to 888.0000 | ETACS Cellular telephones |
| 922.75000 926.06000 928.40000 | | Mir/Salyut TV picture downlinks Mir/Salyut Voice & Telecommand (NFM) Venera deep-space planetary probe |
| 933.00000 to 935.00000 | | New UK personal radio system |
| **935.0000-960.0000** | | Mobile (Cellular telephone) |

**Table 5.1/2**  *continued*

| From-to | Pairing | Allocation |
|---------|---------|------------|
| 935.0125 to 949.9875 | 890.0125 to 904.9875 | Cellular telephone bases (Full Duplex NFM) |
| 950.0000 to 960.0000 | 905.0000 to 915.0000 | GSM Pan-European Cellular telephone system |
| 960.0000–1215.0000 | | Aeronavigation (Distance measuring equipment - DME) & TACANS (radar transponders - IFF) |
| 1215.0000–1240.0000 | | Radiolocation and radionavigation by satellite |
| 1240.0000–1296.0000 | | Radiolocation |
| 1296.0000–1300.0000 | | Amateur Radio 23cm band (NFM, SSB, WBTV, etc) |
| 1300.0000–1365.0000 | | Amateur Radio 23cm band & Radiolocation (government) |
| 1365.0000–1427.0000 | | Radiolocation, Space research & satellite exploration |
| 1400.0000 to 1427.0000 | | Earth exploration satellites, astronomy & space research |
| 1427.0000–1429.0000 | | Fixed & Mobile (Government) & Earth-Space satellite links |
| 1429.0000–1450.0000 | | Fixed & Mobile (Government) |
| 1450.0000–1525.0000 | | Fixed & Mobile (telephony, telecontrol & telemetry) |
| 1525.0000–1530.0000 | | Fixed & land mobile & satellites (space-earth) |

**Table 5.1/2**  *continued*

| From-to | Pairing | Allocation |
|---|---|---|
| **1530.0000–1544.0000** | | Land mobile & maritime mobile satellite services (space-earth) |
| **1544.0000–1545.0000** | | Mobile satellite services |
| 1544.0000 to 1545.0000 | 1645.0000 to 1646.0000 | Space-Earth distress service |
| 1544.5000 | | NOAA9/10 Search & rescue beacon locator downlink |
| **1545.0000–1559.9000** | | Aeronautical mobile satellite service |
| **1559.0000–1626.5000** | | Aeronautical radionavigation & navigation satellites & radio astronomy |
| **1626.5000–1645.0000** | | Maritime mobile satellite service |
| **1645.0000–1646.5000** | | Mobile satellite service |
| 1645.0000 to 1646.0000 | 1544.0000 to 1545.0000 | Earth-Space distress |
| **1646.5000–1660.0000** | | Aeronautical mobile, satellite services (uplinks) & astronomy |
| **1660.0000–1668.0000** | | Fixed & mobile & astronomy |
| **1668.0000–1670.0000** | | Fixed links (government) & astronomy |
| **1670.0000–1700.0000** | | Fixed (PTO & government) & land mobile & meteorological satellites. Goes, NOAA and Meteosat transmissions - for details see satellite section |
| **1700.0000–2000.0000** | | Fixed & land mobile (PTO & government), satellite operations & astronomy |

There follows a glossary of abbreviations and definitions used in Table 5.1/2.

*Aeronautical Distress* Frequencies allocated solely for use by aircraft in distress.

*Aeronautical mobile* Allocations for communication between aircraft and ground stations. The main international band lies between 118-137MHz.

*Aeronautical Radionavigation* Radio beacons for aircraft navigation. They include VHF omni-range (VOR), doppler VOR (DVOR), distance measuring equipment (DME), instrument landing systems (ILS), tactical navigation (TACAN), outer, middle and inner fan markers (OM, MM, IM), etc.

*Aeronautical search and rescue* Frequencies allocated solely for aircraft involved in search and rescue (SAR) duties.

*Amateur* The amateur service is for use by licensed individuals for the purpose of self-training and experimentation.

*Astronomy* Frequencies allocated for research into radio emissions from sources such as other galaxies.

*Broadcast* Transmissions intended for reception by a large group or even the general public.

*BT* British Telecom.

*Carphone* A communication system fitted to a vehicle which communicates with a base station connected to the public telephone system.

*Citizens Band* A low powered communications service available to the public.

*Cordless 'phone* A telephone handset that does not require direct connection to the exchange line.

*COSPAS/SARSAT* Joint US, USSR, Canadian and French rescue service using weather satellite to fix the position of emergency rescue beacons.

*ELINT* Electronic intelligence gathering (typically spy satellites).

*Emergency service* Allocations for police, fire and ambulance services.

*EPIRB* Emergency position indicating rescue beacon.

*Fixed* A base station linked to another base station or non-mobile facility such as a repeater. Often known as point-to-point services.

*FSK* Frequency shift keying.

*IFF* Identify — friend or foe.

*ILR* Independent local radio.

*ISM* Industrial, scientific and medical. These allocations are for equipment which use radio waves to function. These allocations are not for communication purposes.

*Land Mobile* Communications between a fixed base and mobile or portable equipment or between the mobile stations themselves.

*Locator* The transmission of signals for navigation, position fixing and tracking.

*Maritime Mobile* Services for ship-to-shore and ship-to-ship communications.

*Message handling* Similar to PMR but many stations operating through a central operator at a base station.

*Meteorology* The transmission of weather data from remote platforms such as sondes, buoys or satellites to ground stations.

*Military* British military allocations cover the army, Royal Air Force, Royal Navy, military police and United States Air Force (USAF).

*Mobile* Any mobile service. Air, marine or land.

*Mobile satellite service* Communication between a mobile station and satellite (usually the satellite is acting as a relay or repeater to a distant ground station).

*MOD* Ministry of Defence.

*Model Control* The use of radio signals to control the movement of model boats, aircraft and cars.

*MOULD* British military communication system making extensive use of repeaters.

*NOAA* National Oceanic and Atmospheric Administration (USA).

*On-site paging* A paging service operating in a restricted area such as a hospital, factory or hotel.

*Pager* A miniature radio receiver which emits a tone when it receives a signal with its individually assigned code.

*Positioning aid* A beacon used to emit a transmission for precise positioning or navigation. Often used for positioning such things as oil rigs.

*PMR* Private mobile radio. Allocations for non-government users for communication between base stations and mobile units.

*Radio altimeter* The use of radio signals to measure the height of an aircraft above ground.

*Radio microphone* A microphone used in broadcast studios, theatres and the film industry where the unit transmits the sound as a low powered radio signal which is picked-up by a remote receiver and then amplified.

*Radiophone* See Carphone.

*SARBE* Search and rescue beacon. A small radio beacon attached to a lifejacket or dinghy.

*Satellite navigation* Position fixing by reference to transmissions from a satellite.

*Selcal* Selective calling system where a receiver only activates when it receives a pre-determined code.

*Slick marker* A low powered floating beacon used to check the movement of oil slicks.

*Standard frequency* Transmission from a highly stable transmitter which is accurate enough to be used for calibration and reference. The signals often include coded signals of highly accurate time as well.

*TACS* Total access communications system (cellular telephones)

*Telecontrol* A signal containing command information to control remote equipment.

*Telemetry* A radio signal containing data in coded form.

*Television* A radio signal containing visual images.

*Weather satellite* A space satellite that sends weather pictures back to an earth station.

*Wide area paging* A paging service not confined to a private site.

## Aeronautical bands

Aeronautical and marine bands, unlike all other bands, are standard world wide. Aircraft transmissions are of two kinds: civilian and military.

Civilian aircraft transmissions use two bands: HF using SSB for long distance communication, and VHF for communications up to distances of several hundred miles. All communications (civilian and military) are amplitude modulated.

A list of civilian and military airports and corresponding transmission frequencies are given and are believed to be current. However, it should be noted that they are occasionally changed.

### Table 5.3 British and Irish airports and air/ground stations

| *Airfield* | | |
|---|---|---|
| **Aberdeen (Dyce)** | EGPD    civ | 7 miles NW of Aberdeen |
| MET | 125.725 (Scottish Volmet) 118.300 (Kirkwall Met) | |
| ATIS | 121.850, 114.300 | |
| APPROACH | 120.400 | |
| TOWER | 118.100 | |
| GROUND | 121.700 | |
| VDF | 120.400, 121.250, 128.300 | |
| RADAR | 120.400, 128.300 | |
| FIRE VEHICLES | 121.600 | |
| **Aberporth** | EGUC    mil | 5 miles NE of Cardigan |
| AFIS | 122.150, 259.000 | |

**Table 5.3**  *continued*

*Airfield*

| | | | |
|---|---|---|---|
| **Abingdon** | EGUD | mil | 5 miles SW of Oxford |
| TOWER | 130.250, 256.500 | | |
| SRE | 122.100, 123.300, 120.900, 256.500 | | |

| | | | |
|---|---|---|---|
| **Alconbury** | EGWZ | mil | 4 miles NW of Huntingdon |
| ATIS | 231.175 | | |
| MATZ | see Wyton | | |
| TOWER | 122.100, 383.45, 257.800, 315.100 | | |
| GROUND | 259.825 | | |
| DISPATCH | 342.225 | | |
| DEPARTURE | 134.050, 375.535 | | |
| COMMAND POST | 278.050, 340.125 | | |
| METRO | 358.600, 284.925 | | |

| | | | |
|---|---|---|---|
| **Alderney** | EGJA | civ | Channel Islands |
| TOWER | 125.350 | | |
| APPROACH | 128.650 (Guernsey) | | |

| | | | |
|---|---|---|---|
| **Andrewsfield** | EGSL | civ | near Braintree (Essex) |
| A/G | 130.550 | | |

| | | | |
|---|---|---|---|
| **Audley End** | EG | civ | near Saffron Walden (Essex) |
| A/G | 122.350 | | |

| | | | |
|---|---|---|---|
| **Badminton** | EG | civ | 6 miles NE of Chipping Sodbury |
| A/G | 123.175 | | |

| | | | |
|---|---|---|---|
| **Bagby** | | civ | Thirsk |
| A/G | 123.250 | | |

| | | | |
|---|---|---|---|
| **Baldonnel/Casement** | EIME | civ | Republic of Ireland |
| APPROACH | 122.000 | | |
| TOWER | 123.500 | | |
| GROUND | 123.100 | | |
| RADAR | 122.800 | | |
| | 122.300 (Dublin Military) | | |
| PAR | 129.700 | | |

| | | | |
|---|---|---|---|
| **Bantry** | EI | civ | Republic of Ireland |
| A/G | 122.400 | | |

| | | | |
|---|---|---|---|
| **Barra** | EGPR | civ | Traigh Mhor (Western Isles) |
| AFIS | 130.650 | | |

**Table 5.3**  *continued*

*Airfield*

| | | | |
|---|---|---|---|
| **Barrow** | EGNL | civ | North end of Walney Island |
| A/G | 123.200 | | |
| TOWER | 123.200 | | |
| | | | |
| **Barton** | EG | | 5 miles W of Manchester |
| A/G | 122.700 | | |
| | | | |
| **Battersea Heliport** | EGLW | civ | River Thames at Battersea |
| TOWER | 122.900 | | |
| | | | |
| **Beccles Heliport** | EGSM | civ | 2 miles SE of Beccles (Suffolk) |
| A/G | 134.600 | | |
| | | | |
| **Bedford** | EGVW | mil | 5 miles N of city at Thurleigh |
| MATZ | 124.400 | | |
| APPROACH | 130.700, 124.400, 265.300, 277.250 | | |
| TOWER | 130.000, 337.925 | | |
| VDF | 130.700, 130.000, 124.400, 277.250 | | |
| PAR | 118.375, 356.700 | | |
| | | | |
| **Belfast Aldergrove** | EGAA | civ | 13 miles NW of Belfast |
| APPROACH | 120.000, 310.000 | | |
| TOWER | 118.300, 310.000 | | |
| DISPATCHER | 241.825 | | |
| GROUND | 121.750 | | |
| VDF | 120.900 | | |
| RADAR | 120.000, 120.900, 310.000 | | |
| FIRE VEHICLES | 121.600 | | |
| | | | |
| **Belfast City** | EGAC | civ | 2 miles E of city centre |
| APPROACH | 130.850 | | |
| TOWER | 130.750 | | |
| SRE | 134.800 | | |
| | | | |
| **Bembridge** | EGHJ | civ | Isle of Wight |
| A/G | 123.250 | | |
| | | | |
| **Benbecula** | EGPL | civ | |
| APPROACH | 119.200 | | |
| TOWER | 119.200 | | |
| | | | |
| **Benson** | EGUB | mil | 10 miles SE Oxford city |
| MATZ | 120.900 | | |
| APPROACH | 120.900, 122.1, 362.3, 358.800 | | |

**Table 5.3**  *continued*

| *Airfield* | | | |
|---|---|---|---|
| TOWER | 122.100, 279.350 | | |
| GROUND | 340.325 | | |
| VDF | 119.000 | | |
| SRE | 119.000 | | |
| **Bentwaters** | EGVJ | mil | 6 miles NE Woodbridge (Suffolk) |
| ATIS | 341.650 | | |
| MATZ | 119.000 | | |
| APPROACH | 119.000, 362.075 | | |
| TOWER | 122.100, 264.925, 257.800 | | |
| GROUND | 244.775 | | |
| DISPATCH | 356.825 | | |
| DEPARTURE | 258.975 | | |
| SRE/PAR | 119.000, 362.075 | | |
| COMMAND POST | 386.900 | | |
| | ** due for closure ** | | |
| **Biggin Hill** | EGKB | civ | 4 miles N Westerham (Kent) |
| ATIS | 121.875 | | |
| APPROACH | 129.400 | | |
| TOWER | 138.400 | | |
| RADAR | 132.700 (Thames) | | |
| **Birmingham** | EGBB | civ | 6 miles SE of city at Elmdon |
| ATIS | 120.725 | | |
| ATC | 131.325 | | |
| APPROACH | 131.325 | | |
| TOWER | 118.300 | | |
| GROUND | 121.800 | | |
| VDF | 131.325 | | |
| RADAR | 131.325, 118.050 | | |
| FIRE VEHICLES | 121.600 | | |
| **Blackbushe** | EGLK | civ | 4 miles W Camberley (Hants) |
| AFIS | 122.300 | | |
| **Blackpool** | EGNH | civ | South of Town at Squire's Gate |
| APPROACH | 135.950 | | |
| TOWER | 118.400 | | |
| VDF | 135.950, 118.400 | | |
| SRE | 119.950 | | |
| **Bodmin** | EG | civ | 2 miles NE Bodmin (Cornwall) |
| A/G | 122.700 | | |

**Table 5.3**  *continued*

*Airfield*

| | | | |
|---|---|---|---|
| **Booker** | see Wymcombe | | |
| **Boscombe Down** | EGDM | mil | 5 miles N Salisbury |
| MATZ | 126.700, 380.025 | | |
| ATIS | 263.500 | | |
| APPROACH | 126.700, 276.850, 291.650 | | |
| TOWER | 130.000, 370.100 | | |
| PAR | 130.750 | | |
| SRE | 126.700 | | |
| **Boulmer** | EGOM | SAR | 8 miles E of Alnwick |
| A/G Boulmer Rescue | 123.100, 254.425, 282.800, 299.100 | | |
| **Bourn** | EGSN | civ | 7 miles W Cambridge |
| A/G | 129.800 | | |
| **Bournemouth** | EGHH | civ | 4 miles NE Bournemouth |
| ATIS | 121.950 | | |
| APPROACH | 119.625 | | |
| TOWER | 125.600 | | |
| GROUND | 121.700 | | |
| RADAR | 119.625, 118.650 | | |
| FIRE VEHICLES | 121.600 | | |
| **Bridlington** | EG | civ | |
| A/G | 123.250 | | |
| **Bristol** | EGGD | civ | 7 miles SW Bristol |
| ATIS | 121.750 | | |
| APPROACH | 132.400 | | |
| TOWER | 133.850 | | |
| VDF | 132.400 | | |
| SRE | 124.350 | | |
| **Brize Norton** | EGVN | mil | 5 miles SW Witney (Oxon) |
| MATZ | 119.000 | | |
| ATIS | 235.150 | | |
| APPROACH | 133.750, 119.000, 342.450, 362.300 | | |
| TOWER | 126.500, 257.800, 381.200 | | |
| GROUND | 126.500, 370.300 | | |
| DIRECTOR | 130.075, 382.550 | | |
| RADAR | 134.300, 257.100 | | |

**Table 5.3**  *continued*

*Airfield*

| | | | |
|---|---|---|---|
| **Brough** | EG | civ | 6 miles W of Hull |
| APPROACH | 118.225 | | |
| TOWER | 130.550 | | |

| | | | |
|---|---|---|---|
| **Caernarfon** | EG | civ | |
| A/G | 122.250 | | |

| | | | |
|---|---|---|---|
| **Cambridge** | EGSC | civ | 2 miles E of city |
| AP/DF | 123.600 | | |
| TOWER | 122.200, 372.450 | | |
| SRE | 130.750 | | |
| FIRE | 121.600 fire vehicles | | |

| | | | |
|---|---|---|---|
| **Cardiff (Rhoose)** | EGFF | civ | 12 miles SW of Cardiff |
| MET | 128.600 London Volmet South | | |
| ATIS | 119.475 | | |
| AP/DF | 125.850, 277.225 | | |
| TOWER | 125.000 | | |
| RAD/PAR | 125.850, 120.050 | | |

| | | | |
|---|---|---|---|
| **Carlisle (Crosby)** | EGNC | civ | 5 miles NE of Carlisle |
| APPROACH/ | | | |
|  TOWER | 123.600 | | |
| DF | 123.600 | | |

| | | | |
|---|---|---|---|
| **Carrickfin** | EI | civ | Republic of Ireland |
| A/G | 129.800 | | |

| | | | |
|---|---|---|---|
| **Chichester** | EGHR | civ | N of Chichester (Sussex) |
| APPROACH | 122.500 | | |
| TOWER | 120.650 | | |
| A/G | 122.450 | | |
| VDF | 122.450 | | |

| | | | |
|---|---|---|---|
| **Chivenor** | EGDC | mil | 4 miles W of Barnstaple (Devon) |
| MATZ/APP | 130.200, 122.100, 362.300, 364.775 | | |
| TOWER/GROUND | 122.100, 362.450 | | |
| GROUND | 122.100, 379.925 | | |
| VDF | 130.200 | | |
| PAR | 123.300 | | |
| SRE | 122.100, 362.300 | | |

| | | | |
|---|---|---|---|
| **Church Fenton** | EGXG | mil | 6 miles NW of Selby (Yorks) |
| MATZ/APPROACH | 126.500, 282.075, 362.300 | | |

**Table 5.3**  *continued*

*Airfield*

| | | | |
|---|---|---|---|
| TOWER | 122.100, 262.700, 257.800 | | |
| GROUND | 122.100, 340.200 | | |
| PAR | 123.300 | | |
| SRE | 231.00, 362.300 | | |
| DEPARTURE | | | |
| (Linton) | 129.150, 381.075, 292.800 | | |

| **Clacton** | EG | civ | West of Clacton (Essex) |
|---|---|---|---|
| A/G | 122.325 | | |

| **Colerne** | EG | mil | near Bath |
|---|---|---|---|
| A/G | 122.100 | | |

| **Coltishall** | EGYC | mil | 9 miles N of Norwich (Norfolk) |
|---|---|---|---|
| MATZ/APPROACH | 125.900, 122.100, 379.275, 293.425, 342.250 | | |
| TOWER | 122.100, 142.290, 288.850 | | |
| GROUND | 269.450 | | |
| VDF | 125.900, 122.100, 293.425, 342.250 | | |
| SRE | 125.900, 123.300, 293.425, 342.250 | | |
| PAR | 123.300 | | |
| DIRECTOR | 244.750 | | |

| **Compton Abbas** | EGHA | civ | 2 miles E of Shaftesbury (Dorset) |
|---|---|---|---|
| A/G | 122.700 | | |

| **Coningsby** | EGXC | mil | 15 miles NE of Sleaford (Lincs) |
|---|---|---|---|
| MATZ | 120.800 | | |
| APPROACH | 120.800, 122.100, 312.225, 362.300 | | |
| TOWER | 121.100, 120.800, 275.875 | | |
| GROUND | 122.100, 318.150 | | |
| SRE | 120.800 | | |
| PAR | 123.300, 312.225, 362.300 | | |
| DEPARTURE | 344.625 | | |

| **Connaught** | EIKN | civ | Republic of Ireland |
|---|---|---|---|
| TOWER | 130.700 | | |
| GROUND | 121.900 | | |

| **Cork** | EICK | civ | Republic of Ireland |
|---|---|---|---|
| MET | 127.000 Dublin Volmet | | |
| APPROACH | 119.900 | | |
| TOWER | 119.300, 121.700 | | |
| GROUND | 121.800 | | |

**Table 5.3** *continued*

---

*Airfield*

---

| | | | |
|---|---|---|---|
| **Cosford** | EGWC | civ | 9 miles NW of Wolverhampton |
| APPROACH | 276.125, 362.300 | | |
| TOWER | 122.100, 357.125 | | |

---

| | | | |
|---|---|---|---|
| **Cottesmore** | EGXJ | mil | 4 miles NE of Oakham (Leics) |
| MATZ | 123.300 | | |
| APPROACH/DF | 123.300, 380.950 | | |
| TOWER | 122.100, 130.200, 370.050, 257.800 | | |
| GROUND | 122.200, 336.375 | | |
| PAR | 123.300 | | |
| SRE | 123.300, 380.950 | | |
| DEPARTURE | 130.200, 376.575 | | |

---

| | | | |
|---|---|---|---|
| **Coventry** | EGBE | civ | 3 miles S of Coventry |
| APROACH | 119.250 | | |
| TOWER | 119.250, 124.800 | | |
| GROUND | 121.700 | | |
| VDF | 119.250, 122.000 | | |
| SRE | 119.250, 122.000 | | |
| FIRE | 121.600 fire vehicles | | |

---

| | | | |
|---|---|---|---|
| **Cranfield** | EGTC | civ | 4 miles E of M1 junctions 13/14 |
| ATIS | 121.875 | | |
| APPROACH | 122.850, 362.150 | | |
| TOWER | 123.200, 122.850, 341.800 | | |
| VDF | 122.850, 123.200, 124.550 | | |
| RAD | 122.850, 372.100 | | |

---

| | | | |
|---|---|---|---|
| **Cranwell** | EGYD | mil | 4 miles NW of Sleaford (Lincs) |
| MATZ | 119.000 | | |
| APPROACH | 122.100, 119.000, 340.475, 362.300 | | |
| TOWER | 122.100, 379.525, 257.800 | | |
| GROUND | 297.900 | | |
| SRE | 123.300 | | |
| PAR | 123.300 | | |

---

| | | | |
|---|---|---|---|
| **Crossland Moor** | EG | civ | 3 miles SW Huddersfield |
| A/G | 122.200 | | |

---

| | | |
|---|---|---|
| **Croughton** | EG | mil |
| A/G | 343.600, 344.850 | |

---

| | | |
|---|---|---|
| **Crowfield** | EG | civ |
| A/G | 122.775 | |

---

**Table 5.3**  *continued*

---

*Airfield*

---

| | | | |
|---|---|---|---|
| **Culdrose** | EGDR | mil | 1 mile SE of Helston (Cornwall) |
| ATIS | 305.600 | | |
| APPROACH/MATZ | 134.050, 241.950 | | |
| TOWER | 122.100, 123.300, 380.225 | | |
| GROUND | 310.200 | | |
| RADAR | 122.100, 134.050, 241.950, 339.950 | | |
| PAR | 122.100, 123.300, 259.750, 339.950 | | |

---

| **Cumbernauld** | EGPG | civ | 6 miles SW of Falkirk (Strathclyde) |
|---|---|---|---|

---

| **Denham** | EGLD | civ | 1 mile N of M1 junction 1 (Bucks) |
|---|---|---|---|
| A/G | 130.725 | | |

---

| **Dishforth** | EGXD | mil | 4 miles E of Ripon (Yorks) |
|---|---|---|---|
| MATZ | Leeming | | |
| APPROACH | 122.100, 379.675, 362.300 | | |
| TOWER | 122.100, 259.825 | | |

---

| **Dounreay Thurso** | EGPY | civ | 8 miles W of Thurso |
|---|---|---|---|
| AFIS | 122.400 (only by prior arrangement) | | |

---

| **Dublin** | EIDW | civ | |
|---|---|---|---|
| MET | 122.700 | | |
| ATIS | 118.250 | | |
| APPROACH | 121.100 | | |
| TOWER | 118.600 | | |
| GROUND | 121.800 | | |
| SRE | 119.550, 118.500, 118.600, 121.100 | | |

---

| **Dundee** | EGPN | civ | 2 Miles W of Dundee |
|---|---|---|---|
| APPROACH/ TOWER | 122.900 | | |

---

| **Dunkeswell** | EG | civ | 5 miles NW of Honiton (Devon) |
|---|---|---|---|
| A/G | 123.475 | | |

---

| **Dunsfold** | EGTD | civ | 9 miles S of Guildford (Surrey) |
|---|---|---|---|
| APPROACH | 122.550, 312.625, 367.375 | | |
| TOWER | 124.325, 375.400 | | |
| VDF | 122.550, 124.325 | | |
| RAD | 119.825,122.550, 291.900 | | |

---

| **Duxford** | EG | civ | 9 miles S of Cambridge |
|---|---|---|---|
| AFIS | 122.075 | | |

---

82 Scanners

**Table 5.3** *continued*

*Airfield*

| | | | |
|---|---|---|---|
| **Earls Colne**<br>A/G | EGSR<br>122.425 | civ | 5 miles SE of Halstead (Essex) |
| **East Midlands**<br>MET<br>APPROACH<br>TOWER<br>GROUND<br>VDF<br>SRE<br>FIRE | EGNX<br>126.600 (London Volmet North)<br>119.650<br>124.000<br>121.900<br>119.650<br>124.000, 120.125<br>121.600 (fire vehicles) | civ | Castle Donnington, off M1 |
| **Edinburgh**<br>MET<br>ATIS<br>APPROACH<br>TOWER<br>GROUND<br>VDF<br>RAD<br>FIRE | EGPH<br>125.725 Scottish Volmet<br>132.075<br>121.200, 130.400 (departing gliders), 257.800<br>118.700, 257.800<br>121.750, 257.800<br>121.200, 118.700<br>121.200, 128.975<br>121.600 (fire vehicles) | civ | 8 miles W of Edinburgh |
| **Elstree**<br>A/G | EGTR<br>122.400 | civ | 12 miles NW London city centre |
| **Elvington**<br>See Church Fenton | EGYK | mil | |
| **Enniskillen St<br> Angelo**<br>A/G | EGAB<br><br>123.200 | civ | 5 miles N Enniskillen (N. Ireland) |
| **Enstone**<br>A/G | EG<br>129.875 | civ | 5 miles SE of Chipping Norton |
| **Exeter**<br>APPROACH/DF<br>TOWER<br>SRE | EGTE<br>128.150<br>119.800<br>128.150, 119.050 | civ | 4 miles E of Exeter |
| **Fairford**<br>MATZ/APPROACH<br>TOWER<br>GROUND | EGVA<br>Brize Norton<br>119.150, 357.575<br>259.975 | mil | N of Swindon |

**Table 5.3**   *continued*

---

*Airfield*

---

| | | | |
|---|---|---|---|
| DISPATCHER | 379.475 | | |
| COMMAND POST | 371.200, 307.800 | | |
| METRO | 358.600 | | |

---

| **Fairoaks** | EGTF | civ | 3 miles N of Woking |
|---|---|---|---|
| AFIS and A/G | 123.425 | | |

---

| **Farnborough** | EGUF | mil | W of A325 |
|---|---|---|---|
| | EGLF | civ | |
| A/G | 130.050 | | |
| APPROACH | 134.350, 336.275 | | |
| TOWER | 122.500, 357.400 | | |
| PAR | 130.050, 353.850 | | |
| DISPATCHER | 254.850 | | |

---

| **Fenland** | EGCL | civ | Holbeach (Lincolnshire) |
|---|---|---|---|
| AFIS and A/G | 122.925 | | |

---

| **Fife** | see Glenrothes | | |
|---|---|---|---|

---

| **Filton (Bristol)** | EGTG | mil | 4 miles N of Bristol |
|---|---|---|---|
| APPROACH | 122.275, 127.975, 256.125 | | |
| TOWER | 124.950, 342.025 | | |
| VDF | 122.275 | | |
| SRE | 132.350 | | |

---

| **Finningly** | EGXI | mil | SE of Doncaster |
|---|---|---|---|
| MATZ | 120.350 | | |
| APPROACH | 120.350, 358.775 | | |
| TOWER | 122.100, 379.550 | | |
| GROUND | 340.175 | | |
| SRE | 120.350, 285.125, 315.500, 344.000 | | |
| PAR | 123.300, 383.500, 385.400 | | |

---

| **Flotta** | EG | civ | Centre of Orkney Island |
|---|---|---|---|
| A/G | 122.150 | | |

---

| **Galway (Carnmore)** | EICM | civ | Republic of Ireland |
|---|---|---|---|
| A/G/TOWER | 122.500 | | |

---

| **Gamston (Retford)** | EGNE | civ | |
|---|---|---|---|
| A/G | 130.475 | | |

---

| **Gatwick** | see London Gatwick | | |
|---|---|---|---|

**Table 5.3** *continued*

| *Airfield* | | | |
|---|---|---|---|
| **Glasgow** | EGPF | Civ | 6 miles W of City Centre |
| MET | 125.725 (Scottish Voomet) | | |
| | 135.375 (London Volmet Main) | | |
| ATIS | 115.400 | | |
| APPROACH | 119.100 | | |
| TOWER | 118.800 | | |
| GROUND | 121.700 | | |
| RADAR | 119.100, 119.300, 121.300 | | |
| FIRE VEHICLES | 121.600 | | |
| **Glenrothes (Fife)** | EGPJ | civ | |
| A/G | 130.450 | | |
| **Goodwood** | see Chichester | | |
| **Gloucester** | | | |
| **(Staverton)** | EGBJ | civ | Gloucester and Cheltenham |
| APPROACH | 125.650, 120.970 | | |
| TOWER | 125.650 | | |
| VDF | 125.650, 122.900 | | |
| SRE | 122.900 | | |
| FIRE VEHICLES | 121.600 | | |
| **Great Yarmouth** | EGSD | gov | North Denes |
| A/G | 120.450, 122.375 | | |
| HF A/G | 3.488, 5.484 MHz | | |
| **Guernsey** | EGJB | civ | 3 miles S of St Peter Port |
| ATIS | 109.400 | | |
| APPROACH | 128.650 | | |
| TOWER | 119.950 | | |
| GROUND | 121.800 | | |
| VDF | 128.650, 124.500 | | |
| SRE | 118.900, 124.500 | | |
| **Halfpenny Green** | EGBO | civ | 6 miles W of Dudley |
| AFIS | 123.000 | | |
| GROUND | 121.950 | | |
| **Hatfield** | EGTH | civ | 2 miles S Welwyn Garden City |
| APPROACH | 123.350, 343.700 | | |
| TOWER | 130.800, 359.450 | | |
| SRE | 123.350, 119.300, 343.700 | | |

**Table 5.3**  *continued*

---

*Airfield*

---

| | | | |
|---|---|---|---|
| **Haverfordwest**<br>**AFIS** | EGFE<br>122.200 | mil | 2 miles N of town |

---

| | | | |
|---|---|---|---|
| **Hawarden**<br>APPROACH<br>TOWER<br>VDF<br>RADAR | EGNR<br>123.350<br>124.950, 336.325<br>123.350, 129.850<br>129.850 | civ | 4 miles W of Chester |

---

| | | |
|---|---|---|
| **Heathrow** | see London Heathrow | |

---

| | | | |
|---|---|---|---|
| **Henstridge**<br>A/G | EGHS<br>130.275 | civ | Somerset S of A30 |

---

| | | | |
|---|---|---|---|
| **Hethel**<br>A/G | EGSK<br>122.350 | civ | 7 miles SW of Norwich |

---

| | | | |
|---|---|---|---|
| **Honington**<br>MATZ<br>APPROACH<br>TOWER<br>GROUND<br>DEPARTURE<br>SRE<br>PAR | EHXH<br>129.050<br>129.050, 309.950, 344.000<br>122.100, 283.275, 257.900<br>241.975<br>123.300, 309.950<br>129.050, 254.875, 309.950, 338.975, 344.000<br>123.300, 358.750, 385.400 | mil | N of Bury St Edmunds (Suffolk) |

---

| | | | |
|---|---|---|---|
| **Hucknall**<br>A/G | EGNA<br>130.800 | civ | 1 miles SW of town (Notts) |

---

| | | | |
|---|---|---|---|
| **Humberside**<br>APPROACH<br>TOWER<br>VDF<br>FIRE VEHICLES | EGNJ<br>123.150<br>118.550<br>123.150<br>121.600 | civ | 15 miles E of Scunthorpe |

---

| | | | |
|---|---|---|---|
| **Inverness (Dalcross)**<br>MET<br>APPROACH/<br>  TOWER | EGPE<br>125.725 (Scottish Volmet)<br><br>122.600 | civ | 8 miles NE Inverness |

---

| | | | |
|---|---|---|---|
| **Ipswich**<br>A/G | EGSE<br>118.325 | civ | 2 miles SE Ipswich |

---

**Table 5.3**  *continued*

---

*Airfield*

---

| | | | |
|---|---|---|---|
| **Islay (port Ellen)** | EGPI | civ | South end of Island |
| **AFIS** | 123.150 | | |

---

| | | | |
|---|---|---|---|
| **Jersey** | EGJJ | civ | 3 miles W of St. Helier |
| MET | 128.600 (London Volmet South) | | |
| ATIS | 112.200 | | |
| APPROACH | 120.300 | | |
| TOWER | 199.450 | | |
| GROUND | 121.900 | | |
| FIRE VEHICLES | 121.600 | | |

---

| | | | |
|---|---|---|---|
| **Kemble** | EGDK | mil | 4 miles SW Cirencester |
| MATZ | 118.900 | | |
| APPROACH | 118.900, 123.300 | | |
| TOWER | 118.900 | | |

---

| | | | |
|---|---|---|---|
| **Kinloss** | EGQK | mil | 3 miles NE of Foress (Grampian) |
| MET | 118.300 | | |
| MATZ | Lossiemouth | | |
| APPROACH | 119.350, 362.300, 376.650 | | |
| TOWER | 122.100, 336.350, 257.800 | | |
| DISPATCHER | 358.475 | | |
| OPERATIONS | 259.825 | | |
| SRE | 123.300, 259.975, 311.325 | | |
| PAR | 123.300, 370.050, 376.525 | | |

---

| | | | |
|---|---|---|---|
| **Kirkwall** | EGPA | civ | Orkney |
| MET | 118.300 | | |
| APPROACH/ | | | |
|   TOWER | 118.300 | | |

---

| | | | |
|---|---|---|---|
| **Lakenheath** | EGUL | mil | 5 miles N of Barton Mills (Suffolk) |
| APPROACH | 123.300, 398.350 | | |
| RAPCON | 398.350 | | |
| TOWER | 122.100, 358.675, 257.800 | | |
| GROUND | 397.975 | | |
| DISPATCHER | 300.825 | | |
| DEPARTURE | 123.300, 315.575 | | |
| COMMAND POST | 269.075 | | |
| METRO | 257.750 | | |
| SRE/PAR | 123.300, 243.600, 262.925, 290.825, 338.675 | | |
| SRE/PAR | 149.650 (NFM) | | |

---

**Table 5.3**  *continued*

---

*Airfield*

---

| | | | |
|---|---|---|---|
| **Lands End (St. Just)** | EGHC | civ | 6 miles W of Penzance |
| A/G | 130.700 | | |
| APPROACH/ | | | |
|   TOWER | 130.700 | | |

---

| | | | |
|---|---|---|---|
| **Lasham** | EGHL | civ | 5 miles S of Basingstoke |
| A/G | 122.875 | | |

---

| | | | |
|---|---|---|---|
| **Lashenden** | EGHK | civ | 10 miles SE of Maidstone |
| A/G | 122.000 | | |

---

| | | | |
|---|---|---|---|
| **Leavesden** | EGTI | civ | 2 miles NW of Watford |
| APPROACH/ | | | |
|   TOWER | 122.150 | | |
| VDF | 122.150 | | |
| SRE | 122.400 | | |

---

| | |
|---|---|
| **Leconfield Rescue** | EGXV  mil |
| A/G | 122.100, 244.875, 282.800 |

---

| | | | |
|---|---|---|---|
| **Leeds-Bradford** | EGNM | civ | Half way between Leeds & Bradford |
| MET | 126.600 (London Volmet North) | | |
| APPROACH/VDF | 123.750 | | |
| TOWER | 120.300 | | |
| SRE | 121.050 | | |
| FIRE VEHICLES | 121.600 | | |

---

| | | | |
|---|---|---|---|
| **Leeming** | EGXE | mil | Northallerton (Yorks) |
| APPROACH | 127.750, 387.800 | | |
| TOWER | 122.100, 382.100, 394.500 | | |
| VDF | 132.400, 122.100, 359.200, 362.300, 387.800 | | |
| PAR | 122.100, 248.000, 352.900 | | |
| SRE | 127.750, 339.400 | | |

---

| | | | |
|---|---|---|---|
| **Lee-on-Solent** | EGUS | mil | 4 miles west of Gosport |
| TOWER | 135.700, 315.650 | | |

---

| | | | |
|---|---|---|---|
| **Leicester** | EGBG | civ | 4 miles S of Leicester |
| A/G/FIS | 122.250 | | |

---

| | | | |
|---|---|---|---|
| **Lerwick Tingwall** | EG | civ | Shetland Isles |
| A/G | 122.600 | | |

---

**Table 5.3**  *continued*

---

*Airfield*

---

| | | | |
|---|---|---|---|
| **Leuchars** | EGQL | mil | 7 miles SE of Dundee |
| MATZ/LARS | 126.500 | | |
| APPROACH | 126.500, 255.400, 362.300 | | |
| TOWER | 122.100, 258.925 | | |
| GROUND | 120.800, 259.850 | | |
| DISPATCHER | 285.025 | | |
| VDF | 126.500 | | |
| SRE | 123.300, 292.475 | | |
| PAR | 123.300, 268.775, 370.075 | | |

---

| | | | |
|---|---|---|---|
| **Linton-on-Ouse** | EGXU | mil | 10 miles NW of York |
| MATZ/LARS | 129.150, 121.100, 292.800, 344.000 | | |
| APPROACH | 129.150, 292.800, 362.675, 362.300 | | |
| TOWER | 122.100, 257.800, 300.425 | | |
| GROUND | 122.100, 340.025 | | |
| DEPARTURE | 129.150, 381.075, 292.800 | | |
| SRE | 129.150, 122.100, 344.000, 344.475 | | |
| PAR | 123.300, 129.150, 259.875, 358.525 | | |

---

| | | | |
|---|---|---|---|
| **Liverpool** | EGGP | civ | 6 miles SE of city |
| MET | 126.600 (London Volmet North) | | |
| APPROACH | 119.850 | | |
| TOWER | 118.100 | | |
| RADAR | 18.450, 119.850 | | |

---

| | | | |
|---|---|---|---|
| **Llanbedr** | EGOD | mil | 3 miles S of Harlech |
| APPROACH | 122.500, 386.675 | | |
| TOWER | 122.500, 380.175 | | |
| RADAR/PAR/VDF | 122.500, 370.300, 386.675 | | |

---

| | | | |
|---|---|---|---|
| **London City** | EGLC | civ | London Dockland |
| TOWER | 119.425, 118.075 | | |
| RADAR | 132.700 (Thames), 128.025 (City) | | |
| FIRE VEHICLES | 121.600 | | |

---

| | | | |
|---|---|---|---|
| **London Gatwick** | EGKK | civ | 28 miles S of London |
| MET | 135.375 (London Volmet Main) | | |
| ATIS | 128.475 | | |
| APPROACH | 125.875, 134.225 | | |
| TOWER | 124.225, 134.225 | | |
| CLEARANCE | 121.950 | | |
| GROUND | 121.800 | | |
| RADAR | 134.225, 118.600, 119.600, 129.275 | | |
| FIRE VEHICLES | 121.600 | | |

---

**Table 5.3**   *continued*

*Airfield*

| | | | |
|---|---|---|---|
| **London Heathrow** | EGLL | civ | 14 miles W of London |
| MET | 135.375 (London Volmet Main) | | |
| ATIS | 115.100 (Biggin), 113.750 (Bovingdon) | | |
| ATIS | 133.075 | | |
| APPROACH | 119.200, 120.400, 119.500, 127.550 | | |
| TOWER | 118.700, 124.475 | | |
| CLEARANCE | 121.700 | | |
| GROUND | 121.900 | | |
| RADAR | 119.200, 119.500, 127.550, 120.400 | | |
| FIRE VEHICLES | 121.600 | | |

| | | | |
|---|---|---|---|
| **London Stansted** | EGSS | civ | 30 miles N of London |
| MET | 135.375 (London Volmet Main) | | |
| ATIS | 127.175 | | |
| APPROACH | 125.550 | | |
| TOWER | 118.150 | | |
| GROUND | 121.700 | | |
| VDF | 125.550, 126.950, 118.150, 123.800 | | |
| RADAR | 125.550, 126.950, 123.800 | | |
| FIRE VEHICLES | 121.600 | | |

| | | | |
|---|---|---|---|
| **Londonderry** | EGAE | civ | Northern Ireland |
| APPROACH | 123.625 | | |
| TOWER | 122.850 | | |
| FIRE | 121.600 | | |

| | | | |
|---|---|---|---|
| **Lossiemouth** | EGQS | mil | 5 miles N of Elgin (Grampian) |
| MATZ/LARS | 119.350, 376.650 | | |
| APPROACH | 119.350, 362.300, 398.100 | | |
| TOWER | 118.900, 122.100, 337.750 | | |
| GROUND | 299.400 | | |
| SRE | 123.300, 259.975, 311.325 | | |
| PAR | 123.300, 250.050, 312.400 | | |
| VDF | 119.350, | | |

| | | | |
|---|---|---|---|
| **Luton** | EGGW | civ | SE of Luton |
| MET | 128.600 (London Volmet South) | | |
| ATIS | 120.575 | | |
| APPROACH | 129.550, 128.750, 127.300, 259.875 | | |
| TOWER | 119.975 | | |
| GROUND | 121.750 | | |
| VDF | 129.550, 127.300, 128.750 | | |
| SRE | 128.750, 127.300 | | |
| FIRE VEHICLES | 121.600 | | |

**Table 5.3**  *continued*

---

*Airfield*

---

| | | | |
|---|---|---|---|
| **Lydd** | EGMD | civ | Off B2075 Lydd/New Romney |
| APPROACH/ | | | Road |
| TOWER | 120.700 | | |
| SRE | 131.300 | | |

---

| | | | |
|---|---|---|---|
| **Lyneham** | EGDL | mil | 8 miles SW M4 junction 16 (Wilts) |
| ATIS | 381.000 | | |
| APPROACH | 118.425, 123.400, 359.500, 362.300 | | |
| TOWER | 118.425, 122.100, 386.825 | | |
| GROUND | 118.425, 122.100, 340.175 | | |
| DISPATCHER | 265.950 | | |
| OPERATIONS | 254.650 | | |
| VDF | 123.400 | | |
| PAR | 123.300, 375.200, 385.400 | | |
| SRE | 123.400, 300.475, 344.000 | | |

---

| | | | |
|---|---|---|---|
| **Macrihanish** | EGQJ | mil | 4 miles W of Campbeltown |
| MATZ | 125.900, 122.100, 344.525, 362.300 | | |
| APPROACH | 125.900, 122.100,3 44.525, 362.300 | | |
| TOWER | 122.100, 358.600, 257.800 | | |
| PAR | 123.300, 337.975, 385.400 | | |
| SRE | 125.900, 123.300, 259.925, 344.000 | | |

---

| | | | |
|---|---|---|---|
| **Manchester** | EGCC | civ | 10 miles S of city centre |
| MET | 135.375, 126.600, 127.000 (Dublin Volmet) | | |
| ATIS | 128.175 | | |
| APPROACH | 119.400, 121.350 | | |
| TOWER | 118.625 | | |
| GROUND | 121.700, 121.850 | | |
| RADAR | 119.400,121.350 | | |
| FIRE VEHICLES | 121.600 | | |

---

| | | | |
|---|---|---|---|
| **Manchester (Barton)** | EGCB | civ | 6 miles W of Manchester |
| A/G | 122.700 | | |

---

| | | | |
|---|---|---|---|
| **Manston** | EGUM | mil | 4 miles NW of Ramsgate (Kent) |
| | EGMH | civ | |
| MATZ | 126.350 | | |
| APPROACH | 126.350, 122.100, 362.300, 379.025 | | |
| TOWER | 128.775, 122.100, 344.350, 257.800 | | |
| VDF | 126.350, 129.450 | | |
| PAR | 123.300, 118.525, 312.350, 385.400 | | |
| SRE | 126.350, 123.300, 338.625, 344.000 | | |

---

**Table 5.3**  *continued*

*Airfield*

| | | | |
|---|---|---|---|
| **Marham** | EGYM | mil | Near Swaffham (Norfolk) |
| MATZ | 124.150 | | |
| APPROACH | 124.150, 291.950, 362.300 (Eastern Radar) | | |
| TOWER | 122.100, 337.900, 257.800 | | |
| DISPATCHER | 241.450 | | |
| OPERATIONS | 312.550 | | |
| VDF | 124.150, 122.100 | | |
| PAR | 123.300, 379.650, 385.400 | | |
| SRE | 124.150, 293.775, 344.000 | | |

| | | | |
|---|---|---|---|
| **Merryfield** | EG | mil | N of Ilminster (Somerset) |
| APPROACH | 127.350, 276.700, 362.300 (Yeovil) | | |
| TOWER | 122.100, 287.100 | | |

| | | | |
|---|---|---|---|
| **Middle Wallop** | EGVP | mil | 6 miles SW of Andover (Hants) |
| MATZ | Boscombe Down | | |
| APPROACH | 126.700, 122.100, 312.000 | | |
| TOWER | 122.100, 372.650 | | |
| PAR | 364.825 | | |
| SRE | 312.675 | | |

| | | | |
|---|---|---|---|
| **Mildenhall** | EGUN | mil | Near Barton Mills (Suffolk) |
| ATIS | 277.075 | | |
| APPROACH | 128.900 | | |
| TOWER | 122.550, 258.825 | | |
| GROUND | 380.150 | | |
| COMMAND POST | 379.850, 312.450 | | |
| MAINTENANCE | 254.625 | | |
| METRO | 257.750 | | |
| NAVY DUTY | 142.850 (NFM) | | |
| AIR MOBILITY | | | |
| COM | 379.850 | | |

See also Honington for MATZ/APP/DEPART

| | | | |
|---|---|---|---|
| **Mona** | EG | mil | 10 miles W of Menai Bridge |
| AFIS | 122.000 | | |
| APPROACH | 379.700 | | |
| TOWER | 358.750 | | |

See also Valley

| | | | |
|---|---|---|---|
| **Netheravon** | EGDN | mil | Near Amesbury (Wilts) |
| A/G/TOWER | 128.300, 253.500 | | |
| APPROACH | 362.225 | | |
| TOWER | 290.950 | | |

**Table 5.3**  *continued*

---

*Airfield*

---

| | | | |
|---|---|---|---|
| **Netherthorpe** | EGNF | civ | 3 miles NW of Worksop |
| **AFIS** | 123.275 | | |
| **A/G** | 123.275 | | |

---

| | | | |
|---|---|---|---|
| **Newcastle** | EGNT | civ | 5 miles NW of Newcastle |
| **MET** | 126.600 (London Volmet North) | | |
| **ATIS** | 114.250 | | |
| **APPROACH** | 124.375, 284.600 | | |
| **TOWER** | 119.700 | | |
| **VDF** | 118.500, 119.700, 126.350 | | |
| **RADAR** | 126.350, 118.500 | | |
| **FIRE** | 121.600 | | |

---

| | |
|---|---|
| **Newquay** | See St Mawgan |

---

| | | | |
|---|---|---|---|
| **Newton** | EGXN | mil | 6 miles E of Nottingham |
| **APPROACH** | 122.100, 251.725, 362.300 | | |
| **TOWER** | 122.100, 257.800, 375.425 | | |

---

| | | | |
|---|---|---|---|
| **Newtownards** | EGAD | civ | 2 miles SE of town centre |
| **A/G** | 123.500 | | |

---

| | | | |
|---|---|---|---|
| **Northampton** | EGBK | civ | 5 miles NE of city |
| **AFIS/A/G** | 122.700 | | |

---

| | |
|---|---|
| **North Denes** | See Great Yarmouth |

---

| | | | |
|---|---|---|---|
| **Northolt** | EGWU | mil | Close to Uxbridge (London area) |
| **ATIS** | 300.350 | | |
| **APPROACH/VDF** | 126.450, 344.975, 362.300 | | |
| **TOWER** | 126.450, 257.800, 312.350 | | |
| **OPERATIONS** | 244.425 | | |
| **SRE** | 375.500, 379.425 | | |
| **PAR** | 130.350, 385.400 | | |

---

| | | | |
|---|---|---|---|
| **North Weald** | EGSX | mil | NE of Epping (Essex) |
| **A/G** | 123.525 | | |

---

| | | | |
|---|---|---|---|
| **Norwich** | EGSH | civ | 3 miles N of Norwich |
| **MET** | 128.600 (London Volmet South) | | |
| **APPROACH** | 119.350 | | |
| **TOWER** | 124.250 | | |
| **SRE** | 119.350, 118.475 | | |
| **FIRE** | 121.600 | | |

**Table 5.3** *continued*

*Airfield*

| | | | |
|---|---|---|---|
| **Nottingham**<br>A/G | EGBN<br>122.800 | civ | Near Tollerton |
| **Odiham**<br>ATIS<br>MATZ<br>APPROACH<br>TOWER<br>PAR<br>SRE | EGVO<br>276.175<br>Farnborough<br>122.100, 125.250, 315.975, 362.300<br>122.100, 309.625, 257.800<br>123.300, 385.400<br>386.775 | mil | 8 miles N of Alton (Hants) |
| **Old Sarum**<br>A/G | EG<br>123.575 | civ | 2 miles N of Salisbury (Wilts) |
| **Old Warden**<br>A/G | EG<br>123.050 | civ | 2 miles W of Biggleswade (Beds) |
| **Oxford (Kidlington)**<br>ATIS<br>AFIS<br>A/G<br>APPROACH<br>TOWER<br>GROUND<br>VDF | EGTK<br>121.950<br>119.800<br>118.875<br>125.325<br>118.875<br>121.750<br>125.325 | civ | 6 miles NW of Oxford |
| **Panshangar**<br>AFIS | EG<br>120.250 | civ | 4 miles W of Hertford |
| **Penzance Heliport**<br>A/G | EGHK<br>118.100 | civ | 1 miles E of Penzance |
| **Perth (Scone)**<br>APPROACH/VDF<br>TOWER | EGPT<br>122.300<br>119.800 | civ | 3 miles NE of Perth |
| **Peterborough (Con)**<br>A/G | EGSF<br>129.725 | civ | 8 miles S of Peterborough |
| **Peterborough (Sib)**<br>A/G | EGSP<br>122.300 | civ | |
| **Plymouth**<br>APPROACH | EGHD<br>133.550 | civ | 4 miles N of Plymouth |

**Table 5.3**  *continued*

*Airfield*

| | | | |
|---|---|---|---|
| TOWER | 122.600 | | |
| VDF | 133.550, 122.600 | | |
| **Pocklington** | EG | civ | |
| A/G | 130.100 | | |
| **Portishead Radio** | EG | civ | B.T. message handling service |
| A/G | 131.625 | | |
| **Popham** | EG | civ | Near junction 8 of M3 (Hants) |
| A/G | 129.800 | | |
| **Portland** | EGDP | mil | 4 miles S of Weymouth |
| MATZ | 124.150, 317.800 | | |
| APPROACH | 124.150, 122.100, 362.300 | | |
| TOWER | 122.100, 123.300, 124.150, 291.000, 362.300 | | |
| SRE | 124.150, 122.100, 317.800, 362.300 | | |
| PAR | 387.500, 362.300 | | |
| **Predannack** | EG | civ | Near Lizard Point (Cornwall) |
| TOWER | 338.975, 370.000 | | |
| | See also Culdrose | | |
| **Prestwick** | EGPK | civ | 28 miles S of Glasgow |
| MET | 125.725 (Scottish Volmet) | | |
| ATIS | 127.125 | | |
| APPROACH | 120.550, 386.925 | | |
| TOWER | 118.150, 121.800 | | |
| RADAR | 120.550, 119.450 | | |
| FIRE | 121.600 | | |
| ROYAL NAVY OPS | 337.750 | | |
| **Redhill** | EGKR | civ | 1 mile E of town (Surrey) |
| AFIS/TOWER | 120.275 | | |
| **Retford (Gamston)** | EGNE | civ | 3 miles S of Town (Notts) |
| A/G | 130.475 | | |
| **Rochester** | EGTO | civ | 2 miles S of Town (Kent) |
| AFIS | 122.250 | | |
| **St Athan** | EGDX | mil | 10 miles W of Barry (S Glamorgan) |
| APPROACH | 122.100, 277.225, 357.175 | | |
| TOWER | 122.100, 257.800, 336.525 | | |

**Table 5.3**   *continued*

| Airfield | | | |
|---|---|---|---|
| SRE | 123.300, 340.100, 344.000, 380.125, 385.400 | | |
| **St Mawgan** | EGDG | mil | 5 miles NE of Newquay |
| MATZ | 126.500 | | |
| APPROACH | 126.500, 122.100, 125.550, 357.200, 362.300 | | |
| TOWER | 123.400, 122.100, 241.825 | | |
| DISPATCHER | 245.600 | | |
| OPERATIONS | 260.000 | | |
| VDF | 126.500, 125.550 | | |
| PAR | 123.300, 336.550, 385.400 | | |
| SRE | 125.550, 344.000, 360.550 | | |
| **Salisbury Plain** | EG | mil | |
| A/G | 122.750, 253.500 | | |
| **Sandown** | EG | civ | Isle of Wight |
| A/G | 123.500 | | |
| **Scampton** | EGXP | mil | 5 miles N of Lincoln |
| APPROACH | 312.500, 362.300 | | |
| TOWER | 122.100, 282.400, 257.800 | | |
| GROUND | 372.500 | | |
| DEPARTURE | 249.850, 362.300 | | |
| VDF | 252.525 | | |
| RADAR | 127.350, 357.050, 344.000 | | |
| **Scatsta** | EGPM | civ | |
| APPROACH | 123.600 | | |
| TOWER | 123.600 | | |
| SRE | 122.400 | | |
| FIRE | 121.600 | | |
| **Scilly Isles** | EGHE | civ | St Mary's Island |
| APPROACH/ | | | |
|   TOWER | 123.150 | | |
| **Seething** | EG | civ | SE of Norwich |
| A/G | 122.600 | | |
| **Shannon** | EINN | civ | Republic of Ireland |
| MET | 127.000 (Dublin Volmet) | | |
| ATIS | 130.950 | | |
| APPROACH | 121.400, 120.200 | | |
| OCEANIC | | | |

**Table 5.3**  *continued*

*Airfield*

| | | | |
|---|---|---|---|
| DEPARTURE | 121.700 | | |
| TOWER | 118.700 | | |
| GROUND | 121.800 | | |
| RADAR | 121.400 | | |
| **Shawbury** | EGOS | mil | 10 miles NE of Shrewsbury |
| MATZ | 124.150, 254.200 | | |
| APPROACH | 124.150, 276.075, 362.300 | | |
| TOWER | 122.100, 269.100, 257.800 | | |
| GROUND | 337.900 | | |
| SRE | 124.150, 344.000 | | |
| PAR | 123.300, 356.975, 385.400 | | |
| **Sherburn-in-Elmet** | EGCL | civ | Sherburn (Yorkshire) |
| A/G | 122.600 | | |
| **Shipham** | EG | civ | 4 miles S East Dereham (Norfolk) |
| AFIS/A/G | 119.950 | | |
| **Sheffield** | EG | civ | 3 miles NE of city |
| **Shobdon** | EGBS | civ | 10 miles W of Leominster |
| A/G | 123.500 | | |
| **Shoreham** | EGKA | civ | 1 mile W of town |
| A/G | 123.150 | | |
| ATIS | 121.750 | | |
| APPROACH | 123.150 | | |
| TOWER | 125.400 | | |
| VDF | 123.150 | | |
| **Sibson** | see Peterborough | | |
| **Silverstone** | EG | civ | Northamptonshire |
| TOWER/A/G | 121.075 9 (by arrangement only) | | |
| **Skegness** | EG | civ | 2 miles N of town |
| A/G | 130.450 | | |
| **Sleap** | EG | civ | 10 miles N of Shrewsbury |
| A/G | 122.450 | | |
| **Sligo** | EISG | civ | Republic of Ireland |
| AFIS/TOWER/A/G | 122.100 | | |

**Table 5.3**  *continued*

*Airfield*

| | | | |
|---|---|---|---|
| **Southampton** | EGHI | civ | 1 mile W of Eastleigh |
| MET | 128.600 (London Volmet South) | | |
| ATIS | 113.350 | | |
| ATC/APPROACH | 120.225, 128.850, 131.000 | | |
| TOWER | 118.200 | | |
| RADAR | 120.225, 128.850 | | |
| FIRE | 121.600 | | |
| **Southend** | EGMC | civ | 2 miles N of town |
| MET | 128.600 (London Volmet South) | | |
| ATIS | 121.800 | | |
| APPROACH | 128.950 | | |
| TOWER | 127.725 | | |
| SRE | 128.950 | | |
| **Stanford** | EG | mil | 1 mile NW M20 junction 11 (Kent) |
| A/G OPERATIONS | 307.800 | | |
| **Stansted** | see London Stansted | | |
| **Stapelford** | EGSG | civ | 5 miles N of Romford (Essex) |
| A/G | 122.800 | | |
| **Stornoway** | EGPO | civ | 3 miles E of town (Hebrides) |
| MET | 125.750 (Scottish Volmet) | | |
| AFIS/APPROACH | 123.500 | | |
| TOWER | 123.500 | | |
| **Strathallan** | EG | civ | Tayside |
| A/G | 129.900 | | |
| **Sturgate** | EGCS | civ | 6 miles SE of Gainsborough |
| A/G | 130.300 | | |
| **Sumburgh** | EGPB | civ | South of Island (Hebrides) |
| MET | 125.725 (Scottish Volmet) | | |
| ATIS | 125.850 | | |
| APPROACH/ | | | |
|  RADAR | 123.150 | | |
| TOWER | 118.250 | | |
| **Swansea** | EGFH | civ | 6 miles W of Swansea |
| A/G/APPROACH | 119.700 | | |
| TOWER | 119.700 | | |

**Table 5.3** *continued*

*Airfield*

| | | | |
|---|---|---|---|
| **Swanton Morley** TOWER | EG 123.500 | mil | 4 miles N of Dereham (Norfolk) |
| **Swinderbury** APPROACH TOWER | EGXS 283.425 122.100, 375.300 | mil | 8 miles NE of Newark (Lincs) |
| **Sywell** | see Northampton | | |
| **Tatenhill** A/G | EGBM 122.200 | civ | 6 miles W of Burton-on-Trent |
| **Teesside** MET APPROACH TOWER VDF/RADAR | EGNV 126.600 (London Volmet North) 118.850 119.800 118.850, 119.800, 128.850 | civ | 6 miles E of Darlington |
| **Ternhill** APPROACH TOWER RADAR | EG 124.150, 122.100, 276.825, 362.300, 365.075 124.150, 338.825, 309.550 (Chetwynd) 123.300, 122.100, 344.375 | mil | 4 miles SW of Market Drayton |
| **Thruxton** A/G | EGHO 130.450 | civ | 6 miles W of Andover (Hants) |
| **Tiree** AFIS | EGPU 122.700 | civ | centre of island |
| **Topcliffe** MATZ APPROACH TOWER SRE | EGXZ Leeming 125.000, 121.100, 357.375, 362.300 125.000, 121.100, 309.725, 257.800 123.300, 344.350, 385.400 | mil | 4 miles SW of Thirsk (Yorkshire) |
| **Truro** A/G | EG 129.800 | civ | near town (Cornwall) |
| **Unst** APPROACH/ TOWER | EGPW 130.350 | civ | Shetland Isles |
| **Upavon** TOWER | EG 275.800 | mil | 8 miles N of Amesbury (Wilts) |

**Table 5.3**  *continued*

*Airfield*

| | | | |
|---|---|---|---|
| **Upper Heyford** | EGUA | mil | 6 miles W of Bicester |
| ATIS | 242.125 | | |
| APPROACH | 128.550, 123.300, 364.875 | | |
| TOWER | 122.100, 257.800, 316.000 | | |
| GROUND | 375.175 | | |
| DISPATCHER | 277.175 | | |
| DEPARTURE | 364.875 | | |
| COMMAND POST | 357.900, 359.850 | | |
| METRO | 257.750, 358.600 | | |
| RADAR | 128.550, 122.100 | | |
| | ★★ On standby for closure ★★ | | |
| **Valley** | EGOV | mil | 6 miles SE of Hollyhead |
| MATZ | 134.350, 268.775 | | |
| SAR | 282.800 | | |
| APPROACH | 134.350, 372.325, 362.300 | | |
| TOWER | 122.100, 340.175, 257.800 | | |
| GROUND | 122.100, 386.900 | | |
| VDF | 134.350 | | |
| SRE | 134.350, 123.200, 268.775, 282.800 | | |
| DIRECTOR | 337.725, 344.000 | | |
| PAR | 123.300, 358.675, 385.400 | | |
| **Waddington** | EGXW | mil | 6 miles S of Lincoln |
| MATZ | 127.350, 296.750 | | |
| APPROACH | 312.500, 362.300 | | |
| TOWER | 122.100, 285.050, 257.800 | | |
| GROUND | 342.125 | | |
| DEPARTURE | 123.300, 249.850 | | |
| DISPATCHER | 291.150 | | |
| VDF | 127.350 | | |
| PAR | 123.300, 309.675, 385.400 | | |
| SRE | 127.350, 123.300, 300.575, 344.000 | | |
| **Warton** | EGNO | civ | 4 miles E of Lytham St Annes |
| APPROACH | 124.450, 130.800, 336.475 | | |
| TOWER | 121.600, 130.800, 254.350 | | |
| SRE | 124.450, 130.800, 336.475, 254.350 | | |
| RADAR | 129.275, 343.700 | | |
| **Waterford** | EIWF | civ | Republic of Ireland |
| A/G/TOWER | 129.850 | | |

**Table 5.3**  *continued*

*Airfield*

| | | | |
|---|---|---|---|
| **Wattisham**<br>APPROACH<br>TOWER<br>SRE<br>PAR | EGUW<br>135.200,<br>122.100, 343.250<br>123.300, 277.475<br>123.300, 356.175, 359.825 | mil | 10 miles NW of Ipswich |
| **Wellesbourne**<br>A/G | EGBW<br>130.450 | civ | 4 miles E of Stratford-upon-Avon |
| **Welshpool**<br>A/G | EG<br>123.250 | civ | 12 miles W of Shrewsbury |
| **West Freugh**<br>MATZ<br>APPROACH<br>TOWER<br>SRE | EGOY<br>130.050<br>130.050, 383.525<br>122.550, 337.925<br>130.725, 383.525 | mil | 4 miles SE of Stranraer |
| **Westland heliport**<br>TOWER | EGLW<br>122.900 | civ | Battersea (London) |
| **West Malling**<br>A/G | EGKM<br>130.875 | civ | 4 miles W of Maidstone |
| **Weston**<br>A/G | EIWT<br>122.400 | civ | Republic of Ireland |
| **Weybridge**<br>A/G | EG<br>122.350 | civ | just S of town (Surrey) |
| **White Waltham**<br>A/G | EGLM<br>122.600 | civ | 4 miles SW of Maidenhead |
| **Wick**<br>MET<br>AFIS/APPROACH<br>TOWER | EGPC<br>118.300 (Kirkwall)<br>119.700<br>119.700 | civ | |
| **Wickenby**<br>A/G | EGNW<br>122.450 | civ | 10 miles NE of Lincoln |
| **Wigtown (Baldoon)**<br>A/G | EG<br>123.050 | civ | Dumfries and Galloway |

**Table 5.3**  *continued*

*Airfield*

| | | | |
|---|---|---|---|
| **Woodbridge** | EGVG | mil | 5 miles NE of Ipswich |
| MATZ/APPROACH | See Bentwaters | | |
| ATIS | 336.000 | | |
| TOWER | 119.150, 122.100, 257.800, 291.350 | | |
| GROUND | 307.400 | | |
| COMMAND POST | 282.150 | | |
| METRO | 259.400 | | |

**★★ Due for closure ★★**

| | | | |
|---|---|---|---|
| **Woodford** | EGCD | civ | 4 miles E of Wilmslow (Lancs) |
| APPROACH | 130.050, 126.925, 269.125, 358.575 | | |
| TOWER | 126.925, 130.050, 358.575, 299.975 | | |
| SRE | 130.750, 130.050, 269.125, 358.575 | | |

| | | | |
|---|---|---|---|
| **Woodvale** | EGOW | mil | 6 miles SW of Southport (Lancs) |
| APPROACH | 122.100, 312.800 | | |
| TOWER | 119.750, 259.950 | | |

| | | | |
|---|---|---|---|
| **Wroughton** | EGDT | civ | 3 miles S of Swindon |
| A/G | 123.225 | | |

| | | | |
|---|---|---|---|
| **Wycombe Air Park** | EGTB | civ | 3 miles SW of High Wycombe |
| TOWER | 126.550 | | |
| GROUND | 121.775 | | |

| | | | |
|---|---|---|---|
| **Wyton** | EGUY | mil | 4 miles NE of Huntingdon |
| MATZ | 134.050 | | |
| APPROACH | 134.050, 362.375, 362.300 | | |
| TOWER | 122.100, 312.275, 257.800 | | |
| DEPARTURE | 134.050, 375.525 | | |
| PAR | 122.100, 292.900, 385.400 | | |
| SRE | 123.300, 249.550, 344.000 | | |

| | | | |
|---|---|---|---|
| **Yeovil** | EGHG | mil | SW of town |
| APPROACH | 130.180, 369.975 | | |
| TOWER | 125.400, 372.425 | | |
| SRE | 130.800 | | |
| RADAR | 127.350, 369.875 | | |

| | | | |
|---|---|---|---|
| **Yeovilton** | EGDY | mil | 2 miles E of Ilchester |
| MATZ | 127.350 | | |
| ATIS | 379.750 | | |
| APPROACH | 127.350, 369.875, 362.300 | | |
| TOWER | 122.100, 372.650 | | |

**Table 5.3**  *continued*

---

*Airfield*

| | |
|---|---|
| GROUND | 311.325 |
| PAR | 123.300, 339.975, 344.350 |
| SRE | 123.300, 338.875, 362.300 |
| RADAR/VDF | 127.350, 369.875 |

---

*What you might hear*
Remember that aircraft transmissions are usually short and there may
be long periods when nothing is heard on a frequency. This applies, in
particular, to smaller airfields where traffic movement may be quite low.

In addition to approach, control tower and radar landing instructions
you may also hear a variety of other messages being passed on other
frequencies in the bands. Many airlines have 'company frequencies' on
which aircraft crews and ground operation staff communicate. You may
also hear transmissions relating to zone, area or sector controllers. These
are the people who control the movements of aircraft as they fly
between airports. Different sectors have different transmission frequencies and so, to follow a particular aircraft as it moves from one
sector to another, you will need to change your reception frequencies,
to suit.

At London Heathrow and similar large airports, the sheer volume of
traffic means that instructions passed to the aircraft must be done by
several controllers and so you may come across frequencies which are
dealing solely with such things as instructions on taxiing on the ground.

*Continuous transmissions*
Some frequencies are allocated solely for transmissions from the
ground. The aircraft never transmit on these frequencies but the crews
may listen to the broadcasts for information. The most common of these
are 'VOLMETS', transmitted round the clock and detailing current
weather conditions for most major airports.

Automatic terminal information service (ATIS) transmissions, on the
other hand, are sent out by individual airports and only include details of
that airport, including current weather, runway and approach patterns
in use, and any other essential information. They, in fact, contain all the
information a pilot needs except actual landing permission. Pilots will
listen to these transmissions and when contacting the controller will
often be heard to say such things as 'information Bravo received'. The
word 'Bravo' standing for the code letter which identifies the start of
an ATIS transmission.

*Range*

Using a reasonable outside aerial it may be possible to hear ground stations up to 20 miles or so away. However, if hills or large buildings are between the scanner and the airport then this range will be considerably reduced. For instance, in my own case I cannot pick up my local airport which is only four miles away and yet can pick up another airport which is some 25 miles away in a different direction.

Air-to-ground range though is a different matter altogether. Aircraft flying at tens of thousands of feet may be heard several hundred miles

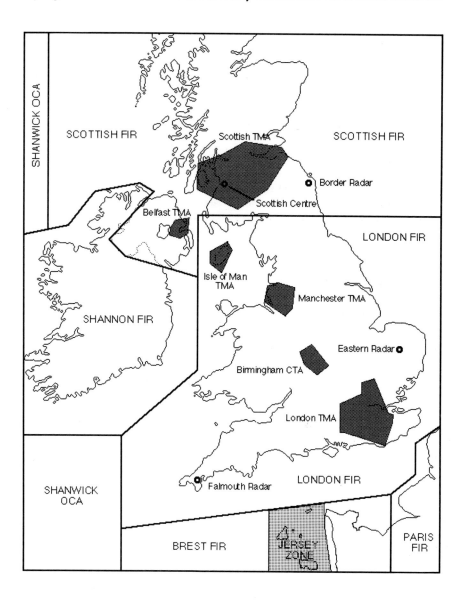

away even though the scanner is only operating on a small telescopic aerial. This is because the line-of-site range is greatly extended by the height of the aircraft which is transmitting from a point where there are no obstructions to block or weaken the signal.

If an aerial is used solely for airband reception then it should be vertically polarised. It is worth noting, by the way, that a simple ground plane aerial of the type described in Chapter 4 is more than adequate for aircraft band-only operation.

You will hear many unfamiliar expressions and considerable use of abbreviations in the airband. If you are not familiar with these, you can look them up in the airband section in Chapter 6.

## Table 5.4 United Kingdom Airways Allocations

| A/way | Sector | Control |
|-------|--------|---------|
| A1 | Turnberry & 54.30N | Scottish Ctl 126.250 & 128.500 |
| | 54.30N & abm Stafford | London Ctl 131.050, 129.100 & 134.425 |
| | 54.30N & abm Stafford | Manchester Ctl 126.650 & 124.210 |
| | Abm Stafford & Birmingham | London Ctl 133.700, 134.425 |
| | Abm Stafford & Birmingham | Manchester Ctl 124.200 |
| | Birmingham & Abm Woodley | London Ctl 133.700 & 133.975 |
| | Daventry area and Birmingham Zone Ctl | Birmingham SRA/SRZ 120.500 |
| A2 | TALLA & 54.30N | Scottish Ctl 128.500 |
| | 54.30N & Abm Lichfield | London Ctl 131.050 & 134.425 |
| | 54.30N & Abm Lichfield | Manchester Ctl 126.65 & 124.200 |
| | Abm Lichfield & Abm Birmingham | London Ctl 121.025, 133.700 & 134.425 |
| | Abm Lichfield & Abm Birmingham | Manchester Ctl 126.65 & 124.200 |
| | Abm Birmingham & London Ctl 121.025, 133.700 | Brookmans Park & 133.975 |
| | South of Brookmans Park | London Ctl 127.100 & 132.450 |
| A20 | FIR Boundary & Biggin | London Ctl 127.100 |
| | Biggin & Abm Birmingham | London Ctl 121.025, 133.700 & 133.975 |
| | Abm Birmingham & Pole Hill | London Ctl 131.050 above FL155 |
| | Abm Birmingham & Pole Hill | Manchester Ctl 124.200 & 126.650 |
| A25 | Dean Cross & 54.30N | Scottish Ctl 126.250 & 128.500 |
| | 54.30N & REXAM | London Ctl 128.050, 129.100 & 134.425 |
| | 54.30N & REXAM | Manchester Ctl 133.050 & 125.100 |
| | REXAM & Cardiff | London Ctl 131.200 |
| | Cardiff & 50.00N | London Ctl 132.600 & 135.250 |
| | 50.00N & Channel Isles Boundary | Jersey Zone 125.200 |
| A30 | London FIR | London Ctl 127.100 |
| A34 | London FIR | London Ctl 127.700 & 124.275 |

**Table 5.4**  *continued*

| A/way | Sector | Control |
|---|---|---|
| A37 | Entire route | London Ctl 129.600, 127.950, 133.450 & 133.525 |
| A47 | Pole Hill & Lichfield | London Ctl 131.050 above FLI55 |
| | Pole Hill & Lichfield | Manchester Ctl 126.65, 124.200 below FL175 |
| | Lichfield & abm Birmingham | London Ctl 133.700 Above FL135 |
| | Lichfield & abm Birmingham | Manchester Ctl 124.200 below FL175 |
| | Abm Birmingham & Woodley | London Ctl 133.700, 121.020 |
| | Daventry CTA below FL130 | London Ctl 133.975 |
| | South of Woodley to FIR Boundary | London Ctl 127.700, 135.050 & 124.275 |
| B1 | West of Wallasey | London Ctl 128.050, 129.100 & 134.425 |
| | West of Wallasey | Manchester Ctl 133.050 below FL175 |
| | Wallasey & BARTN | London Ctl 128.050 & 134.425 |
| | Wallasey & BARTN | Manchester Ctl 125.100 below FL175 |
| | BARTN & Ottringham | London Ctl 131.050 & 134.425 |
| | BARTN & Ottringham | Manchester Ctl 126.650 & 124.200 |
| | East of Ottringham | London Ctl 134.250, 127.950 & 133.525 |
| B2 | North of TMA | Scottish Ctl 124.500 |
| | South of TMA | Scottish Ctl 135.675 |
| B3 | Belfast & 5W | Scottish Ctl 135.675 |
| | 5W & Wallasey | London Ctl 128.050 & 129.100 |
| | Wallasey & Stafford | London Ctl 128.050 & 129.100 |
| | Wallasey & Stafford | Manchester Ctl 125.100 & 124.200 |
| | Stafford & abm Birmingham | London Ctl 133.7 & 121.025 above FL135 |
| | Stafford & abm Birmingham | Manchester Ctl 125.1 & 124.200 below FL175 |
| | Daventry CTA within A1 | Birmingham Zone Ctl on 120.500 below FL80 |
| | Abm Birmingham & Brookmans Park | London Ctl 133.700, 121.025 & 133.975 |
| | South of Brookmans Park to FIR boundary | London Ctl 127.100 & 134.900 |
| B4 | Detling & Brookmans Park | London Ctl 127.100 & 134.900 |
| | Brookmans Park & abm Birmingham | London Ctl 121.025, 133.700 & 133.975 |
| | Abm Birmingham & ROBIN | London Ctl 121.025, 133.700 & 134.425 above FL135 |
| | Abm Birmingham & ROBIN | Manchester Ctl 124.200 & 126.650 below FL175 |
| | ROBIN & Pole Hill | London Ctl 131.050, 134.425 above FL155 |
| | ROBIN & Pole Hill | Manchester Ctl 124.200 & 126.650 below FL175 |

**Table 5.4**  *continued*

| A/way | Sector | Control |
|-------|--------|---------|
| | Pole Hill & 54.30N | London Ctl 131.050 & 134.425 above FL155 |
| | Pole Hill & 54.30N | Manchester Ctl 126.65 124.200 below FL175 |
| | 54.30N & GRICE | Scottish Ctl 135.675 (night) & 128.500 (day) |
| B5 | Entire route | London Ctl 134.250, 127.950 & 133.525 |
| B11 | Within London FIR | London Ctl 134.450, 127.700 & 124.275 |
| B29 | Within London FIR | London Ctl 129.600 & 127.950 |
| B39 | MALBY & RADNO | London Ctl 131.200 |
| | RADNO & TOLKA | London Ctl 128.050 |
| B53 | Entire route | London Ctl 128.050 & 129.100 above FL155 |
| | Entire route | Manchester Ctl 125.100 & 124.200 below FL175 |
| B226 | Entire route | Scottish Ctl 124.500 |
| G1 | West of Brecon | London Ctl 131.200 |
| | Brecon & abm Woodley | London Ctl 132.800 & 131.200 |
| | East of abm Woodley to FIR Boundary | London Ctl 134.900 & 127.100 |
| G27 | North of 50.00N | London Ctl 127.700 & 124.275R1 |
| R1 | ORTAC to Ockham | London Ctl 134.450, 132.300, 127.700 & 124.275 |
| | Ockham to FIR Boundary | London Ctl 129.600, 127.950, 133.450 & 133.520 |
| R3 | Wallasey & ROBIN | London Ctl 128.050, 129.100 & 134.425 above FL155 |
| | Wallasey & ROBIN | Manchester Ctl 125.100 & 124.200 below FL175 |
| R8 | BRIPO to Southampton | London Ctl 132.600 & 124.275 |
| | Southampton to Midhurst | London Ctl 134.450, 132.300, 127.700 & 124.270 |
| | Midhurst & Dover | London Ctl 134.900, 127.100 & 124.275 |
| R12 | Entire route | London Ctl 129.600, 127.950, 133.450 & 133.520 |
| R123 | Entire route | London Ctl 129.600, 127.950, 133.450 & 133.520 |
| R14 | Within London FIR | London Ctl 131.200 |
| R25 | Entire route | London Ctl 127.700 |
| R41 | ORTAC & Southampton | London Ctl 134.450, 132.300, 127.700 & 124.275 |
| | Southampton & abm Compton | London Ctl 132.800, 131.200, & 124.275 |
| | Abm Compton & Westcott | London Ctl 133.700 & 121.025 |
| R84 | Entire route | London Ctl 134.450, 132.300, 127.700 & 124.275 |

**Table 5.4**   *continued*

| A/way | Sector | Control |
|---|---|---|
| R126 | Within London FIR | London Ctl 129.600 & 127.940 |
| R803 | Entire route | London Ctl 127.700 & 124.275 |
| W1 | Daventry to Abm Barkway | London Ctl 121.025, 133.700, & 133.975 |
| | Abm Barkway to 20nm N of Dover | London Ctl 129.600, 127.950, & 133.450 |
| | 20nm North of Dover to Dover | London Ctl 132.900 & 127.100 |
| W923 | Entire route | London Ctl 131.050, 129.100, & 134.425 above FL155 |
| | Entire route | Manchester Ctl 126.650 & 124.200 below FL175 |
| W934 | Within London FIR | London Ctl 127.700 & 124.275 |

*Lower ATS Advisory Routes*

| A/way | Sector | Control |
|---|---|---|
| A1D | 60N 10W to Stornoway | Scottish Ctl 127.275 |
| | Stornoway to Glasgow | Scottish Ctl 127.275 |
| B1D | Within Scottish FIR | Scottish Ctl 131.300 |
| G4D | Within London FIR | London Ctl 132.600 |
| N552D | Entire route | Scottish Ctl 127.275 |
| N562 | Entire route | Scottish Ctl 127.275 |
| N571D | Entire route | Scottish Ctl 127.275 |
| R8D | Within London FIR | London Ctl 132.600 |
| W2D | West of Fleetwood | London Ctl 128.050, 129.200, & 134.425 above FL155 |
| | West of Fleetwood | Manchester Ctl 133.050 below FL175 |
| | East of Fleetwood | London Ctl 131.050 & 134.425 above FL155 |
| | East of Fleetwood | Manchester Ctl 126.650 & 124.200 below FL175 |
| W3 | South of Inverness | Scottish Ctl 124.500 |
| | Between Inverness & Sumburgh | Scottish Ctl 131.300 |
| W4D | Within Scottish FIR | Scottish Ctl 131.300 |
| W5D | Within Scottish FIR | Scottish Ctl 131.300 |
| W6D | Glasgow to Benbecula to Stornoway to 05.00W to Inverness | Scottish Ctl 127.275 |
| W910D | Entire route | Scottish Ctl 127 275 |
| W911D | South of 54.30N | Scottish Ctl 128.500 & Border Radar on 132.900 |
| | South of 54.30N | London Ctl 128.050, 129.100, & 134.425 above FL155 |
| | South of 54.30N | Manchester Ctl 133.050 below FL175 |
| W927D | West of North light | London Ctl 128.050, 129.100 & 134.425 above FL 155 |
| | West of North light | Manchester Ctl 133.050 below FL175 |

**Table 5.4**  *continued*

| A/way | Sector | Control |
|---|---|---|
| | East of North light | London Ctl 128.050, 134.425, above FL155 |
| | East of North light | Manchester Ctl 133.050 below FL175 |
| W928D | Entire route | Scottish Ctl 135.675 |
| W985D | Entire route | Scottish Ctl 127.275 |

*Upper ATS allocations*

| A/way | Sector | Control |
|---|---|---|
| UA1 | North of 54.30N | Scottish Ctl 135.850 |
| | Between 54.30N & abm Lichfield | London Ctl 131.050, 129.100 & 134.425 |
| | Abm Lichfield & abm Woodley | London Ctl 133.700 |
| | South of Woodley to UIR Boundary | London Ctl 127.700, 124.275 & 127.425 |
| UA2 | Machrihanish & 54.30N | Scottish Ctl 135.850 |
| | 54.30N & Trent | London Ctl 131.050, 129.100 & 134.425 |
| | Trent & Lambourne | London Ctl 133.700 & 121.025 |
| | South of Lambourne to UIR Boundary | London Ctl 127.100, 132.450 & 127.425 |
| UA20 | Entire route | London Ctl 127.100 & 127.425 |
| UA25 | GRICE to 54.30N | Scottish Ctl 135.850 |
| | 54.30N & South of Wallasey | London Ctl 128.050, 129.100 & 134.425 |
| | South of Wallasey & S of Brecon | London Ctl 133.600 |
| | South of Brecon to UIR Boundary | London Ctl 132.600, 131.050 & 134.425 |
| UA29 | BAKUR & MERLY | London Ctl 133.600 |
| | MERLY & SALCO | London Ctl 132.600 |
| UA30 | Entire route | London Ctl 127.100 & 127.425 |
| UA34 | Wallasey & TELBA | London Ctl 128.050 & 129.100 |
| | TELBA & Abm Woodley | London Ctl 133.700 |
| | Abm Woodley & UIR Boundary | London Ctl 127.700, 124.270 & 127.425 |
| UA37 | DANDI & GABAD | London Ctl 134.250, 128.125 & 133.525 |
| | GABAD & Detling | London Ctl 129.600, 127.950, 133.525 & 127.400 |
| UA47 | Daventry & Woodley | London Ctl 133.700 & 121.025 |
| | South of Woodley to UIR Boundary | London Ctl 127.700, 135.050, & 127.425 |
| UA251 | Pole Hill & TELBA | London Ctl 131.050 & 129.100 |
| | TELBA & EXMOR | London Ctl 133.600 |
| UB1 | Liffey to Wallasey | London Ctl 128.050 & 134.425 |
| | Wallasey to Ottringham | London Ctl 131.050 & 134.425 |
| | East of Ottringham | London Ctl 134.250, 128.125 & 133.525 |

**Table 5.4** *continued*

| A/way | Sector | Control |
|---|---|---|
| UB2 | DALKY to Perth | Scottish Ctl 135.850, & 126.850 |
| | Perth to KLONN | Scottish Ctl 124.050 |
| UB3 | Belfast to 05.00W | Scottish Ctl 135.85 & 126.850 |
| | 05.00W to 53.00N | London Ctl 128.050 & 121.025 |
| | Brookmans Park & Dover | London Ctl 127.100, 134.900 & 127.425 |
| UB4 | FINDO & 54.30N | Scottish Ctl 135.850 |
| | 54.30N & ROBIN | London Ctl 131.050 & 134.425 |
| | ROBIN & Brookmans Park | London Ctl 121.025 & 133.700 |
| | South of Brookmans Park to UIR Boundary | London Ctl 127.100, 132.450 & 127.425 |
| UB5 | North of FAMBO | Scottish Ctl 135.850 |
| | South of FAMBO | London Ctl 134.250, 128.125 & 133.525 |
| UB10 | Within London UIR | London Ctl 133.600 |
| UB11 | Within London UIR | London Ctl 134.450, 127 700, 124.275 & 127.400 |
| UB29 | Compton & Abm Brookmans Park | London Ctl 133.600 & 132.800 |
| | East of Abm Brookmans Park to UIR Boundary | London Ctl 129.600, 127.950, 133.525 & 127.400 |
| UB39 | Midhurst & RADNO | London Ctl 133.600 & 132.600 |
| | RADNO & TOLKA | London Ctl 128.050 & 127.425 |
| UB40 | Entire route | London Ctl 133.600 & 132.600 |
| UB105 | Within London UIR | London Ctl 134.250,128.125 & 133.525 |
| UG1 | West of Abm Woodley to UIR Boundary | London Ctl 133.600 & 132.800 |
| | East of Abm Woodley to UIR Boundary | London Ctl 134.900, 127.100 & 127.425 |
| UG4 | Within London UIR | London Ctl 132.600 |
| UG11 | Within Scottish UIR | Scottish Ctl 124.050 |
| UG106 | Within London UIR | London Ctl 134.900, 127.100 & 127.425 |
| UH71 | Sumburgh to LIRKI | Scottish Ctl 124.050 & 134.775 |
| UH73 | GRICE to Machrihanish | Scottish Ctl 135.850 & 126.850 |
| UL1 | West of abm Woodley to UIR Boundary | London Ctl 133.600 & 132.800 |
| | East of abm Woodley to UIR Boundary | London Ctl 134.900, 127.100 & 127.425 |
| UL74 | Entire route | London Ctl 134.250 & 128.125 |
| UL7 | North of SKATE | Scottish Ctl 124.050 |
| | South of SKATE | London Ctl 134.250 & 128.125 |

**Table 5.4**    *continued*

| A/way  Sector | Control |
|---|---|
| UL722 Entire route | London Ctl 132.600 & 132.950 |
| UN490 UIR Boundary to TAKAS | Brest Control 129.500 |
| UN491 UIR Boundary to TAKAS | Brest Control 129.500 |
| UN500 Entire route | London Ctl 132.600 & 132.950 |
| UN508 UIR Boundary to TAKAS | Brest Control 129.500 |
| UN510 RATKA to OMIMI | Shannon Ctl 135.600 |
| UN520 OMIMI to UIR Boundary | Brest Ctl 129.5 |
| UN549 Strumble to BAKUR | London Ctl 133.600 & 132 800 |
| UN550 ERNAN to 55.00N 01.00W | Scottish Ctl 135.850 & 126.850 |
| UN551 Belfast to 55.00N 01.00W | Scottish Ctl 135.850 & 126.850 |
| UN552 TALLA to Machrihanish to 55.00N 01.00W | Scottish Ctl 135.850 & 126.850 |
| UN560 ERNAN to 55.00N 01.00W | Scottish Ctl 135.850 |
| UN561 Belfast to 55.00N 01.00W | Scottish Ctl 135.850 & 126.850 |
| UN562 Machrihanish to 55.00N 01.00W | Scottish Ctl 135.850 & 126.850 |
| UN563 Glasgow to 55.00N 01.00W | Scottish Ctl 135.850 & 126.850 |
| UN564 GRICE to 55.00N 01.00W | Scottish Ctl 135.850 & 126.850 |
| UN570 GRICE to 56.00N 01.00W | Scottish Ctl 135.850 & 126.850 |
| UN571 Machrihanish to 57.00N 01.00W | Scottish Ctl 135.850 & 126.850 |
| UN572 Tiree to 57.00N 01.00W | Scottish Ctl 135.850 & 126.850 |
| UN580 Glasgow to Tiree to 57.20N | Scottish Ctl 135.850 & 126.850 |
| 57.20N to 58.00N 01.00W | Scottish Ctl 124.050 & 134.775 |
| UN581 Aberdeen to Benbecula to 58.00N 01.00W | Scottish Ctl 124.050 & 134.775 |
| UN582 ASPIT to 57.20N | Scottish Ctl 135.850 & 126.850 |
| 57.20N to Stornoway | Scottish Ctl 124.050 & 134.775 |
| UN58  Sumburgh to Stornoway to 58.00N 01.00W | Scottish Ctl 124.050 & 134.775 |
| UN584 Sumburgh to 58.00N 01.00W | Scottish Ctl 124.050 & 134.775 |
| UN590 MARGO to Glasgow & Benbecula | Scottish Ctl 135.850 & 126.850 |
| Benbecula to 59.00N 01.00W | Scottish Ctl 124.050 & 134.775 |
| UN593 Sumburgh to 59.00N 01.00W | Scottish Ctl 124.050 & 134.775 |
| UN601 TALLA to 57.20N | Scottish Ctl 135.850 & 126.850 |
| 57.20N to Stornoway to 60.00N to 01.00W | Scottish Ctl 124.050 & 134.775 |

**Table 5.4** *continued*

| A/way | Sector | Control |
|---|---|---|
| UN602 | Glasgow to 57.20N | Scottish Ctl 135.850 & 126.850 |
| | 57.20N to RONAK to 60.00N 01.00W | Scottish Ctl 124.050 & 134.775 |
| UN603 | Sumburgh to 60.00N 01.00W | Scottish Ctl 124.050 & 134.775 |
| UN610 | Stornoway to 60.00N 01.00W | Scottish Ctl 124.050 & 134.775 |
| UN611 | BATSU to Aberdeen to RONAK to 60.10N 01.00W | Scottish Ctl 124.050 & 134.775 |
| UN612 | Sumburgh to 60.10N 01.00W | Scottish Ctl 124.050 & 134.775 |
| UN615 | Glasgow to 57.20N | Scottish Ctl 135.850 & 126.850 |
| | 57.20N to Stornoway to MATIK | Scottish Ctl 124.050 & 134.775 |
| UR1 | ORTAC/Midhurst to Lambourne | London Ctl 134.450, 127.700 |
| UR12 | abm Lambourne | 132.300 & 124.275 |
| UR123 | Lambourne to Clacton to UIR Boundary | London Ctl 129.600, 127.950, 133.450, 133.525 & 127.425 |
| UR3 | Entire route | London Ctl 128.050 & 134.425 |
| UR4 | IOM to Pole Hill | London Ctl 128.050 & 134.425 |
| | Pole Hill to Ottringham | London Ctl 131.050 & 134.425 |
| | Ottringham to DANDI | London Ctl 134.250, 128.125 & 133.525 |
| UR8 | From Lands End to Southampton | London Ctl 132.600, 124.275, 134.450, 132.300 & 127.700 |
| | From Southampton to Midhurst | London Ctl 124.275 & 127.425 |
| UR14 | Within London UIR | London Ctl 132.600 & 133.600 |
| UR23 | Glasgow to SAB | Scottish Ctl 135.850 |
| | SAB to GORDO | Scottish Ctl 124.050 |
| UR24 | ORIST to ASPEN | London Ctl 134.450, 132.300 & 127.700 |
| UR25 | Entire route | London Ctl 127.700 & 124.275 |
| UR37 | NORLA to Southampton | London Ctl 132.600 & 124.275 |
| | Between Southampton & abm Midhurst | London Ctl 134.450, 127.700, 132.310 & 124.27 |
| | Abm Midhurst to DONER | London Ctl 134.900, 127.100 124.275 & 127.425 |
| UR38 | Newcastle to 57.15N | Scottish Ctl 135.850 & 126.850 |
| | 57.15N to Stornoway | Scottish Ctl 124.050 & 134.775 |
| UR41 | Between ORTAC & Southampton | London Ctl 134.450, 132.300 & 127.700 |
| | Between Southampton & abeam Woodley | London Ctl 132.800 & 131.200 |

**Table 5.4** *continued*

| A/way | Sector | Control |
|-------|--------|---------|
| | Between Abm Woodley & Westcott | 133.700, 121.025 & 127.425 |
| UR84 | ORTAC to Midhurst | London Ctl 132.300, 127.700 & 127.425 |
| UR126 | Entire route | London Ctl 129.600, 127.950 & 133.525 |
| UR168 | Lands End to CAVAL | London Ctl 132.600 |
| UT7 | From Lands End to NOTRO | London Ctl 132.600 |
| | From NOTRO to ASKIL | Brest Ctl 129.500 |
| UW1 | Between Daventry & abm Barkway | London Ctl 121.025 & 133.700 |
| | Between abm Barkway & Clacton | London Ctl 129.600, 127.950, 133.450 & 133.500 |
| UW2 | Between Compton & Brookmans Park | London Ctl 133.600, 132.600 & 127.425 |
| *Northern Radar Advisory Service area* | | |
| | North of W911D | Scottish Control 124.500 |
| | South of W911D | Pennine Radar 128.675 |
| *Hebrides Upper Control Area* | | |
| | South of a line 57.30N 10.00W & TIR & 65.36N & 00.41W | Scottish Ctl 135.850 & 126.850 |
| | North of a line 57.30N 10.00W & TIR & 65.36N & 00.41W | Scottish Ctl 124.050 |

*Notes on civilian airport frequencies*

Occasionally frequencies may be interchanged and, for instance, approach control will be handled by the tower. However, all the air-fields shown do have their main frequencies listed. A/G (Air/Ground stations) are for the most part communication stations available at smaller airfields. Pilots can call these facilities to obtain current weather information and the operator may well also warn of any other aircraft that are in the circuit. However, unlike an air traffic controller, the operator is not licensed to give the pilot landing instructions and it is up to the pilot to keep a look-out and make sure that he is not going to endanger any other aircraft during landing or take-off.

**Military airport transmissions**

Military airport transmissions use the same frequencies as civilian airports, but also have frequency allocations between 240 and 350MHz.

## Table 5.5 Special military allocations

| Facility | Frequency (MHz) | | |
|---|---|---|---|
| Aces High Ops (N. Weald) | 130.175 | | |
| Boulmer Rescue | 123.100 | | |
| Dalcross Tower (range) | 122.600 | | |
| Distress (army) | 40.0500 | | |
| Distress (including beacons) | 243.000 | | |
| Donna Nook Range | 123.050 | | |
| Lee-on-Solent rescue | 132.650 | | |
| NATO emergency | 243.000 | | 40.050 |
| NATO low level manouvres | 273.900 | | |
| NATO SAR training | 253.800 | | |
| Neatishead (range warning) | 123.100 | | |
| SAR co-ordination air/sea | 123.100 | | |
| Spadeadam Range | 122.100 | | |
| Standard Mil Field frequency | 122.100 | 123.300 | |
| Wembury Range control | 122.100 | | |

## Table 5.5b UK military danger area activity information service (DAAIS)

| Aberdeen | 120.400 | Donna Nook | 123.050 | Neatishead | 123.100 |
|---|---|---|---|---|---|
| Aberporth | 122.150 | Edinburgh | 121.200 | Newcastle | 126.350 |
| Bentwaters | 119.000 | Farnborough | 125.250 | Portland | 124.150 |
| Border Info | 134.850 | Goodwood | 122.450 | St. Mawgan | 126.500 |
| Border Info | 132.900 | Leeming | 132.400 | Salisbury Plain | 130.150 |
| Boscombe Down | 126.700 | Leuchars | 126.500 | Scottish Mil | 124.900 |
| Brawdy | 124.400 | Liverpool | 119.850 | Scottish Mil | 133.200 |
| Bristol | 127.750 | Llanbedr Radar | 122.500 | Train Range | 118.900 |
| Brize Radar | 134.300 | London Info | 124.600 | Waddington | 127.350 |
| Chivenor | 130.200 | London Info | 134.700 | Wembury Range | 122.100 |
| Culdrose | 134.050 | Lydd | 120.700 | West Freugh | 130.050 |
| Dalcross Tower | 122.600 | Lyneham | 123.400 | Yeovilton | 127.350 |

These stations provide information on the military training areas closest to them. Training ranges are used for a variety of purposes including gunnery on the ground, at sea and in the air. The airspace above the ranges is often closed to non-military aircraft and civilian pilots will call the above stations to determine whether or not they can fly through the areas.

MATZ stands for 'military aerodrome traffic zone' and civilian aircraft are not allowed in these areas without permission. Calls to obtain permission will be made on the MATZ frequency shown.

As with the civilian listing, many of the frequencies are inter-changeable and it is not unusual for, say, the MATZ frequency to also be used for approach control or radar services.

## Miscellaneous airband services

In addition to general airport approach, take off and landing services, there are a wide variety of other services. Aircraft need to be passed from one region to another and their use of designated airways needs to be controlled. When an aircraft is approaching London, for instance, it will have to change frequencies several times as it is handed from one sector to another. Crossing the borders of different countries also means a change of frequency to a new ground controller. Following an aircraft is easy as it is standard procedure in airband communication for the ground controller to tell the pilot which frequency to change to and for the pilot to repeat the frequency he has been given.

### Emergency frequencies

Table 5.6 lists the allocated UK emergency frequencies and services.

In addition to being allocated for emergency communications use, frequencies 121.5MHz and 243.0MHz are also used for search and rescue beacons of three forms. The first is a small transmitter emitting a radio bleep. It is triggered automatically when a crash occurs, or may be switched on manually. The second type contains a voice transmitter. The third type also includes a receiver, so turning it onto a full, two-way communications transceiver. These beacons are either hand-held or, in the case of SARBE versions, fitted to lifejackets.

Frequencies 156.0MHz and 156.8MHz (both marine frequencies) are used by search and rescue aircraft to communicate with lifeboats, etc.

### Table 5.6 Emergency frequencies and services

| Service | Frequencies (MHz) |
| --- | --- |
| Civilian | 121.500 |
| Boulmer Rescue | 123.100-254.425-282.800-299.100 |
| Leconfield Rescue | 122.100-244.875-282.800 |
| Lifeboat/coastguard | 156.000 (FM) |
| Marine distress | 156.800 (FM) |
| Military | 243.000-40.0500 |
| NATO (scene of search) | 282.800 |
| Search and rescue (air) | 123.100 |

*Navigational aids*

Between the frequencies 108MHz and 117.95MHz you will hear a variety of navigational aids. These are VHF omni-range beacons (VOR) and instrument landing systems (ILS). Some of these services are paired with navigational aids on other bands to give additional services such as distance measuring (DME). Combined VOR/DME services are called VORTACS — the TAC part being a shortening of TACAN which in turn stands for 'tactical navigation'.

*VOLMETS*

These are transmit-only stations providing constantly updated weather information for a variety of major airports.

**Table 5.7 VOLMETS providing weather information**

| *Service* | *Frequency (MHz)* |
| --- | --- |
| London VOLMET main | 135.375 |
| London VOLMET north | 126.600 |
| London VOLMET south | 128.600 |
| Dublin VOLMET | 127.000 |
| Scottish VOLMET | 125.725 |

**Table 5.7b Miscellaneous airband allocations**

| *Service* | *Frequency (MHz)* |
| --- | --- |
| Air-to-Air | 123.450 |
| Air-to-Air (North Atlantic only) | 131.800 |
| Balloons (hot air) | 129.900 |
| Distress | 121.500 |
| Fisheries protection surveillance | 122.100 (North Sea) |
|  | 131.800 (S.W approaches and Channel) |
| Fire vehicles | 121.600 |
| Gliders | 130.100, 130.125, 130.400 |
| Ground control | 121.700, 121.800, 121.900 |
| Hang gliders | 129.900 |
| Lighthouse helipads | 129.700 |
| Search and Rescue (SAR) | 123.100 |

## Table 5.7c Airline and handling agent frequencies

| Operator | Frequency (MHz) | | | | |
|---|---|---|---|---|---|
| Aceair | 130.175 | | | | |
| Aer Lingus | 131.500 | 131.750 | | | |
| Air Atlantique | 130.625 | | | | |
| Air Bridge Carriers | 122.350 | | | | |
| Air Canada | 131.450 | | | | |
| Air Foyle | 131.775 | | | | |
| Air France | 131.500 | | | | |
| Air Hanson | 130.375 | | | | |
| Air India | 131.600 | | | | |
| Air Jamaica | 131.450 | | | | |
| Air Kilroe | 122.350 | | | | |
| Air Malta | 131.650 | | | | |
| Air UK | 129.750 | 131.750 | | | |
| Alitalia | 131.450 | | | | |
| Aurigny Aviation | 122.350 | | | | |
| British Aerospace | 123.050 | | | | |
| Beauport Aviation | 129.700 | | | | |
| Britannia Airways | 131.675 | | | | |
| British Air Ferries | 130.625 | | | | |
| British Airways | 123.650 | 131.475 | 131.800 | 131.550 | 131.625 |
| | 131.850 | 131.900 | | | |
| British Island Airways | 129.750 | | | | |
| British Midland | 129.750 | 131.575 | | | |
| British West Indian | 131.450 | | | | |
| Brymon | 123.650 | | | | |
| Channel Express | 130.600 | | | | |
| C.S.E. Oxford | 129.700 | | | | |
| Connectair | 130.175 | | | | |
| Cyprus Airways | 131.775 | | | | |
| Danair | 131.875 | | | | |
| Delta | 130.600 | | | | |
| Diamond Air | 129.700 | | | | |
| Eastern Airlines | 131.900 | | | | |
| El Al | 131.575 | | | | |
| Eurojet | 131.875 | | | | |
| Execair | 122.350 | | | | |
| Fields Heathrow | 130.600 | | | | |
| Finnair | 131.950 | | | | |
| Gatwick Handling | 130.650 | | | | |
| Genavco | 130.375 | | | | |
| Hatair | 123.650 | | | | |
| Iberia | 131.950 | | | | |
| Inflight | 130.625 | | | | |

**Table 5.7c**  *continued*

| Operator | Frequency (MHz) | |
|---|---|---|
| Interflight | 130.575 | |
| Iran Air | 131.575 | |
| Japanese Airlines | 131.650 | |
| Jet centre | 130.375 | |
| K.L.M. | 131.650 | |
| Kuwait Airlines | 131.500 | |
| Loganair | 130.650 | |
| Lufthansa | 131.925 | |
| Luxair | 131.550 | |
| Magec | 123.650 | |
| M.A.M. | 129.700 | |
| Manx Airlines | 129.750 | |
| M.A.S. | 131.575 | |
| McAlpine Aviation | 123.650 | |
| Monarch | 131,525 | |
| Nigerian Airways | 131.775 | |
| Northern | 130.650 | |
| Pakistan International | 131.450 | |
| Qantas | 131,875 | |
| Royal Jordanian | 131.425 | |
| S.A.S. | 131.700 | |
| Sabena | 131.475 | |
| Saudia | 131.425 | |
| Servisair | 130.075 | 130.600 |
| Singapore Airlines | 131.950 | |
| Skycare | 122.050 | 130.025 |
| Spurnair | 122.050 | |
| Swissair | 131.700 | |
| T.A.P. | 131.750 | |
| Thai-Inter | 131.450 | |
| T.W.A. | 131.600 | |
| Uni Avco | 130.575 | |
| Veritair | 129.900 | |
| Wardair | 129.700 | |

# Marine band

This, like the VHF airband, is one of the few international bands; it is common to *all* ITU regions.

It is channelized in that radio equipment made for marine VHF use does not usually have facilities to tune to a given frequency, instead it has a channel selector which goes from channel 1 to channel 88. A list of marine band channels and their transmission frequencies is given in Table 5.8.

Channels are designated for specific uses in that some are for ship-to-shore use, others for ship-to-ship, and so forth. The method of operating on marine band is very different from airband. On marine bands there is a common calling frequency which is also the main distress frequency: channel 16, at 156.8MHz. When a ship wishes to call a shore station, even though the operator may know the channel that is used by that shore station, he will still make first contact on channel 16. Once contact is made the ship and shore station will then move to a 'working channel' — in most instances this will be the station's 'prime' channel for general transmissions, or 'link' channel for link calls (ie, ship-to-shore telephone calls).

Channels 0 and 67 are used by lifeboats and the coast guard. Some search and rescue aircraft also have the facility to work these channels.

Table 5.8 shows that many channels have two frequencies. This is to enable duplex operation. Because these *are* duplex transmissions, it is impossible for a scanner to simultaneously monitor both frequencies. Two scanners would have to be used, each tuned to one of the two frequencies, if the whole transmission was to be received.

### Range
The useful range for marine VHF communications tends to be somewhat better than for the same type of frequencies and power levels used across land. Quite simply, there are few obstructions at sea and maximum ranges of 50-100 miles are not unusual. However, while signals from a ship may be quite strong at a coastal station, the signals may deteriorate even a mile or two inland.

## Table 5.8 International marine channels

| Channel | Ship | Coast | Service |
|---|---|---|---|
| 0 | 156.000 | | Coastguard/lifeboat |
| 00 | 160.600 | | Coastguard/lifeboat |
| 01 | 156.050 | 160.650 | Port operations/link calls |
| 02 | 156.100 | 160.700 | Port operations/link calls |
| 03 | 156.150 | 160.750 | Port operations/link calls |
| 04 | 156.200 | 160.800 | Port operations/link calls |
| 05 | 156.250 | 160.850 | Port operations/link calls |
| 06 | 156.300 | | Intership primary/search and rescue |
| 07 | 156.350 | 160.950 | Port operations/link calls |
| 08 | 156.400 | | Intership |
| 09 | 156.450 | | Intership |

**Table 5.8**  *continued*

| Channel | Ship | Coast | Service |
|---|---|---|---|
| 10 | 156.500 | | Intership/pollution control |
| 11 | 156.550 | | Port operations |
| 12 | 156.600 | | Port operations primary |
| 13 | 156.650 | | Port operations |
| 14 | 156.700 | | Port operations primary |
| 15 | 156.750 | | Port operations |
| 16 | 156.800 | ****** | Distress and calling |
| 17 | 156.850 | | Port operations |
| 18 | 156.900 | 161.500 | Port operations |
| 19 | 156.950 | 161.550 | Port operations |
| 20 | 157.000 | 161.600 | Port operations |
| 21 | 157.050 | 161.650 | Port operations |
| 22 | 157.100 | 161.700 | Port operations |
| 23 | 157.150 | 161.750 | Link calls |
| 24 | 157.200 | 161.800 | Link calls |
| 25 | 157.250 | 161.850 | Link calls |
| 26 | 157.300 | 161.900 | Link calls |
| 27 | 157.350 | 161.950 | Link calls |
| 28 | 157.400 | 161.200 | Link calls |
| 29 | 157.450 | 162.050 | Private channel |
| 30 | 157.500 | 162.100 | Private channel |
| 31 | 157.550 | 162.150 | Private channel |
| 32 | 157.600 | 162.200 | Private channel |
| 33 | 157.650 | 162.250 | Private channel |
| 34 | 157.700 | 162.300 | Private channel |
| 35 | 157.750 | 162.350 | Private channel |
| 36 | 157.800 | 162.400 | Private channel |
| 37 | 157.850 | 162.450 | Private channel |
| 38 | 157.900 | 162.500 | Private channel |
| 39 | 157.950 | 162.550 | Private channel |
| 40 | 158.000 | 162.600 | Private channel |
| 41 | 158.050 | 162.650 | Private channel |
| 42 | 158.100 | 162.700 | Private channel |
| 43 | 158.150 | 162.750 | Private channel |
| 44 | 158.200 | 162.800 | Private channel |
| 45 | 158.250 | 162.850 | Private channel |
| 46 | 158.300 | 162.900 | Private channel |
| 47 | 158.350 | 162.950 | Private channel |
| 48 | 158.400 | 163.000 | Private channel |
| 49 | 158.450 | 163.050 | Private channel |
| 50 | 158.500 | 163.100 | Private channel |
| 51 | 158.550 | 163.150 | Private channel |
| 52 | 158.600 | 163.200 | Private channel |
| 53 | 158.650 | 163.250 | Private channel |
| 54 | 158.700 | 163.300 | Private channel |
| 55 | 158.750 | 163.350 | Private channel |
| 56 | 158.800 | 163.400 | Private channel |
| 60 | 156.025 | 160.625 | Link calls |

**Table 5.8**  *continued*

| Channel | Ship | Coast | Service |
|---|---|---|---|
| 61 | 156.075 | 160.675 | Link calls |
| 62 | 156.125 | 160.725 | Link calls |
| 63 | 156.175 | 160.775 | Link calls |
| 64 | 156.225 | 160.825 | Link calls |
| 65 | 156.275 | 160.875 | Link calls |
| 66 | 156.325 | 160.925 | Link calls |
| 67 | 156.375 |  | Intership/small yacht safety/coastguard |
| 68 | 156.425 |  | Intership |
| 69 | 156.475 |  | Intership |
| 70 | 156.525 |  | Digital selective calling/Distress |
| 71 | 156.575 |  | Port operations |
| 72 | 156.625 |  | Intership |
| 73 | 156.675 |  | Intership/pollution control/Coastguard |
| 74 | 156.725 |  | Ports/lock keepers/swing bridges |
| 77 | 156.875 |  | Intership |
| 78 | 156.925 | 161.525 | Port operations |
| 79 | 156.975 | 161.575 | Port operations |
| 80 | 157.025 | 161.625 | Port operations |
| 81 | 157.075 | 161.675 | Port operations |
| 82 | 157.125 | 161.725 | Port operations |
| 83 | 157.175 | 161.775 | Port operations |
| 84 | 157.225 | 161.825 | Port operations |
| 85 | 157.275 | 161.875 | Port operations |
| 86 | 157.325 | 161.925 | Link calls |
| 87 | 157.375 | 161.975 | Link calls |
| 88 | 157.425 | 162.025 | calls calls |
| M1 | 157.850 |  | Marinas |
| M2 | 161.675 |  | Marinas & yacht clubs |

On-board-ship UHF handset frequencies (FM-split frequency simplex)
CH1    457.525 paired with 467.525
CH2    457.550 paired with 467.550
CH3    457.575 paired with 467.675

**Table 5.9 General marine services and channel allocations**

| Service | Channels |
|---|---|
| Ship-to-ship | 6, 8, 9, 10, 13, 15, 17, 67, 68, 70, 72, 75, 76, 77, 78 |
| Port operations (simplex) | 9, 10, 11, 12, 13, 14, 15, 17, 67, 69, 71, 73, 74 |
| Port operations (duplex) | 1, 2, 3, 4, 5, 7, 18, 19, 20, 21, 22, 60, 61, 62, 63, 64, 65, 66, 78, 79, 80, 81, 82, 84 |
| Public correspondence (link calls) | 1, 2, 3, 4, 5, 7, 23, 24, 25, 26, 27, 28, 60, 61, 62, 63, 64, 65, 66, 82, 83, 84, 85, 86, 87, 88 |

## Shore stations

Table 5.10 lists UK shore stations, together with their broadcast and working channels. All stations transmit local area navigation warnings (beacons out of action, hazardous floating objects, etc). Most, but not all, transmit local area weather forecasts and storm warnings.

## Table 5.10 British and Irish Coastal Stations

| | *Traffic* | | *Nav lists* | *Wx warn* | *Gale warn* |
|---|---|---|---|---|---|
| Cullercoats | 0103 | 1303 | 0233 | | |
| Chs: 16 26 | 0303 | 1503 | 0633 | 0703 | 0303 |
| | 0503 | 1703 | 1033 | | 0903 |
| | 0703 | 1903 | 1433 | | 1503 |
| | 0903 | 2103 | 1833 | 1903 | 2103 |
| | 1103 | 2303 | 2233 | | |
| Hebrides | 0103 | 1303 | 0203 | | |
| Chs: 16 26 | 0303 | 1503 | 0603 | 0703 | 0303 |
| | 0503 | 1703 | 1003 | | 0903 |
| | 0703 | 1903 | 1403 | | 1503 |
| | 0903 | 2103 | 1803 | 1903 | 2103 |
| | 1103 | 2303 | 2203 | | |
| Humber | 0103 | 1503 | 0133 | | 0303 |
| Chs: 16 24 26 85 | 0303 | 1703 | 0533 | 0733 | 0903 |
| | 0503 | 1903 | 0933 | | 1503 |
| | 0903 | 2103 | 1333 | | 2103 |
| | 1103 | 2303 | 1733 | 1933 | |
| | 1303 | | 2133 | | |
| Ilfracombe | 0133 | 1533 | 0233 | | 0303 |
| Chs: 16 05 07 | 0533 | 1733 | 0633 | 0833 | 0933 |
| | 0733 | 1933 | 1033 | | 1503 |
| | 0933 | 2133 | 1433 | | 2103 |
| | 1133 | 2333 | 1833 | 2033 | |
| | 1333 | | 2233 | | |
| Jersey | After | | 0433 | 0645 | as |
| Chs: 16 82 25 67 | wx | | 0645 | 0745 | req + |
| | | | 0745 | 1245 | |
| | | | 0833 | 1845 | 0307 |
| | | | 1245 | 2245 | 0907 |
| | | 1633 | 1845 | | 1507 |
| | | 2033 | 2245 | | 2107 |

**Table 5.10**  *continued*

| | Traffic | | Nav lists | Wx warn | Gale warn |
|---|---|---|---|---|---|
| **Land's End** | 0103 | 1503 | 0233 | | 0303 |
| Chs: 16 27 88 85 64 | 0303 | 1703 | 0633 | 0733 | 0903 |
| | 0503 | 1903 | 1033 | | 1503 |
| | 0903 | 2103 | 1433 | | 2103 |
| | 1103 | 2303 | 1833 | 1933 | |
| | 1303 | | 2233 | | |
| **Malin Head** | 0103 | 1503 | 0033 | | |
| Chs: 16 23 67 85 | 0503 | 1703 | 0433 | | |
| | 0903 | 1903 | 0833 | | |
| | 1103 | 2103 | 1233 | | |
| | 1303 | 2303 | 1633 | | |
| **Niton** | 0103 | 1503 | 0233 | | 0303 |
| Chs: 16 04 28 81 | 0303 | 1703 | 0633 | 0733 | 0903 |
| 85 64 87 | 0503 | 1903 | 1033 | | 1503 |
| | 0903 | 2103 | 1433 | | 2103 |
| | 1103 | 2303 | 1833 | 1933 | |
| | 1303 | | 2233 | | |
| **North Foreland** | 0103 | 1503 | 0233 | | 0303 |
| Chs: 16 05 26 66 65 | 0303 | 1703 | 0633 | 0733 | 0903 |
| | 0503 | 1903 | 1033 | | 1503 |
| | 0903 | 2103 | 1433 | | 2103 |
| | 1103 | 2303 | 1833 | 1933 | |
| | 1303 | | 2233 | | |
| **Portpatrick** | 0103 | 1303 | 0203 | | |
| Chs: 16 27 | 0303 | 1503 | 0603 | 0733 | 0303 |
| | 0503 | 1703 | 1003 | | 0903 |
| | 0703 | 1903 | 1403 | | 1503 |
| | 0903 | 2103 | 1803 | 1903 | 2103 |
| | 1103 | 2303 | 2203 | | |
| **St Peter Port** | After | | 0133 | | |
| Chs: 16 12 62 78 | navi- | 0533 | | | |
| | gation | 0933 | 1333 | | |
| | warnings | | 1733 | | |
| | | | 2133 | | |
| **Shetland** | 0103 | 1303 | 0233 | | |
| Chs: 16 27 | 0303 | 1503 | 0633 | 0703 | 0303 |

**Table 5.10**  *continued*

|  | Traffic | Nav lists | Wx warn | Gale warn |
|---|---|---|---|---|
| Remote control from | 0503 | 1703 | 1033 | 0903 |
| Wick | 0703 | 1903 | 1433 | 1503 |
|  | 0903 | 2103 | 1833 | 1903 | 2103 |
|  | 1103 | 2303 | 2233 |  |  |
| Stonehaven | 0103 | 1303 | 0233 |  |  |
| Chs: 16 26 | 0303 | 1503 | 0633 | 0733 | 0303 |
|  | 0503 | 1703 | 1033 |  | 0903 |
|  | 0703 | 1903 | 1433 |  | 1503 |
|  | 0903 | 2103 | 1833 | 1933 | 2103 |
|  | 1103 | 2303 | 2233 |  |  |
| Valentia | 0333 | 1533 | 0233 |  | 0033 |
| Chs: 16 24 28 67 | 0733 | 1733 | 0633 |  |  |
|  | 0933 | 1933 | 1033 |  | 0633 |
|  | 1333 | 2333 | 1833 |  | 1233 |
|  | 2233 | 2033 | 1833 |  |  |

Anglesey Chs: 16 26 28 61 remote control by Portpatrick

Bacton Chs: 16 07 63 64 03 remote control by Humber

Bantry Chs: 16 23 67 85 remote control by Valentia

Belmullet Chs: 16 67 83 remote control by Malin Head

Buchan Chs: 16 25 87 remote control by Stonehaven

Cardigan Bay Chs: 16 03 remote control by Portpatrick

Celtic Chs: 16 24 remote control by Ilfracombe

Clyde Chs: 16 26 remote control by Portpatrick

Collafirth Chs: 16 24 remote control by Wick

Cork Chs: 16 26 67 remote control by Valentia

Cromarty Chs: 16 28 84 remote control by Wick

Dublin Chs: 16 83 remote control by Malin Head

Forth Chs: 16 24 62 remote control by Stonehaven

**Table 5.10**   *continued*

---

Glen Head Chs: 16 24 67 remote control by Malin Head

---

Grimsby Chs: 16 04 27 remote control by Humber

---

Hastings Chs: 16 07 63 remote control by North Foreland

---

Islay Chs: 16 25 60 remote control by Portpatrick

---

Lewis Chs: 16 05 remote control by Stonehaven

---

Mine Head Chs: 16 67 83 remote control by Valentia

---

Morcambe Bay Chs: 16 04 82 remote control by Portpatrick

---

Orfordness Chs: 16 62 82 remote control by North Foreland

---

Orkney Chs: 16 26 remote control by Wick

---

Pendennis Chs: 16 62 66 remote control by Land's End

---

Rosslare Chs: 16 23 67 remote control by Valentia

---

Shannon Chs: 16 24 28 67 remote control by Valentia

---

Skye Chs: 16 24 remote control by Stonehaven

---

Start Point Chs: 16 26 65 60 remote control by Land's End

---

Thames Chs: 16 02 83 remote control by North Foreland

---

Weymouth Bay Chs: 16 05 remote control by Niton

---

Whitby Chs: 16 25 28 remote control by Cullercoats

---

Wick See Shetland

---

*Remote stations broadcast at the same time as their control stations.

## Table 5.10b Ports, harbours and marinas in Great Britain

| Port/Harbour | Channels |
| --- | --- |
| **Aberdeen** (Aberdeen) | |
| Aberdeen Radio | 10 11 12 13 16 |
| **Aberdovey** (Gwynedd) | |
| Aberdovey Harbour | 12 16 |
| **Abersoch** (Gwynedd) | |
| South Caernarfon Yacht Club | 37 80 |
| **Aberystwyth** (Dyfed) | |
| Harbour Control | 14 16 |
| **Alderney** | see Braye |
| **Amble** (Northumberland) | |
| Amble Harbour | 14 16 |
| Amble Braid Marina | 37 80 |
| **Appledore** (Devon) | see River Taw |
| **Ardrishaig** (Argyll) | |
| Harbour | 16 74 |
| **Avonmouth** (Avon) | see Bristol |
| **Barmouth** (Gwynedd) | |
| Barmouth Harbour | 10 16 |
| **Barry** (South Glamorgan) | |
| Barry Radio | 10 12 |
| **Beaucette** (Guernsey) | |
| Marina | 16 37 80 |
| **Bembridge** (Isle of Wight) | |
| Bembridge Marina | 16 37 80 |
| **Berwick-on-Tweed** (Northumberland) | |
| Pilots and Harbourmaster | 12 16 |
| **Blackwater River** (Essex) | |
| Bradwell & Tollesbury Marinas | 37 80 |
| **Blyth** (Northumberland) | |
| Blythe Harbour Control | 12 16 |

**Table 5.10b** *continued*

| Port/Harbour | Channels |
|---|---|
| **Boston** (Lincolnshire) | |
| Boston Dock | 12 |
| Grand Sluice | 74 |
| **Braye** (Alderney) | |
| Alderney Radio | 16 74 |
| Mainbryce Marina (summer only) | 37 80 |
| **Bridlington** (Humberside) | |
| Bridlington Harbour | 12 14 16 |
| **Bridport** (Dorset) | |
| Bridport Radio | 11 12 14 16 |
| **Brighton** (East Sussex) | |
| Brighton Control | 11 16 68 |
| Marina | 37 80 |
| **Bristol** (Avon) | |
| Avonmouth Radio | 12 |
| South Pier & Royal Edward Dock | 12 |
| Port Operations | 09 11 14 16 |
| Pilots | 06 08 09 12 14 |
| Royal Portbury, Portishead & City Docks | 12 14 16 |
| Floating Harbour | 16 73 |
| Newport | 09 11 16 |
| **Brixham** (Devon) | |
| Harbour | 14 16 |
| Pilots | 09 10 13 16 |
| Brixham Coastguard | 10 16 67 73 |
| **Bude** (Cornwall) | |
| Bude Radio | 12 16 |
| **Burghead** (Moray) | |
| Harbour | 14 16 |
| **Burnham-on-Crouch** (Essex) | |
| Essex and West Wick Marinas | 37 80 |
| **Burnham-on-Sea** (Somerset) | |
| Harbour Master and Pilots | 08 16 |

**Table 5.10b**  *continued*

| Port/Harbour | Channels |
|---|---|
| Watchet | 09 12 14 16 |
| Marina | 37 80 |
| **Caernarfon** (Gwynedd) | |
| Caernarfon Radio (day only) | 12 14 16 |
| **Caledonian Canal** (Inverness) | see also Inverness |
| All locks | 74 |
| **Campbelltown** (Argyll) | |
| Harbour | 12 14 16 |
| **Cardiff** (South Glamorgan) | |
| Docks | 11 14 16 |
| Marina | 37 80 |
| **Cattewater Harbour** (Devon) | see Plymouth-Devonport |
| **Charlestown** (Cornwall) | see Fowey |
| **Chichester** (West Sussex) | |
| Harbour | 14 16 |
| Marinas | 37 80 |
| **Colchester** (Essex) | |
| Colchester Harbour Radio | 11 14 16 |
| **Conwy** (Gwnedd) | |
| Conway | 06 08 12 14 16 72 |
| Llanddulas | 14 16 |
| Cruising Club | 37 80 |
| **Cowes** (Isle of Wight) | |
| Cowes | 06 11 16 |
| Island Harbour and marinas | 37 80 |
| Chain Ferry | 10 |
| **Craobh Haven/Loch Shuna** (Argyll) | |
| Marina | 16 37 80 |
| **Crinan** (Argyll) | |
| Harbour | 16 74 |
| **Cromarty Firth** | see Inverness |

**Table 5.10b** *continued*

| Port/Harbour | Channels |
|---|---|
| **Dartmouth** (Devon) | |
| Harbour/Pilots | 14 |
| Dart Marina & Sailing Centre | 37 80 |
| Kingswear Marina ('Marina Four') | 37 80 |
| Fuel barge | 16 |
| Water taxi | 16 37 80 |
| **Devonport** (Devon) | see Plymouth-Devonport |
| **Douglas** (Isle of Man) | |
| Douglas Harbour | 12 16 |
| **Dover** (Kent) | |
| Dover Port Control | 12 74 |
| Channel Navigation Information Service | 11 16 67 69 80 |
| Information broadcasts (H + 40) | 11 |
| **Dundee/River Tay** (Fife/Angus) | |
| Dundee Harbour Radio | 10 11 12 13 14 16 |
| Perth Harbour | 09 |
| **East Loch Tarbert** (Argyll) | |
| Harbour | 16 |
| **Exeter** (Devon) | |
| Harbour | 06 12 16 |
| Pilots | 09 12 14 16 |
| **Eyemouth** (Berwick) | |
| No regular watch | 12 16 |
| **Falmouth** (Cornwall) | see also River Fal |
| Falmouth Harbour Radio | 11 16 |
| **Felixstowe** (Suffolk) | see Harwich |
| **Firth of Forth** (Lothian Fife) | |
| North Queensferry Naval Station | 13 16 71 |
| Rosyth Naval Base ('QHM') | 13 |
| Forth Navigation Service | 12 16 20 71 |
| Grangemouth Docks | 14 16 |
| Port Edgar Marina | 37 80 |
| BP Grangemouth Terminal | 14 16 19 |

**Table 5.10b**  *continued*

| Port/Harbour | Channels |
|---|---|
| Braefoot Terminal | 15 16 69 73 |
| Hound Point Terminal | 09 10 12 16 19 |
| **Fishguard** (Dyfed) | |
| Fishguard Radio | 14 16 |
| Marina | 37 80 |
| **Fleetwood** (Lancashire) | |
| Fleetwood Harbour Control | 11 12 16 |
| Fleetwood Docks | 12 16 |
| Ramsden Docks | 12 16 |
| **Folkestone** (Kent) | |
| Harbour | 16 22 |
| Pilot Station | 09 |
| **Fowey** (Cornwall) | |
| Fowey Harbour Radio | 12 16 |
| Pilots | 09 |
| Water taxi | 06 |
| Boat Marshall Patrol | 12 16 |
| Charlestown | 14 16 |
| Par Port Radio | 12 16 |
| **Fraserburgh** (Aberdeen) | |
| Harbour | 12 16 |
| **Glasson Dock** (Lancashire) | |
| Glasson Radio | 08 16 |
| Marina | M |
| **Gorey** (Jersey) | |
| Gorey Harbour (summer only) | 74 |
| **Gravesend** (Essex) | |
| Gravesend Radio | 12 16 |
| **Great Yarmouth** (Norfolk) | |
| Yarmouth Radio | 09 11 12 16 |
| Breydon Bridge | 12 |
| **Greenock** (Renfrew) | |
| Clydeport Estuary Radio | 12 14 16 |
| Dunoon Pier | 12 16 31 |

**Table 5.10b**  *continued*

| Port/Harbour | Channels |
|---|---|
| **Grimsby** (Humberside) | see also River Humber |
| Grimsby (Royal Dock) | 09 16 18 |
| **Guernsey** | see St Peter Port, St Sampsons & Beaucette |
| **Hamble** (Hampshire) | |
| Hamble Harbour Radio | 16 68 |
| Marinas | 37 80 |
| **Hartlepool** (Cleveland) | |
| Hartlepool Dock Radio | 11 12 16 |
| **Harwich** (Essex) | |
| Harwich Harbour Control | 11 14 16 71 |
| Harbour Board patrol launch | 11 |
| Shotley Poin Marina | 37 80 |
| **Havengore** (Essex) | see Shoeburyness |
| **Helensburgh** (Dumbarton) | |
| Rhu Marina | 37 80 |
| Faslane (nuclear sub base) Patrol Boats | 16 |
| **Helford River** (Cornwall) | |
| Helford River SC & Gweek Quay Marina | 37 80 |
| **Heysham** (Lancashire) | |
| Heysham | 14 16 |
| **Holyhead** (Gwynedd) | |
| Holyhead Radio | 14 16 |
| Anglesey Marine Terminal | 10 12 16 19 |
| **Ilfracombe** (Devon) | |
| Ilfracombe Harbour (summer only) | 12 16 37 80 |
| **Immingham** (Humberside) | see also River Humber |
| Immingham Docks | 09 16 22 |
| **Inverkip** (Renfrew) | |
| Kip Marina | 37 80 |
| **Inverness** (Inverness) | |

**Table 5.10b**  *continued*

| Port/Harbour | Channels |
|---|---|
| Inverness Harbour Office | 06 12 14 16 |
| Inverness Boat Centre & Caley Marina | 37 80 |
| Cromarty Firth Port Control | 06 08 11 12 13 14 16 |
| Clachnaharry Sea Lock & Caledonian Canal | 74 |
| **Ipswich** (Suffolk) | |
| Ipswich Port Radio | 12 14 16 |
| Marinas and yacht harbour | 37 80 |
| **Isle of Man** | see also I.O.M. ports |
| Radio/Landline link to Liverpool | 12 16 |
| **Isles of Scilly** | |
| Land's End Radio | 64 |
| St Mary's Harbour | 14 16 |
| **Jersey** | see St Helier & Gorey |
| **King's Lynn** (Norfolk) | |
| King's Lynn Radio | 11 1416 |
| Docks | 11 14 16 |
| Wisbech | 09 14 16 |
| **Kirkcudbright** (Kirkcudbrightshire) | |
| Harbour | 12 16 |
| **Kirkwall** (Orkney Islands) | |
| Kirkwall Radio | 12 16 |
| Orkney Harbour Radio | 09 11 16 20 |
| **Langstone** (Hampshire) | |
| Langstone | 12 16 |
| Marina | 37 80 |
| **Largs** (Ayr) | |
| Yacht Haven | 37 80 |
| **Lerwick** (Shetland Islands) | |
| Lerwick | 11 12 16 |
| Sullom Voe | 12 14 16 19 20 |
| Scalloway | 12 16 |
| Balta Sound (no regular watch) | 16 20 |

**Table 5.10b**  *continued*

| Port/Harbour | Channels |
|---|---|
| **Littlehampton** (West Sussex) | |
| Littlehampton | 14 16 |
| Marina | 37 80 |
| **Liverpool** (Merseyside) | |
| Mersey Radio | 09 12 16 18 19 22 |
| Alfred & Gladstone Docks | 05 |
| Tranmere Stages | 09 |
| Gartson & Waterloo Docks | 20 |
| Langton Dock | 21 |
| Eastham Locks (Manchester Ship Canal) | 07 14 |
| Latchford Locks (Manchester Ship Canal) | 14 20 |
| Weaver Navigation & Weston Point | 74 |
| Marsh, Dutton & Saltisford Locks | 74 |
| Anderton Depot | 74 |
| **Loch Craignish** (Argyll) | |
| Yachting Centre | 16 37 80 |
| **Loch Maddy** (North Uinst) | |
| Harbour | 12 16 |
| **Loch Melfort** (Argyll) | |
| Camus Marine | 16 37 80 |
| **London** | see River Thames |
| **Looe** (Cornwall) | |
| Only occasional watch | 16 |
| **Lossiemouth** (Moray) | |
| Lossiemouth Radio | 12 16 |
| **Lowestoft** (Suffolk) | |
| Harbour | 14 16 |
| Pilots | 14 |
| **Lyme Regis** (Dorset) | |
| Lyme Regis Harbour Radio | 14 16 |
| **Lymington** (Hampshire) | |
| Marinas | 37 80 |

**Table 5.10b**  *continued*

| Port/Harbour | Channels |
|---|---|
| **Lulworth Gunnery Range** (Dorset) | |
| Range Safety Boats | 08 |
| Portland Naval Base | 13 14 |
| Portland Coastguard | 67 |
| **Macduff** (Banff) | |
| Harbour | 12 16 |
| **Mallaig** (Inverness) | |
| Mallaig Harbour Radio | 09 16 |
| **Manchester** (Lancashire) | |
| Ship canal | 14 16 |
| Barton & Irlham Docks & Mode Wheel Lock | 14 18 |
| Stanlow Oil Docks & Latchford Lock | 14 20 |
| Eastham Lock | 07 14 |
| Tugs inbound | 08 |
| Tugs outbound | 10 |
| Weaver Navigation Service | 14 71 73 |
| **Maryport** (Cumbria) | |
| Maryport Harbour (occasional watch) | 12 16 |
| **Methil** (Fife) | |
| Methil Radio | 14 16 |
| **Mevagissey** (Cornwall) | |
| Harbour | 16 56 |
| **Milford Haven** (Dyfed) | |
| Milford Haven Radio | 09 10 11 12 14 16 67 |
| Patrol & Pilot launches | 06 08 11 12 14 16 67 |
| Milford Docks | 09 12 14 16 |
| Amoco/Gulf Terminals | 14 16 18 |
| Esso Terminal | 14 16 19 |
| Texaco Terminal | 14 16 21 |
| Marina and Yacht Station | 37 80 |
| **Minehead** (Somerset) | |
| Minehead Radio (occasional watch only) | 12 14 16 |
| **Montrose** (Angus) | |
| Montrose Radio | 12 16 |

**Table 5.10b**  *continued*

| Port/Harbour | Channels |
|---|---|
| **Newhaven** (East Sussex) | |
| Harbour | 12 16 |
| Marina | 37 80 |
| **Newlyn** (Cornwall) | |
| Newlyn Harbour | 12 16 |
| Pilots | 09 12 16 |
| **Newquay** (Cornwall) | |
| Newquay Radio | 14 16 |
| **North Shields** (Tyne and Wear) | see River Tyne |
| **Oban** (Argyll) | |
| Coastguard | 16 |
| **Padstow** (Cornwall) | |
| Padstow Radio | 16 14 |
| **Par Port Radio** (Cornwall) | see Fowey |
| **Peel** (Isle of Man) | |
| Peel | 12 16 |
| **Penzance** (Cornwall) | |
| Harbour/Pilots | 09 12 16 |
| **Peterhead** (Aberdeen) | |
| Peterhead Radio | 09 11 14 16 |
| **Plymouth – Devonport** (Devon) | |
| Long Room Port Control | 08 12 14 16 |
| Mill Bay Docks | 12 14 16 |
| Sutton Harbour Radio | 12 16 37 80 |
| Marinas, Yacht harbour & Clubs | 37 80 |
| Cattewater Harbour Office | 12 16 |
| **Poole** (Dorset) | |
| Poole Harbour Control | 14 16 |
| Pilots | 06 09 14 16 |
| Salterns Marina ('Gulliver Base') | 37 80 |
| Cobb's Quay | 37 80 |
| **Porthmadog** (Caernarfon) | |
| Harbour Master | 12 16 |

**Table 5.10b**  *continued*

| Port/Harbour | Channels |
|---|---|
| Madoc Yacht Club | 16 37 |
| **Portland** (Dorset) | |
| Portland Naval Station | 13 14 |
| Portland Coastguard | 16 67 69 |
| **Port of London** | see River Thames |
| **Portpatrick** (Wigtown) | |
| Portpatrick Coast Radio Station | 16 27 |
| Stranraer | 14 16 |
| **Portree** (Skye) | |
| Port (no regular watch) | 08 16 |
| **Port Saint Mary** (Isle of Man) | |
| Port Saint Mary Harbour | 12 16 |
| **Portsmouth** (Hampshire) | see also Solent |
| Portsmouth Harbour Radio | 11 13 |
| Queens Harbour Master | 11 |
| Portsmouth Naval | 13 |
| Marina ('Camper Base') & yacht harbour | 37 80 |
| Fort Gilkicker | 16 |
| **Ramsey** (Isle of Man) | |
| Ramsey | 12 16 |
| **Ramsgate** (Kent) | |
| Harbour & Marina | 14 16 |
| **River Avon** | see Bristol |
| **River Deben** (Suffolk) | |
| Tide Mill Yacht Harbour | 37 80 |
| Pilot | 08 |
| **River Exe** (Devon) | |
| Exeter | 06 12 16 |
| **River Fal** (Cornwall) | |
| Falmouth Harbour Radio | 11 16 |
| Pilots | 06 08 09 10 11 12 14 16 |
| Coastguard | 10 16 67 73 |
| Customs Launch | 06 09 12 16 |

**Table 5.10b**  *continued*

| Port/Harbour | Channels |
| --- | --- |
| Port Health | 06 12 16 |
| Yacht harbour, marina and club | 37 80 |
| **River Humber** (Humberside) | |
| Humber Vessel Traffic Service | 12 16 |
| Grimsby (Royal Dock) | 09 16 18 |
| Immingham Docks | 09 16 22 |
| River Hull Port Operations ('Drypool Radio') | 06 14 16 |
| Tetney Oil Terminal | 16 19 |
| Goole Docks | 14 16 |
| Booth Ferry Bridge | 12 16 |
| Selby Bridges | 09 12 16 |
| Marinas and yacht harbour | 37 80 |
| **River Medway** (Kent) | see also The Swale |
| Medway Radio | 09 11 16 22 74 |
| Marinas | 37 80 |
| **River Ore** (Suffolk) | |
| Orford | 16 67 |
| **River Orwell** (Suffolk) | see Ipswich |
| **River Taw** (Devon) | |
| Pilots | 06 09 12 16 |
| **River Tees** (Cleveland) | |
| Tees Harbour Radio | 08 11 12 14 16 22 |
| **River Thames** (London) | |
| Woolwich Radio | 14 16 22 |
| Gravesend Radio | 12 14 16 18 20 |
| Thames Radio | 02 |
| Thames Patrol | 06 12 14 16 |
| Thames Barrier | 14 |
| Thames Navigation Service | 12 |
| St Katherines Yacht Haven | 37 80 |
| Chelsea Harbour Marina | 14 16 37 |
| Brentford Dock Marina | 14 16 |
| North Foreland | 26 |
| Hastings | 07 |
| Orfordness Radio | 62 |
| Shellhaven | 16 19 |

**Table 5.10b**  *continued*

| Port/Harbour | Channels |
|---|---|
| **River Tyne** (Tyne and Wear) | |
| Tyne Harbour Radio | 11 12 14 16 |
| **Rona Naval Base** (Rona) | |
| Base | 16 |
| **Rothesay** (Isle of Bute) | |
| Harbour | 12 16 |
| **Rye** (East Sussex) | |
| Harbour | 14 16 |
| **Saint Helier** (Jersey) | |
| Saint Helier Port Control | 14 |
| Jersey Radio | 16 25 82 |
| Lifeboat | 00 16 14 |
| **Saint Kilda** (Saint Kilda Island) | |
| Kilda Radio | 08 16 |
| **Saint Peter Port** (Guernsey) | |
| Port Control | 12 16 21 |
| Lifeboat | 00 12 16 |
| **Saint Sampsons** (Guernsey) | |
| Harbour | 12 16 |
| **Salcombe** (Devon) | |
| Salcombe Harbour | 14 |
| ICC Clubhouse & Floating HQ | 37 80 |
| Fuel barge | 06 |
| Water taxi | 14 |
| **Scarborough** (North Yorkshire) | |
| Scarborough Lighthouse | 12 14 16 |
| **Scrabster** (Caithness) | |
| Harbour | 12 16 |
| **Seaham** (Durham) | |
| Seaham Harbour | 06 12 16 |
| **Sharpness** (Gloucestershire) | |
| Sharpness Control | 14 16 |
| Bridges | 74 |

**Table 5.10b**  *continued*

| Port/Harbour | Channels |
|---|---|
| **Sheerness** (Kent) | see River Medway |
| **Shetland Islands** | |
| Shetland Radio | 16 27 |
| Collafirth Radio | 16 24 |
| **Shoeburyness** (Essex) | |
| Gunnery Range Operations Officer | 16 |
| Gravesend Radio | 12 |
| **Shoreham** (West Sussex) | |
| Marinas | 37 80 |
| **Solent** (Hampshire) | |
| Solent Coastguard | 00 06 10 16 67 73 |
| Southampton Port Radio | 12 14 16 18 20 22 |
| Pilots | 06 08 09 10 12 14 16 18 |
| Queen's Harbour Master (Portsmouth) | 11 13 |
| Commercial Harbour Master (Portsmouth) | 11 |
| Pilots | 09 |
| Ships, tugs, & berthing | 71 74 |
| BP Terminal | 06 16 18 |
| Esso Terminal | 14 16 18 |
| **Southampton** (Hampshire) | see also Solent |
| Vessel Traffic Services | 12 14 16 |
| Harbour Patrol | 10 12 14 16 18 22 71 74 |
| Marinas | 37 80 |
| **Southwold** (Suffolk) | |
| Southwold Port Radio | 12 16 |
| Pilots | 09 12 |
| **Stornoway** (Outer Hebrides-Lewis) | |
| Harbour | 12 16 |
| **Stromness** (Orkney Islands) | |
| Stromness Radio | 12 16 |
| **Sullom Voe** | see Lerwick |
| **Sunderland** (Tyne and Wear) | |
| Sunderland Docks | 14 16 |

**Table 5.10b** *continued*

| Port/Harbour | Channels |
|---|---|
| **Sutton Harbour** (Devon) | see Plymouth-Devonport |
| **Swansea** (West Glamorgan) | |
| Swansea Docks Radio | 14 16 |
| Marina | 37 80 |
| **Teignmouth** (Devon) | |
| Harbour/Pilots | 12 16 |
| **Tenby** (Dyfed) | |
| Listening watch days only | 16 |
| **The Swale** (Kent) | |
| Medway Radio | 09 11 16 22 74 |
| Kingsferry Bridge | 10 |
| **Torquay** (Devon) | |
| Harbour | 14 16 |
| **Troon** (Ayr) | |
| Marina | 37 80 |
| Androssan | 12 14 16 |
| Girvan | 12 16 |
| **Ullapool** (Ross and Cromarty) | |
| Port | 12 16 |
| **Watchet** (Somerset) | |
| Port/Pilots | 09 12 14 16 |
| **Wells-next-the-Sea** (Norfolk) | |
| Wells Radio | 06 08 12 16 |
| **Weymouth** (Dorset) | |
| Harbour | 12 16 |
| Pilots | 09 16 |
| **Whitby** (North Yorkshire) | |
| Whitby Harbour | 11 12 16 |
| Whittby Bridge | 06 11 16 |
| **Whitehills** (Banff) | |
| Whitehills Harbour Radio | 09 16 |

**Table 5.10b** *continued*

| Port/Harbour | Channels |
|---|---|
| **Whitstable** (Kent) | |
| Harbour | 09 12 16 |
| **Wick** (Caithness) | |
| Harbour | 14 16 |
| **Wisbech** (Cambridgeshire) | |
| Wisbech Cut | 09 14 12 |
| **Workington** (Cumbria) | |
| Workington Docks | 14 16 |

### Principal simplex allocations

Table 5.11 lists principal simplex services' allocated channels.

**Table 5.11 Principal simplex services' channel allocations**

| Service | Channel |
|---|---|
| Calling and distress | 16 |
| Port operations (prime) | 12 |
| Port operations (alternative) | 14 |
| Small yacht safety | 67 |
| Marinas | M/M2 |
| Inter-ship (prime) | 06 |
| Inter-ship (alternative) | 08 |

## Amateur bands

Most general-purpose scanners will cover at least one of the VHF/UHF amateur bands. Although many scanner users may look to such things as air and marine bands as being the more exciting listening, amateur bands do have an attraction in that the operators are not subject to the same power restrictions, and so even at VHF and UHF amateur radio becomes international in its coverage. During the summer months, in particular, effects such as sporadic-E and tropospheric ducting can mean that signals can be picked up over several hundreds of miles.

British amateurs are restricted at VHF and UHF to five bands; 6 metre, 4 metre, 2 metre, 70 centimetres and 23 centimetres. There are other bands but these are often beyond the coverage of most scanners.

## 6 metre band
The 6 metre band became available to British amateurs on the 1st of February, 1985, on an allocation between 50.0 and 52.00MHz.

**Table 5.12 Recommended UK frequency allocations in the 6 metre band**

| Frequency (MHz) | Allocation |
| --- | --- |
| 50.000—50.100 | CW only |
| | 50.020—50.080MHz – beacons |
| 50.100—50.500 | SSB and CW only |
| | 50.110MHz – intercontinental calling |
| 50.500—51.000 | All modes |
| | 50.630—50.750MHz – packet radio in 20kHz steps |
| 51.000—51.525 | SSB and CW only |
| | 51.110MHz – Australia/New Zealand calling |
| 51.525—51.410 | All modes |
| 51.410—51.830 | FM simplex channels in 20kHz steps |
| 51.830—52.00 | All modes (emergency communications priority) |

This particular band is also available to amateurs in countries in Regions 2 and 3 (including the USA). There, the band lies between 50—54MHz and many amateurs claim that because it is lower in frequency than 2 metre and 4 metre bands it should be possible at times at achieve very good distances. The Gibraltar beacon for example ZB2VHF, on 50.035MHz, is regularly heard in Britain. Transatlantic communications have also been achieved, at these frequencies, in the past.

## 4 metre band
This band is one of the least used by amateurs, although it is actively used for packet digital communications as well as various amateur emergency communication groups. Possibly one reason why it is not popular is that Britain is one of the few countries in the world with an allocation at these frequencies and so little if any international

working is possible. The band extends from 70.025 to 70.5MHz and the only allocations are as given in Table 5.13.

**Table 5.13 Recommended UK frequency allocations in the 4 metre band**

| Frequency (MHz) | Allocation |
|---|---|
| 70.000—70.030 | Beacons<br>70.030MHz – personal beacons |
| 70.030—70.250 | SSB and CW only<br>70.200MHz – SSB and CW calling |
| 70.250—70.300 | All modes<br>70.260MHz – AM/FM calling |
| 70.300—70.500 | Channelized operation in 12.5kHz steps<br>70.3125, 70.3250, 70.3375MHz – packet radio<br>70.3500, 70.3750, 70.4000MHz – emergency communications priority<br>70.4500MHz – FM calling<br>70.4875MHz – packet radio |

**2 metre band**

This is without a doubt the most popular amateur VHF band and signals can usually be heard on it in most areas at any time of day. The UK band extends from 144—146MHz but in other regions the band is extended even higher. Equipment for this band is relatively cheap and portable which makes it a favourite with amateurs for local contact work.

Range on the band varies enormously. Varying conditions can mean that a transmission of several hundred watts output may only be heard 20 or 30 miles away at one time, while a signal of a few watts could be picked up hundreds of miles away at another time. Peak propagation tends to be in the summer when sporadic-E activity is at its highest. The band is used for a whole range of transmission types and several modes are used. Frequency allocation, listed in Table 5.14, is more by a sort of gentlemen's agreement than anything else. The band is organised into blocks of transmission types.

The abbreviation 'ms', used in Table 5.14, stands for 'meteor scatter', a method of bouncing a radio signal off the tail of a meteor or a meteor shower. A similar method of communication is involved in 'moonbounce'. These types of communications are generally beyond the scope of scanner users as highly sensitive equipment and massive aerial arrays are required.

## Table 5.14 UK frequency allocations on the 2 metre band

| Frequency (MHz) | Allocation |
| --- | --- |
| 144.000—144.150 | CW only<br>144.000—144.030MHz – Moonbounce<br>144.050MHz – CW calling<br>144.100MHz – CW MS reference freq.<br>144.140—144.150 – CW FAI working |
| 144.150—144.500 | SSB and CW only<br>144.150—144.160MHz – SSB FAI working<br>144.195—144.205MHz – SSB random MS<br>144.250MHz – used for slow Morse transmissions and weekend news broadcasts<br>144.260MHz – used for slow Morse transmissions<br>144.300MHz – SSB calling frequency<br>144.395—144.405MHz – SSB random MS |
| 144.500—144.845 | All modes non-channelized<br>144.500MHz – SSTV calling<br>144.600MHz – RTTY calling<br>144.625MHz – Packet radio<br>144.650MHz – Packet radio<br>144.675MHz – Packet radio<br>144.700MHz – FAX calling<br>144.750MHz – FSTV calling and talkback<br>144.775—144.825MHz – Emergency communications priority |
| 144.845—144.990 | Beacons<br>(144.850MHz may be used by emergency communications) |
| 144.990—145.200 | FM repeater inputs<br>145.000MHz – R0<br>145.025MHz – R1<br>145.050MHz – R2<br>145.075MHz – R3<br>145.100MHz – R4<br>145.125MHz – R5<br>145.150MHz – R6<br>145.175MHz – R7 |
| 145.200—145.600 | FM simplex channels<br>145.200MHz – S8 Emergency communications priority<br>145.225MHz – S9 Emergency |

**Table 5.14**   *continued*

| Frequency (MHz) | Allocation |
|---|---|
| | communications priority |
| | 145.250MHz – S10 Use for slow Morse transmissions |
| | 145.275MHz – S11 |
| | 145.300MHz – S12 RTTY/AFSK |
| | 145.325MHz – S13 |
| | 145.350MHz – S14 |
| | 145.375MHz – S15 |
| | 145.400MHz – S16 |
| | 145.425MHz – S17 |
| | 145.450MHz – S18 |
| | 145.475MHz – S19 |
| | 145.500MHz – S20 FM Calling channel |
| | 145.525MHz – S21 Used for weekend news broadcasts |
| | 145.550MHz – S22 Used for rally and exhibition talk-in |
| | 145.575MHz – S23 |
| 145.600—145.800 | FM repeater outputs |
| | 145.600MHz – R0 |
| | 145.625MHz – R1 |
| | 145.650MHz – R2 |
| | 145.675MHz – R3 |
| | 145.700MHz – R4 |
| | 145.725MHz – R5 |
| | 145.750MHz – R6 |
| | 145.775MHz – R7 |
| 145.800—146.000 | Satellite service |

### 70 centimetre band

This band is allocated between 430.00 and 440MHz. It is allocated on a 'secondary' basis which means that amateurs using it must not interfere with other services on the band. The other services are mainly the military, the navigational positioning beacons known as 'SYLEDIS', and, in the London area, two-way commercial PMR.

The characteristics of the band are very similar to those of the 2 metre band with the exception that operators do not get the extreme ranges achieved at times on the 2 metre band. By and large the band is less used than the 2 metre band although in densely populated areas there can be a fairly high level of activity.

Like the 2 metre band, the 70 centimetre band also has repeaters, throughout the country, which considerably increase the range of operation.

Frequency allocations, again divided into blocks of transmission types, is listed in Table 5.15.

**Table 5.15 Recommended UK frequency allocations in the 70 centimetre band**

| Frequency (MHz) | Allocation |
| --- | --- |
| 430.000—432.000 | All modes (a section of this range is used for PMR in the London Area) |
| 432.000—432.150 | CW only<br>423.000—432.025MHz – moonbounce<br>432.050MHz – CW centre of activity |
| 432.150—432.500 | SSB and CW only<br>432.200MHz – SSB centre of activity<br>432.350MHz – Microwave talk-back |
| 432.500—432.800 | All modes non-channelized<br>432.500MHz – SSTV activity centre<br>432.625, 432.650, 432.675MHz – packet radio<br>432.700MHz – FAX activity centre |
| 432.800—432.990 | Beacons |
| 433.000—433.400 | FM repeater outputs<br>433.000MHz – RB0<br>433.025MHz – RB1<br>433.050MHz – RB2<br>433.075MHz – RB3<br>433.100MHz – RB4<br>433.125MHz – RB5<br>433.150MHz – RB6<br>433.175MHz – RB7<br>433.200MHz – RB8<br>433.225MHz – RB9<br>433.250MHz – RB10<br>433.275MHz – RB11<br>433.300MHz – RB12<br>433.325MHz – RB13<br>433.350MHz – RB14<br>433.375MHz – RB15 |

**Table 5.15**  *continued*

| Frequency (MHz) | Allocation |
| --- | --- |
| 433.400—434.600 | FM simplex channels |
| | 433.400MHz – SU16 |
| | 433.425MHz – SU17 |
| | 433.450MHz – SU18 |
| | 433.475MHz – SU19 |
| | 433.500MHz – SU20 FM calling channel |
| | 433.525MHz – SU21 |
| | 433.550MHz – SU22 |
| | 433.575MHz – SU23 |
| | 433.600MHz – SU24 RTTY AFSK |
| | 433.625—433.675MHz – packet radio |
| | 433.700—433.775MHz – Emergency communications priority |
| 434.600—435.000 | FM repeater inputs |
| | 434.600MHz – RB0 |
| | 434.625MHz – RB1 |
| | 434.650MHz – RB2 |
| | 434.675MHz – RB3 |
| | 434.700MHz – RB4 |
| | 434.725MHz – RB5 |
| | 434.750MHz – RB6 |
| | 434.775MHz – RB7 |
| | 434.800MHz – RB8 |
| | 434.825MHz – RB9 |
| | 434.850MHz – RB10 |
| | 434.875MHz – RB11 |
| | 434.900MHz – RB12 |
| | 434.925MHz – RB13 |
| | 434.950MHz – RB14 |
| | 434.975MHz – RB15 |
| 435.000—438.000 | Satellite service and FSTV |
| 438.000—439.800 | FSTV |
| 438.900—440.00 | Packet radio |

**23 centimetre band**

Since the 3rd edition of *Scanners*, a wide range of scanners, even the tiniest handheld types, now give coverage up to 1300MHz. This allows reception of the sections of the 23cm band used for FM simplex and repeater communication, as well as DX communication.

The latter you will normally only hear during VHF/UHF contests, such as the annual VHF National Field Day. However 23cm repeaters are horizontally polarized, although this may change in the future. A number of amateurs use 23cm to get away from the relatively congested 2m and 70cm bands, although activity is currently very low due to the high cost of equipment. However, as this comes down in price, occupancy is likely to increase.

**Table 5.15a Recommended UK frequency allocations in the 23 centimetre band**

| Frequency (MHz) | Allocation |
|---|---|
| 1240.000—1243.250 | All modes<br>1240.150—1240.750MHz digital communications |
| 1243.250—1260.000 | ATV<br>1248.000MHz RMT3 TV repeater input<br>1249.000MHz RMT2/2R TV repeater input |
| 1260.000—1270.000 | Satellite service |
| 1270.000—1272.000 | All modes |
| 1272.000—1291.000 | ATV<br>1276.500 RMT1 AM TV repeater light |
| 1291.000—1291.500 | Repeater inputs<br>1291.000MHz – RM0<br>1291.025MHz – RM1<br>1291.050MHz – RM2<br>1291.075MHz – RM3<br>1291.100MHz – RM4<br>1291.125MHz – RM5<br>1291.150MHz – RM6<br>1291.175MHz – RM7<br>1291.200MHz – RM8<br>1291.225MHz – RM9<br>1291.250MHz – RM10<br>1291.275MHz – RM11<br>1291.300MHz – RM12<br>1291.325MHz – RM13<br>1291.350MHz – RM14<br>1291.375MHz – RM15 |
| 1291.500—1296.000 | All modes |
| 1296.000—1296.150 | CW |
| 1296.150—1296.800 | SSB<br>1296.200MHz centre of narrowband activity |

**Table 5.15a**  *continued*

| Frequency (MHz) | Allocation |
|---|---|
| 1296.800—1297.990 | Beacons |
| 1297.000—1297.475 | Repeater outputs |
| | 1296.000MHz – RM0 |
| | 1296.025MHz – RM1 |
| | 1296.050MHz – RM2 |
| | 1296.075MHz – RM3 |
| | 1296.100MHz – RM4 |
| | 1296.125MHz – RM5 |
| | 1296.150MHz – RM6 |
| | 1296.175MHz – RM7 |
| | 1296.200MHz – RM8 |
| | 1296.225MHz – RM9 |
| | 1296.250MHz – RM10 |
| | 1296.275MHz – RM11 |
| | 1296.300MHz – RM12 |
| | 1296.325MHz – RM13 |
| | 1296.350MHz – RM14 |
| | 1296.375MHz – RM15 |
| 1297.500—1298.000 | FM Simplex |
| | 1297.500MHz – SM20 |
| | 1297.525MHz – SM21 |
| | 1297.550MHz – SM22 |
| | 1297.575MHz – SM23 |
| | 1297.600MHz – SM24 |
| | 1297.625MHz – SM25 |
| | 1297.650MHz – SM26 |
| | 1297.675MHz – SM27 |
| | 1297.700MHz – SM28 |
| | 1297.725MHz – SM29 |
| | 1297.750MHz – SM30 |
| 1298.000—1298.500 | All modes (digital communications) |
| 1298.500—1300.000 | Packet radio |
| | 1299.000MHz Packet radio 25kHz bandwidth |
| | 1299.425MHz Packet radio 150kHz bandwidth |
| | 1299.575MHz Packet radio 150kHz bandwidth |
| | 1299.725MHz Packet radio 150kHz bandwidth |

**Table 5.15a**  *continued*

| Frequency (MHz) | Allocation |
| --- | --- |
| 1300.000—1325.000 | TV repeater outputs<br>1308.000MHz RMT3 FM TV repeater output<br>1311.500MHz RMT1 AM TV repeater output<br>1316.000MHz RMT2R FM TV repeater output<br>1318.500MHz RMT2 FM TV repeater output |

## Land mobile services

Under the banner of land mobile services is a varied range of communications users. In the following section you will find listed private mobile radio, emergency services, message handling and paging.

The term 'land mobile' applies to any radio communications that takes place between either mobile-to-mobile or mobile-to-base, across land as opposed to air or marine. The mobile can either be a vehicle installation or a portable transceiver of the walkie-talkie type.

Ranges of such equipment vary enormously. In open country ranges of 20 or 30 miles are not unusual but in built-up areas this may be cut to considerably less. Users of mobile radio equipment operating in towns and cities often use aerials on very high buildings well away from the actual point of operation. Connection between the operator and the remote aerial site is usually through a dedicated landline or a radio/microwave link. Emergency services may have even more sophisticated arrangements with several aerial/transmitter sites to give total coverage of an area. This becomes particularly important when communication is to and from low powered handsets with limited aerial facilities.

### Private mobile radio (PMR)

Private mobile radio is a form of communication between a base station and one or more mobile or portable units. Typical examples are the transceivers used by taxi firms. PMR is not to be confused with the government allocations, emergency services or car radiophones, all of which fall into different categories and are listed elsewhere.

Communication in the PMR bands can be either FM or AM and may be split frequency, or single frequency simplex.

Table 5.16 shows bands allocated to PMR communications, listing them with respect to frequency and service allocations.

**Cellular telephones**
The cellular radio telephone system relies on a whole network of base stations. The 'cellphone' system is computer-controlled and as the vehicle moves out of range of one base station it is automatically switched to the frequency of the next closest cell. All the radio traffic is connected to the public telephone network.

**Table 5.16 UK private mobile radio bands and frequency allocations**

*Band: VHF low (12.5kHz channel spacing)*

| Frequency (MHz) | Allocation |
|---|---|
| 71.5125—72.7875 | Mobile Tx |
| 76.9625—77.5000 | Mobile Tx |
| 85.0125—86.2875 | Base Tx |
| 86.9625—87.5000 | Base Tx |
| 86.3000—86.7000 | Single Simplex |

COMMENT: Split frequency simplex separation usually either 10MHz or 13.5MHz

*Band: VHF mid (12.5kHz channel spacing)*

| Frequency (MHz) | Allocation |
|---|---|
| 105.00626—107.89375 | Base Tx |
| 138.00625—140.99375 | Mobile Tx |

COMMENT: Split frequency separation usually 33MHz. This band will be phased out by the end of 1995 to make way for FM broadcasting.

*Band: VHF high (12.5kHz channel spacing)*

| Frequency (MHz) | Allocation |
|---|---|
| 165.0625—168.2500 | Base Tx |
| 169.8625—173.0500 | Mobile Tx |
| 168.9500—169.8500 | Single simplex |

**Table 5.16**  *continued*

COMMENT: Split frequency separation usually 4.8MHz

*Band: VHF Band III (12.5kHz channel spacing)*
*Frequency (MHz)*                          *Allocation*

| | |
|---|---|
| 184.50—191.50 | Mobile Tx |
| 192.50—199.50 | Mobile Tx |
| 216.50—223.50 | Mobile Tx |
| 176.50—183.50 | Base Tx |
| 200.50—207.50 | Base Tx |
| 208.50—215.50 | Base Tx |
| 174.00—176.50 | Single simplex |
| 183.50—184.50 | Single simplex |
| 191.50—192.50 | Single simplex |
| 199.50—200.50 | Single simplex |
| 207.50—208.50 | Single simplex |
| 215.50—216.50 | Single simplex |
| 223.50—225.00 | Single simplex |

COMMENT: Split frequency separation is 8.0MHz.

*Band: UHF band (12.5kHz channel spacing)*
*Frequency (MHz)*                          *Allocation*

| | |
|---|---|
| 425.025—425.475 | Mobile Tx |
| 425.525—428.975 | |
| 445.525—445.975 | Base Tx |
| 440.025—443.475 | |
| 446.025—446.475 | Single simplex |

COMMENT: Split frequency separation either 14.5MHz or 20.5MHz.

*Band: UHF London (12.5kHz channel spacing)*
*Frequency (MHz)*                          *Allocation*

| | |
|---|---|
| 431.00625—431.99375 | Mobile Tx |

**Table 5.16**  *continued*

| | |
|---|---|
| 448.00625—448.99375 | Base Tx |

COMMENT: This band is only available in the London area. Split frequency separation is 17MHz

**Table 5.17 UHF cellular band allocated frequencies (25kHz channel spacing — 45.0MHz separation)**

| Frequency (MHz) | Allocation |
|---|---|
| 890.0125—904.9875 | Mobile Tx |
| 935.0125—949.9875 | Base Tx |

**Wide area paging**
This service provides for one way transmissions from a base station to a small pocket receiver. The transmission is coded to activate only the required pager. The simplest form of pagers merely emit a bleeping sound to alert the holder that they are wanted. Some of the more sophisticated types can receive a short digital message that appears on a small liquid crystal display. Wide area pagers usually cover a specific area such as a town but a number of services also cover most of the country. Wide area paging should not be confused with 'on-site' paging.

Table 5.18 lists wide area paging allocated frequencies

**Table 5.18 Wide area paging allocated frequencies**

| Band | Frequency (MHz) |
|---|---|
| VHF (12.5kHz spacing) | 153.025—153.475 |
| UHF (25kHz spacing) | 454.0125—454.825 |

**On-site paging**
Similar to wide area paging but low powered and operating over a small area such as a factory, building site, etc. Sometimes the pager has a small

and simple transmitter which allows the user to acknowledge that the paging signal has been received. AM or FM modes may be transmitted, and data communications are possible.

Table 5.19 lists on-site paging allocated frequencies and services. At VHF a 12.5kHz channel spacing is used, at UHF 25kHz.

### Table 5.19 On-site paging allocated frequencies

| Band | Frequency (MHz) | Allocation |
|------|-----------------|------------|
| VHF | 26.957—27.283 | Private paging |
| | 31.725—31.775 | Hospital paging |
| | 161.000—161.100 | (acknowledge) |
| UHF | 459.100—459.500 | Private paging |

### Message handling

Many smaller companies may not be able to justify the cost of their own radio-telephone network and so, instead, may make use of a message handling service in which messages are verbally passed between mobile and portable transceivers, through a central contractor. Some message handling services work in a restricted area such as a town or city, but some do span most of the country by using base stations in strategic places.

Table 5.20 lists allocated frequencies for message handling services.

### Table 5.20 Message handling services' allocated frequencies

| Frequency (MHz) | Allocation |
|-----------------|------------|
| 157.4500—158.4000 | Mobile Tx |
| 159.9375—160.5375 | |
| 162.0500—163.0000 | Base Tx |
| 164.4375—165.0375 | |

### Land emergency services

Land emergency services are normally police, fire and ambulance services. Some services are also found on bands allocated to PMR but nearly all police forces operate in bands allocated to the UK Home Office. In addition to the bands listed in Table 5.21, emergency services in some areas may be located in government mobile allocations (see Tables 5.1 and 5.2). Note that, in accordance with international agreements, the allocation between 97.60 and 102.10MHz has now been reallocated for broadcast use. Most services have already moved off this band and others will do so shortly.

**Table 5.21 Land emergency services' band and allocated frequencies**

*Band: VHF low (12.5kHz channel spacing, AM)*

| Frequency (MHz) | Allocation |
|---|---|
| 70.5000—71.5000 | Fire bases |
| 81.9000—83.9000 | Fire mobiles |
| 80.00—84.00 | Mobile Tx |
| 97.60—102.10 | Base Tx |

*Band: VHF high (12.5kHz channel spacing, AM/FM)*

| Frequency (MHz) | Allocation |
|---|---|
| 143.00—144.0000 | Mobile Tx |
| 152.00—153.0000 | Base Tx |
| 147.2000—148.0000 | Mobile Tx |
| 155.2000—156.0000 | Base Tx |
| 146.0000—147.2000 | Fixed links |
| 166.2750—166.5250 | Ambulances |

*Band: UHF low (12.5kHz channel spacing, FM)*

| Frequency (MHz) | Allocation |
|---|---|
| 420.00—425.00 | |
| 429.00—432.00 | |
| 443.50—445.00 | |
| 446.00—450.00 | |
| 451.000—453.000 | |
| 459.50—470.00 | |
| 464.9000—467.0000 | |

*Band: UHF high (25 kHz channel spacing, FM)*

| Frequency (MHz) | Allocation |
|---|---|

**Table 5.21**  *continued*

*Band: VHF mid (12.5kHz channel spacing, FM)*
*Frequency (MHz)* | *Allocation*

862.00—864.00

COMMENT: Usually split frequency simplex but channel pairings vary.

## Table 5.22 Ambulance services

| Area | Base | Mobile | Call | Channel |
|------|------|--------|------|---------|
| Avon | 166.5000 | 171.3000 | | 117 |
| Bedfordshire | 166.3375 | 171.1375 | | 104 |
| Bedfordshire | 166.4625 | 171.2625 | | 114 |
| Bedfordshire | 166.7750 | 171.5750 | | 139 |
| Berkshire | 166.3875 | 171.1875 | | 108 |
| Berkshire | 166.6125 | 171.4125 | | 126 |
| Buckinghamshire | 166.2875 | 171.0870 | | 100 |
| Buckinghamshire | 166.5625 | 171.3625 | | 122 |
| Cambridgeshire | 166.3125 | 171.1125 | | 102 |
| Cambridgeshire | 166.3500 | 171.1500 | | 105 |
| Cheshire | 166.3625 | 171.1625 | | 106 |
| Cleveland | 166.2000 | 171.0000 | | 93 |
| Cleveland | 166.3500 | 171.1500 | | 105 |
| Clwyd | 166.4125 | 171.2125 | | 110 |
| Clwyd | 166.4625 | 171.2625 | | 114 |
| Clwyd | 166.5625 | 171.3625 | | 122 |
| Cornwall | 166.2875 | 171.0870 | | 100 |
| Cornwall | 166.5000 | 171.3000 | | 117 |
| County Durham | 166.5875 | 171.3875 | | 124 |
| Cumbria | 166.3000 | 171.1000 | | 101 |
| Cumbria | 166.3500 | 171.1500 | | 105 |
| Cumbria | 166.3750 | 171.1750 | | 107 |
| Derby | 166.2875 | 171.0870 | | 100 |
| Derby | 166.3125 | 171.1125 | | 102 |
| Derbyshire | 166.3750 | 171.1750 | | 107 |
| Devon | 166.3125 | 171.1125 | | 102 |
| Devon | 166.5625 | 171.3625 | | 122 |
| Doctors common | 166.8125 | 171.6125 | | 1 |

**Table 5.22**  *continued*

| Area | Base | Mobile | Call | Channel |
|------|------|--------|------|---------|
| Dorset | 166.2000 | 171.0000 | | 93 |
| Dorset | 166.3000 | 171.1000 | | 101 |
| Dorset | 166.4875 | 171.2875 | | 116 |
| Dorset | 166.5250 | 171.3250 | | 119 |
| Dorset | 166.8375 | 171.6375 | | 144 |
| East Anglia | 166.0500 | 170.8500 | | |
| East Anglia | 166.3500 | 171.1500 | | 105 |
| East Anglia | 166.3625 | 171.1625 | | 106 |
| East Anglia | 166.4375 | 171.2375 | | 112 |
| East Anglia | 166.5250 | 171.3250 | | 119 |
| Essex | 166.3625 | 171.1625 | | 106 |
| Essex | 166.4875 | 171.2875 | | 116 |
| Essex | 166.5500 | 171.3500 | | 121 |
| Glamorgan | 166.7750 | 171.5750 | | 139 |
| Glamorgan (mid) | 166.3250 | 171.1250 | | 103 |
| Glamorgan (mid) | 166.5250 | 171.3250 | | 119 |
| Glamorgan (S) | 166.3000 | 171.1000 | | 101 |
| Glamorgan (S) | 166.4750 | 171.2750 | | 115 |
| Glamorgan (S) | 166.5875 | 171.3875 | | 124 |
| Glamorgan (W) | 166.3500 | 171.1500 | | 105 |
| Glamorgan (W) | 166.8250 | 171.6250 | | 143 |
| Gloucestershire | 166.3625 | 171.1625 | | 106 |
| Gloucestershire | 166.8000 | 171.6000 | | 142 |
| Gloucestershire | 166.8375 | 171.6375 | | 144 |
| Guernsey | 86.4250 | | | |
| Gwent | 166.4000 | 171.2000 | | 109 |
| Gwent | 166.5750 | 171.3750 | | 123 |
| Gwynedd | 166.4750 | 171.2750 | | 115 |
| Hampshire | 166.3625 | 171.1625 | | 106 |
| Hampshire | 166.5750 | 171.3750 | | 123 |
| Hampshire | 166.5875 | 171.3875 | | 124 |
| Hampshire | 166.7750 | 171.5750 | | 139 |
| Hatfield | 166.6125 | 171.4125 | | 2 |
| Hatfield | 166.8125 | 171.6125 | | 1 |
| Herefordshire | 166.3750 | 171.1750 | | 107 |
| Herefordshire | 166.4750 | 171.2750 | | 115 |
| Herefordshire | 166.5625 | 171.3625 | | 122 |
| Herefordshire | 166.6125 | 171.4125 | | 126 |
| Herefordshire | 166.8250 | 171.6250 | | 143 |
| Hertfordshire | 166.5875 | 171.3875 | | 124 |

**Table 5.22**  *continued*

| Area | Base | Mobile | Call | Channel |
|------|------|--------|------|---------|
| Humberside | 166.3000 | 171.1000 | | 101 |
| Humberside | 166.3250 | 171.1250 | | 103 |
| Humberside | 166.4000 | 171.2000 | | 109 |
| Humberside | 166.5250 | 171.3250 | | 119 |
| Humberside | 166.5750 | 171.3750 | | 123 |
| Humberside | 166.6125 | 171.4125 | | 126 |
| Isle of Wight | 166.3375 | 171.1375 | | 104 |
| Isles of Scilly | 166.5000 | 171.3000 | | 117 |
| Jersey | 154.6625 | 146.1125 | Jersam | 1 |
| Jersey | 154.7500 | 146.2250 | Jersam | 2 |
| Kent | 166.2875 | 171.0875 | | 100 |
| Kent | 166.3375 | 171.1375 | | 104 |
| Kent | 166.3875 | 171.1875 | | 108 |
| Kent | 166.8250 | 171.6250 | | 143 |
| Lancashire | 166.2750 | 171.0750 | | 99 |
| Lancashire. | 166.3875 | 171.1875 | | 108 |
| Lancashire. | 166.5500 | 171.3500 | | 121 |
| Leicestershire | 166.4125 | 171.2125 | | 110 |
| Leicestershire | 166.5375 | 171.3375 | | 120 |
| Leicestershire | 166.3000 | 171.1000 | | 101 |
| Lincolnshire | 166.2000 | 171.0000 | | 93 |
| Lincolnshire | 166.2750 | 171.0750 | | 99 |
| Lincolnshire | 166.3625 | 171.1625 | | 106 |
| Lincolnshire | 166.4000 | 171.2000 | | 109 |
| London | 165.6250 | 170.4250 | | 3 |
| London | 165.6375 | 170.4750 | | 2 |
| London | 165.6500 | 170.8500 | | 1 |
| London | 166.1000 | 170.9000 | | 6 |
| London | 166.1250 | 170.9250 | Red | 5 |
| London | 166.3125 | 171.1125 | Red | 1 |
| London | 166.4375 | 171.2375 | Red | 15 |
| London | 166.5250 | 171.3250 | Red | 4 |
| London | 166.5750 | 171.3750 | White | 10 |
| London (E) | 166.3500 | 171.1500 | Red | 2 |
| London (NE) | 166.3000 | 171.1000 | Gold | 9 |
| London (NE) | 166.4250 | 171.2250 | Gold | 7 |
| London (NE) | 166.5000 | 171.3000 | Gold | 8 |
| London (NW) | 166.4500 | 171.2500 | Blue | 6 |
| London (NW) | 166.4750 | 171.2750 | Blue | 5 |
| London (S) | 166.4125 | 171.2125 | Red | 3 |

**Table 5.22**   *continued*

| Area | Base | Mobile | Call | Channel |
|------|------|--------|------|---------|
| London (SE) | 166.2000 | 171.0000 | Green | 13 |
| London (SE) | 166.3250 | 171.1250 | Orange | 12 |
| London (SE) | 166.3750 | 171.1750 | Green | 14 |
| London (SW) | 166.2750 | 171.0750 | Orange | 11 |
| Manchester | 166.2875 | 171.0870 | | 100 |
| Manchester | 166.3000 | 171.1000 | | 101 |
| Manchester | 166.4875 | 171.2875 | | 116 |
| Manchester | 166.5000 | 171.3000 | | 117 |
| Manchester | 166.5125 | 171.3125 | | 118 |
| Manchester. | 166.6000 | 171.4000 | | 125 |
| Merseyside | 166.3250 | 171.1250 | | 103 |
| Merseyside | 166.3375 | 171.1375 | | 104 |
| Merseyside | 166.4750 | 171.2750 | | 115 |
| Merseyside | 166.5875 | 171.3875 | | 124 |
| Midlands (W) | 166.2750 | 171.0750 | | 99 |
| Midlands (W) | 166.3500 | 171.1500 | | 105 |
| Midlands (W) | 166.4625 | 171.2625 | | 114 |
| Midlands (W) | 166.5500 | 171.3500 | | 121 |
| Midlands (W) | 166.6000 | 171.4000 | | 125 |
| National | 87.6500 | 77.6500 | | |
| National | 166.1000 | 170.9000 | | |
| National | 166.6000 | 171.4000 | | |
| National | 166.6125 | 171.4125 | | |
| Norfolk | 166.4375 | 171.2375 | | 1 |
| Norfolk | 166.5625 | 171.3625 | | 2 |
| Northern Ireland | 87.5500 | 77.5500 | | |
| Northern Ireland | 87.5750 | 77.5750 | | |
| Northern Ireland | 87.6250 | 77.6250 | | |
| Northern Ireland | 87.6500 | 77.6500 | | |
| Northern Ireland | 87.6750 | 77.6750 | | |
| Northern Ireland | 87.5250 | 77.5250 | | |
| Northumbria | 166.2875 | 171.0870 | | 100 |
| Northumbria | 166.4000 | 171.2000 | | 109 |
| Northumbria | 166.4875 | 171.2875 | | 116 |
| Northumbria | 166.5125 | 171.3125 | | 118 |
| Northumbria | 166.5750 | 171.3750 | | 123 |
| Northumbria | 166.6000 | 171.4000 | | 125 |
| Nothamptonshire | 166.5500 | 171.3500 | | 121 |
| Nothamptonshire | 166.5750 | 171.3750 | | 123 |
| Nottinghamshire | 166.4125 | 171.2125 | | 110 |

**Table 5.22**   *continued*

| Area | Base | Mobile | Call | Channel |
|------|------|--------|------|---------|
| Oxfordshire | 166.4875 | 171.2875 | | 116 |
| Oxfordshire | 166.6125 | 171.4125 | | 126 |
| Pembrokeshire | 166.3625 | 171.1625 | | 106 |
| Powys | 166.2875 | 171.0870 | | 100 |
| Powys. | 166.3125 | 171.1125 | | 102 |
| Private national | 72.5375 | | | |
| Private national | 86.0375 | | | |
| Red Cross | 86.3250 | | | |
| Red Cross | 86.4125 | | | |
| Somerset | 166.2750 | 171.0750 | | 99 |
| Somerset | 166.3375 | 171.1375 | | 104 |
| St Johns | 86.3250 | | | |
| St Johns | 86.4125 | | | |
| St Johns | 169.3625 | | | |
| Staffordshire | 166.3875 | 171.1875 | | 108 |
| Staffordshire | 166.5000 | 171.3000 | | 117 |
| Staffordshire | 166.5875 | 171.3875 | | 124 |
| Staffordshire | 166.6125 | 171.4125 | | 126 |
| Staffordshire | 166.7500 | 171.7500 | | 137 |
| Suffolk | 166.5250 | 171.3250 | | 119 |
| Suffolk | 166.3500 | 171.1500 | | 105 |
| Suffolk (W) | 166.3375 | 171.1375 | | 104 |
| Surrey | 166.2875 | 171.0870 | | 100 |
| Surrey | 166.5125 | 171.3125 | | 118 |
| Surrey | 166.5375 | 171.3375 | | 120 |
| Surrey | 166.7500 | 171.7500 | | 137 |
| Sussex (E) | 166.4000 | 171.2000 | | 109 |
| Sussex (W) | 166.4625 | 171.2625 | | 114 |
| Sussex (W) | 166.5625 | 171.3625 | | 122 |
| Welwyn | 166.6125 | 171.4125 | | 2 |
| Welwyn | 166.8125 | 171.6125 | | 1 |
| Wiltshire | 166.4125 | 171.2125 | | 110 |
| Wiltshire | 166.6125 | 171.4125 | | 126 |
| Worcestershire | 166.3750 | 171.1750 | | 107 |
| Worcestershire | 166.4750 | 171.2750 | | 115 |
| Worcestershire | 166.5625 | 171.3625 | | 122 |
| Worcestershire | 166.8250 | 171.6250 | | 143 |
| Yorkshire | 166.2000 | 171.0000 | | 93 |
| Yorkshire | 166.3875 | 171.1875 | | 108 |
| Yorkshire (N) | 166.3375 | 171.1375 | | 104 |

**Table 5.22** *continued*

| Area | Base | Mobile | Call | Channel |
|------|------|--------|------|---------|
| Yorkshire (N) | 166.4625 | 171.2625 | | 114 |
| Yorkshire (N) | 166.4750 | 171.2750 | | 115 |
| Yorkshire (N) | 166.5000 | 171.3000 | | 117 |
| Yorkshire (N) | 166.5250 | 171.3250 | | 119 |
| Yorkshire (N) | 166.5375 | 171.3375 | | 120 |
| Yorkshire (N) | 166.6125 | 171.4125 | | 126 |
| Yorkshire (S) | 166.4000 | 171.2000 | | 109 |
| Yorkshire (S) | 166.4875 | 171.2875 | | 116 |
| Yorkshire (S) | 166.5500 | 171.3500 | | 121 |
| Yorkshire (S) | 166.5625 | 171.3625 | | 122 |
| Yorkshire (W) | 166.3000 | 171.1000 | | 101 |
| Yorkshire (W) | 166.4000 | 171.2000 | | 109 |
| Yorkshire (W) | 166.4125 | 171.2125 | | 110 |
| Yorkshire (W) | 166.4625 | 171.2625 | | 114 |
| Yorkshire (W) | 166.5375 | 171.3375 | | 120 |

**UHF allocations for Regional Health Authorities**

| | | |
|------|------|------|
| 457.4002 | | Yorkshire |
| 457.4250 | 2 | Yorkshire |
| | 4 | East Anglia |
| 457.4500 | 1 | Northern |
| 457.4750 | 4 | East Anglia |
| 457.5000 | 4 | East Anglia |
| 457.5250 | 12 | West Midlands |
| 457.5750 | 12 | West Midlands |
| 457.6250 | | Wales |
| 457.6750 166.335 | 4 | East Anglia |
| 457.7250 | 1 | Northern |
| 457.7500 | | Wales |
| 457.7750 | 4 | East Anglia |
| 457.9750 | 4 | East Anglia |
| 458.0000 | 2 | Yorkshire |
| 458.0250 | 5 | |
| | 6 | |
| | 7 | |
| | 8 | Thames |
| 458.0500 | 3 | Trent |
| | 11 | South West |
| 458.1250 | 1 | Northern |
| 458.1500 | 12 | West Midlands |

**Table 5.22**  *continued*

*UHF allocations for Regional Health Authorities*

| | | |
|---|---|---|
| 458.1750 | 2 | Yorkshire |
| | 12 | West Midlands |
| | | Wales |
| 458.2250 | 4 | East Anglia |
| | | Wales |
| 458.2500 | 2 | Yorkshire |
| 458.3000 | | Wales |
| 458.3250 | 1 | Northern |
| | 5 6 7 8 | Thames |
| 458.3500 | 1 | Northern |
| 458.4250 | 5 6 7 8 | Thames |
| 458.4750 | | Wales |
| 459.7750 | | Jersey |
| 460.5750 | 5 6 7 8 | Thames |
| | 11 | South West |
| 460.6000 | 10 | Oxford |
| 460.6250 | 1 | Northern |
| | 10 | Oxford |
| 460.6500 | | Wales |
| 460.675 | 1 | Northern |
| | 2 | Yorkshire |
| 460.725 | 11 | South West |
| 460.750 | 1 | Northern |
| 461.275 | 1 | Northern |
| | 2 | Yorkshire |
| | 5 6 7 8 | Thames |
| | 12 | West Midlands |
| | | Wales |
| 461.300 | 2 | Yorkshire |
| | 5 6 7 8 | Thames |
| | 10 | Oxford Wales |
| 461.325 | 10 | Oxford |
| 461.350 | 10 | Oxford |
| | | Wales |
| 461.375 | 10 | Oxford |
| 461.475 | 10 | Oxford |
| | | Wales |
| 462.925 | 4 | East Anglia |
| 462.950 | 1 | Northern |
| | 9 | Wessex |

**Table 5.22**   *continued*

*UHF allocations for Regional Health Authorities*

|  |  |  |
|---|---|---|
|  |  | Wales |
| 462.975 | 4 | East Anglia |
| 463.000 166.525 | 4 | East Anglia |
| 463.050 | 10 | Oxford |
| 463.075 | 4 | East Anglia |
| 463.100 | 1 | Northern |
|  |  | Wales |
| 463.150 | 1 | Northern |
|  |  | Wales |
| 463.175 166.3375 | 4 | East Anglia |
| 463.225 |  | Wales |
| 463.250 | 4 | East Anglia |
| 463.500 | 9 | Wessex |
| 463.525 | 1 | Northern |
|  | 4 | East Anglia |
| 463.550 |  | Wales |
| 463.600 | 9 | Wessex |
|  |  | Wales |
| 463.625 | 1 | Northern |
|  | 9 | Wessex |
|  | 12 | West Midlands |
| 463.650 | 5 6 7 8 | Thames |
| 463.700 | 12 | West Midlands |
| 463.750 | 9 | Wessex |
|  | 12 | West Midlands |
| 463.825 | 1 | Northern |
|  |  | Wales |
| 463.850 | 1 | Northern |
|  |  | Wales |
| 463.900 | 5 6 7 8 | Thames |
| 463.925 | 1 | Northern |
|  |  | Wales |
| 463.950 | 5 6 7 8 | Thames |
|  | 9 | Wessex |
|  | 12 | West Midlands |
| 463.975 | 12 | West Midlands |
| 467.025 | 12 | West Midlands |
| 467.050 |  | Wales |
| 467.125 | 1 | Northern |
| 467.175 | 1 | Northern |

**Table 5.22** *continued*

*UHF allocations for Regional Health Authorities*

| 467.225 | 11 | South West |
|---|---|---|
| 467.250 | 1 | Northern Wales |
| 467.475 | | Wales |
| 467.775 | | Wales |
| 467.800 | | Wales |
| 467.825 | | Wales |
| 467.900 | | Wales |
| 467.925 | | Wales |

| 1 Northern: | Cleveland, Cumbria, Durham, Northumbria |
|---|---|
| 2 Yorkshire: | Yorkshire, Humberside |
| 3 Trent: | Derbyshire, Leicestershire, Lincolnshire, Nottinghamshire, S. Yorkshire |
| 4 East Anglia: | Cambridgeshire, Norfolk, E. Suffolk |
| 5 NW Thames: | N. Bedfordshire, E. Hertfordshire |
| 6 NE Thames: | Mid Essex |
| 7 SE Thames: | Eastbourne, Medway, Kent |
| 8 SW Thames: | Mid Surrey, W. Sussex |
| 9 Wessex: | E. Dorset, Hampshire, Isle of Wight |
| 10 Oxford: | W. Berkshire, Buckinghamshire, Northamptonshire, Oxford |
| 11 South West: | Avon, Cornwall, Devon, Gloucester, Scilly Isles, Somerset |
| 12 West Midlands: | Hereford, Mid Staffordshire, Salop, South Warwickshire, Worcestershire |
| 13 Mersey: | Cheshire, Merseyside |

**Table 5.22a Fire Brigades V.H.F.**

*Band: V.H.F. High (12.5kHz channel spacing (AM/FM)*

| Band | Allocation |
|---|---|
| 70.5125—71.5000 | Fire bases |
| 80.0000—82.5000 | Fire mobiles |
| 146.0000—148.000 | Fire mobiles |
| 154.0000—156.000 | Fire bases |

**Table 5.22a**  *continued*

| Area | Base | Mobile | Call | Channel |
|------|------|--------|------|---------|
| Avon & Somerset | 71.0125 | 80.1750 | M2QG | |
| Avon & Somerset | 154.5000 | | M2QC | |
| Bedfordshire | 71.1125 | | M2VM | |
| Berkshire | 154.0750 | 146.1750 | M2HD | |
| Berkshire | 71.2000 | | M2HD | |
| Buckinghamshire | 71.1375 | 80.1125 | M2HK | |
| Cambridgeshire | 154.1250 | 146.1750 | M2VP | |
| Cambridgeshire | 70.8375 | | M2VC | |
| Cambridgeshire | 71.4250 | | M2VC | |
| Cheshire | 154.2250 | | M2CF | |
| Cheshire | 154.6500 | | M2CF | |
| Cheshire | 155.5750 | 146.2875 | M2CF | |
| Cheshire | 70.7750 | 80.5000 | M2CF | |
| Cleveland | 71.1125 | | M2LT | |
| Clwyd | 71.1625 | 80.8750 | M2WK | |
| Cornwall | 70.7875 | 80.8000 | M2QA | |
| County Durham | 70.8875 | 80.2125 | M2LF | |
| Cumbria | 70.8375 | 80.0375 | M2BC | |
| Derbyshire | 154.0500 | 146.5375 | M2ND | |
| Derbyshire | 70.7125 | 80.8000 | M2ND | |
| Devon | 70.7250 | 80.0375 | M2QD | |
| Devon | 70.8250 | 80.0375 | M2QD | |
| Devon & Cornwall | 154.0750 | 146.1750 | M2QA | |
| Dorset | 70.8625 | 80.5500 | M2QK | |
| Dyfed | 70.6125 | 80.1250 | M2WV | |
| East Anglia | 154.6500 | 146.1125 | | |
| East London | 70.7625 | 80.1500 | M2FE | 3 |
| Essex | 70.6250 | 80.6125 | M2VD | 1 |
| Essex | 70.7250 | 80.6750 | M2VD | 2 |
| Essex | 70.9125 | | M2VD | |
| Gloucestershire | 71.0750 | 80.6250 | M2QF | |
| Gloucestershire | 71.3875 | | M2QC | |
| Gloucestershire | 154.3125 | | M2QF2 | |
| Greater Manchester | 70.5875 | 80.7625 | M2FT | 3 |
| Greater Manchester | 70.5250 | 80.7375 | M2FT | 2 |
| Greater Manchester | 70.5500 | | M2FT | |
| Greater Manchester | 70.8250 | 80.7875 | M2FT | 4 |
| Gwent | 70.7000 | 81.1250 | M2WP | |
| Gwynedd | 70.8125 | 81.2125 | M2WC | |
| Hampshire | 154.5750 | | M2HX | |

**Table 5.22a** *continued*

| Area | Base | Mobile | Call | Channel |
|---|---|---|---|---|
| Hampshire | 154.7625 | | M2HX | |
| Hampshire | 155.3375 | | M2HX | |
| Hampshire | 70.5875 | 80.1875 | M2HX | 2 |
| Hampshire | 70.7750 | 80.5000 | M2HX | 1 |
| Hampshire (N) | 154.8750 | | M2ND | |
| Handsets | 154.6875 | | | |
| Hereford & Worcester | 70.6875 | 81.1250 | M2YB | |
| Hereford & Worcester | 154.3000 | | M2YB | |
| Hereford & Worcester | 155.4000 | | M2YB | |
| Hertfordshire | 70.9000 | 80.0375 | M2VI | |
| Humberside | 154.6000 | | M2XT | |
| Humberside | 154.8250 | 146.7000 | M2XT | |
| Humberside | 71.0750 | | M2XT | |
| Humberside | 71.1000 | 80.6625 | M2XT | |
| Humberside (N) | 154.7750 | | XT | |
| Isle of Wight | 71.2750 | 81.0625 | M2HP | |
| Kent | 154.4750 | 146.1750 | M2HO5 | |
| Kent | 154.7500 | | M2KA1 | |
| Kent | 70.8375 | 80.0375 | M2KF | |
| Lancashire | 70.5250 | 80.9625 | M2MP | 2 |
| Lancashire | 71.3875 | | M2BE | 3 |
| Lancashire | 70.6750 | 80.5500 | M2BE | 1 |
| Lancashire | 70.9000 | 80.6000 | M2BE | 4 |
| Leamington | 155.2250 | | M2YS | |
| Leicestershire | 70.6625 | 81.0000 | M2NK | |
| Lincolnshire | 70.5625 | 80.6000 | M2NV | |
| London | 154.1250 | 146.1750 | M2FN | |
| London | 154.1750 | 146.3500 | M2FS2 | |
| London | 154.6750 | 146.2750 | M2FE3 | |
| London | 154.8250 | 147.6125 | M2FN4 | |
| London | 71.3000 | | M2FH | 5 |
| London (N) | 71.1750 | 80.2125 | M2FN | 4 |
| London (S) | 70.9626 | 80.1125 | M2FS | 2 |
| London Central | 70.5250 | 80.9625 | M2FH | 1 |
| Merseyside | 70.6250 | | M2F0 | 3 |
| Merseyside | 70.7000 | | M2F0 | 4 |
| Merseyside | 70.9625 | 81.0875 | M2FO | 2 |
| Merseyside | 71.0375 | 81.0625 | M2FO | |
| Mid Glamorgan | 70.5625 | 80.6000 | M2WF | |
| Norfolk | 70.7000 | | M2VF | |

**Table 5.22a**  *continued*

| Area | Base | Mobile | Call | Channel |
| --- | --- | --- | --- | --- |
| Norfolk | 154.4000 | | M2VF | |
| Norfolk | 154.7250 | | M2VF | |
| Norfolk | 154.8500 | | M2VF | |
| North Yorkshire | 71.1375 | 80.4375 | M2LY | |
| North Yorkshire | 71.1750 | | M2LY | |
| Northamptonshire | 70.7500 | 80.7500 | M2N0 | |
| Northumberland | 70.5125 | 80.1875 | M2LJ | |
| Nottinghamshire | 154.6750 | 146.2750 | M2NZ | |
| Nottinghamshire | 70.5375 | 80.1875 | M2NZ | |
| Oxfordshire | 71.1000 | 80.6625 | M2HI | |
| Powys | 70.8500 | 80.9625 | M2WB | |
| Shropshire | 70.9750 | 80.6500 | M2YU | |
| Somerset | 71.1250 | 80.1125 | M2QI | |
| South Glamorgan | 70.6750 | 80.5250 | M2WD | |
| South Yorkshire | 70.6375 | 80.2125 | M2XY | |
| Staffordshire | 154.1250 | 146.1750 | M2YG | |
| Staffordshire | 154.2250 | 146.7000 | M2YG | |
| Staffordshire | 154.4750 | 146.1750 | M2YG | |
| Staffordshire | 155.6000 | | M2YG | |
| Staffordshire | 70.8875 | 80.9375 | M2YG | |
| Suffolk | 71.2750 | 81.0875 | M2VN | |
| Surrey | 70.6125 | 80.1250 | M2HF | |
| Surrey | 146.0250 | | M2HF | |
| Sussex | 70.6375 | 80.2125 | M2KD | |
| Sussex (E) | 154.8250 | 146.6125 | M2KW | |
| Sussex (W) | 70.8000 | 80.5125 | M2KW | |
| Sussex (W) | 154.8000 | 146.7250 | M2KW | |
| Thames Valley | 154.0750 | 146.1750 | M2HI | |
| Thames Valley | 154.5500 | | M2HI | |
| Tyne and Wear | 71.3000 | | M2LP | |
| Tyne and Wear | 71.3000 | | M2LP | 2 |
| Wales | 154.8750 | 146.0375 | M2WP | |
| Wales | 154.9500 | 146.0125 | M2WP | |
| Warwickshire | 70.6000 | 80.2625 | M2YS | |
| West Glamorgan | 70.9500 | | M2WZ | |
| West Midlands | 70.5125 | 80.4375 | M2BW | 1 |
| West Midlands | 154.2500 | | M2FB | |
| West Midlands | 155.4500 | | M2FB | |
| West Midlands | 70.5750 | 80.4625 | M2F0 | 3 |
| West Midlands | 71.1500 | 80.5125 | M2EW | 2 |

**Table 5.22a**   *continued*

| Area | Base | Mobile | Call | Channel |
|------|------|--------|------|---------|
| West Yorkshire | 70.7625 | | M2XF | |
| West Yorkshire | 70.6125 | | M2XF | |
| West Yorkshire | 70.8750 | | M2XF | |
| Wiltshire | 154.1250 | 146.1750 | M2QM | |
| Wiltshire | 154.4750 | 146.1750 | M2QM | |
| Wiltshire | 70.6500 | 80.9875 | M2QM | |
| Yorkshire | 154.0500 | 146.5375 | M2XK | |

**Table 5.22b Police U.H.F. Allocations**

| Band: UHF (25kHz channel spacing, FM) Frequency (MHz) | Allocation |
|------|------|
| 451.0000—453.0000 | Base transmit |
| 464.9000—466.9000 | Mobile transmit |
| 455.0000—456.0000 | Base transmit (shared) |
| 468.0000—469.0000 | Mobile transmit (shared) |

Comment: The two shared bands are used by forces connected with transportation and are regularly in use at railway stations, harbours and airports. The DTI channel number is shown with this list.

**Table 5.22c Police VHF allocations**

| Band VHF mid (special police 'Helitell' airborne units) Frequency (MHz) | Allocation |
|------|------|
| 138.09375 | Ch 1 |
| 138.10500 | Ch 40 |
| 138.10625 | Ch 2 |
| 138.29375 | Ch 3 |
| 138.30625 | Ch 4 |

**Table 5.22c**  *continued*

---

*Band: VHF high (12.5kHz channel spacing mostly AM but some FM)*
*Frequency (MHz)*                                    *Allocation*

---

143.0000—144.0000                          Mobile transmit
152.0000—153.0000                          Base transmit
146.0000—149.0000                          Mobile transmit
154.0000—156.0000                          Base transmit

---

**Citizens' band radio**

Citizens' band radio communications originated in the USA where it was felt there was a need for a low powered, short distance communication system. The idea was for a low cost service with the minimum of regulations where the user did not have to comply with strict licensing conditions to prove an essential use for two-way radio. Originally it was to give such people as small businesses, servicemen, truckers, farmers and social organisations as a means of communications.

Later, CB acquired a cult following and a colourful slang language all of its own. These days it bears little resemblance to its original aims.

*Legal and illegal*

The UK started off with an illegal CB service using the same channel allocations as those in the USA. AM equipment, designed for America, was smuggled into Britain. CB became such a craze that thousands of illegal transceivers were in use and often caused havoc to legitimate users of the frequencies which included radio modellers, paging systems and meteorological equipment. Finally, the Government, which appeared reluctant to establish a legal service, gave in. The service introduced in November 1981 had slightly different frequencies to the American equipment and used frequency modulation.

Britain has three CB allocations, two at HF the other at UHF (see Table 5.23). Even so, American equipment, still illegal in the UK, is used from time to time, particularly when conditions favour long distance contact. The UHF allocation tends not to attract many users because of the high cost of the equipment involved. Aerial systems are also more critical and costly at these frequencies.

No more equpment is now being manufactured for this band, which now has a limited life.

*Range*

Across open country usable HF ranges of up to 20 or more miles can be expected but a lot will depend on circumstances, ie, base/base, base/mobile or mobile/mobile working. Ranges are considerably reduced in built-up areas but under lift conditions ranges may become almost global. The band is very prone to the effects of the 11 year sunspot cycle and when that happens it is not unusual to hear transmissions from the USA, Australia, Asia, South America, etc.

On the UHF band, activity is usually limited to local conditions, but even at these high frequencies lift conditions do occur. For instance, cross channel contacts between stations in southern England and the Channel Islands (distances of more than 100 miles) regularly take place in the summer months.

Note that HF ranges quoted are only likely to be achieved by using a proper CB aerial. Most discone-type aerials, favoured for scanner operation, operate quite poorly at lower frequencies. The same, in fact, goes for UHF ranges, where an ordinary discone cannot compete with a multi-element Yagi pointed at the transmitting station.

**Table 5.23 UK CB channels and allocated frequencies**

| | | Frequencies (MHz) | |
| *Channel* | *UK/HF (FM)* | *UK/UHF (FM)* | *CEPT (FM)* |
|---|---|---|---|
| 01 | 27.60125 | 934.0125 | 26.965 |
| 02 | 27.61125 | 934.0625 | 26.975 |
| 03 | 27.62125 | 934.1125 | 26.985 |
| 04 | 27.63125 | 934.1626 | 27.005 |
| 05 | 27.64125 | 934.2125 | 27.015 |
| 06 | 27.65125 | 934.2625 | 27.025 |
| 07 | 27.66125 | 934.3125 | 27.035 |
| 08 | 27.67125 | 934.3625 | 27.055 |
| 09 | 27.68125 | 934.4125 | 27.065 |
| 10 | 27.69125 | 934.4625 | 27.075 |
| 11 | 27.70125 | 934.5125 | 27.085 |
| 12 | 27.71125 | 934.5625 | 27.105 |
| 13 | 27.72125 | 934.6125 | 27.115 |
| 14 | 27.73125 | 934.6625 | 27.125 |
| 15 | 27.74125 | 934.7125 | 27.135 |
| 16 | 27.75125 | 934.7625 | 27.155 |
| 17 | 27.76125 | 934.8125 | 27.165 |
| 18 | 27.77125 | 934.8625 | 27.175 |
| 19 | 27.78125 | 934.9125 | 27.185 |
| 20 | 27.79125 | 934.9625 | 27.205 |

**Table 5.23**  *continued*

| Channel | Frequencies (MHz) UK/HF (FM) | UK/UHF (FM) | CEPT (FM) |
|---|---|---|---|
| 21 | 27.80125 | | 27.215 |
| 22 | 27.81125 | | 27.225 |
| 23 | 27.82125 | | 27.255 |
| 24 | 27.83125 | | 27.235 |
| 25 | 27.84125 | | 27.245 |
| 26 | 27.85125 | | 27.265 |
| 27 | 27.86125 | | 27.275 |
| 28 | 27.87125 | | 27.285 |
| 29 | 27.88125 | | 27.295 |
| 30 | 27.89125 | | 27.305 |
| 31 | 27.90125 | | 27.315 |
| 32 | 27.91125 | | 27.325 |
| 33 | 27.92125 | | 27.335 |
| 34 | 27.93125 | | 27.345 |
| 35 | 27.94125 | | 27.355 |
| 36 | 27.95125 | | 27.365 |
| 37 | 27.96125 | | 27.375 |
| 38 | 27.97125 | | 27.385 |
| 39 | 27.98125 | | 27.395 |
| 40 | 27.99125 | | 27.405 |

## Space satellites

Even old hands at scanning, like myself, still get a kick out of hearing
signals from space — even if they are not voice transmissions. For that
reason I have included here a wide range of frequency allocations which
should enable scanner users to pick up at least some signals.

A large amount of hardware now circles the earth in the form of man-
made satellites. Some of these devices stay permanently in space
(communication, weather and navigation vehicles); others, such as the
American space shuttle, only stay up for a pre-determined period. The
latter are usually manned with crews; astronauts in the case of the
Americans, cosmonauts in the case of the Russians.

For the scanner user, not all forms of transmission can be received
from these space vehicles as many of the frequencies used are in the SHF
band (3—30GHz). However *some* VHF and UHF frequencies are used
and those likely to be of interest to scanner users are some of the voice
communications for the astronauts/cosmonauts, amateur communications relays and weather satellites. The latter transmit pictures back to

earth in digital form which, unfortunately, means the received signal cannot just be fed straight into a television set. However, some home computers can be used with suitable software programs to convert the signals into a picture.

### Various other transmissions

Many of the 'space' allocations shown in Tables 5.1 and 5.2 do not contain voice transmissions. Many satellites transmit streams of data from on-board sensors, used for a variety of scientific measurements, and without suitable decoding equipment these signals are meaningless. The same is true of satellites used for navigation purposes. Also, most of the communications and television satellites, both for relay and broadcasting, operate at frequencies well removed from the coverage of most scanners.

### Satellite reception problems

By the time satellite transmissions reach earth they can be very weak. In some instances it is necessary to use special aerials to receive the signals. Remembering the comments in Chapter 4 about aerials and polarisation, one problem in the reception of an orbiting satellite's transmissions is that, as the satellite moves, its aerial effectively changes polarity in relation to the aerial of the ground station, causing the received signal to, apparently, fade away and then come back again, every few minutes. This can be overcome, though, by using a crossed dipole aerial.

Movement of the space craft also causes an effect, known as doppler shift, which slightly alters the received frequency of the radio signal. This can be a nuisance as it means a scanner must be tuned off the centre frequency to track the shifting signal. On some scanners, with small frequency step controls, this presents no great problem as, fortunately, the manual tuning control can be used to track the signal. On the AOR-2001 and similar scanners it may be possible to completely overcome the effect by switching to wide FM reception mode, although this will not work if other signals are present on adjacent channels.

## Amateur satellites

Amateur satellite transmissions are among some of the easiest to receive as the satellites are designed to transmit on frequencies that are easily picked up by unsophisticated equipment. Two satellites that can be received with just a simple aerial are UoSAT 2 and 'Dove' on 145.825MHz. UoSATs were built by amateurs at the University of Surrey and, although they are mostly used for sending down data in ASCII computer code, they also have an interesting on-board synthesiser. This can be heard as a robot-type voice listing strings of numbers.

UoSAT transmissions might not be very exciting but they do make a good starting point to get the feel of satellite reception. Aerial phasing and doppler shift problems will all become apparent. Bear in mind that UoSATs are orbiting satellites and so transmissions can only be received for a few minutes at a time unless sophisticated trackable beam aerials are used to follow them from horizon to horizon. Occasionally their orbits take them well away from the UK and, at such times, it might not be possible to receive transmissions at all. In addition to their VHF transmission they also transmit signals on UHF, but in my experience these are much more difficult to receive.

Amateur communications satellite transmissions are more interesting but they are also harder to receive. It is necessary to, at least, use a set of crossed dipoles, if not a Yagi aerial, with motors to control direction and elevation.

The way communications take place using these communications satellites is that an amateur transmits up to the satellite on an 'uplink' frequency. The satellite then re-transmits the signal back on a different, 'downlink', frequency. In this way it is quite easy to span large distances using VHF and UHF: communications between Europe and the Americas are quite normal.

This method of re-transmitting the signal is known as 'transponding', which can be either analogue or digital. The UoSATs do not have transponders as they are experimental scientific satellites and their job is merely to transmit data from on-board sensors.

## Table 5.24 Amateur satellites

| Satellite | Beacons | Uplinks | Downlinks |
|-----------|---------|---------|-----------|
| RS-10 | 29.357 | 145.860—145.900 | 29.360—29.400 |
|  | 29.403 | 21.160—21.200 | 29.360—29.400 |
|  | 145.857 | 21.160—21.200 | 145.860—145.900 |
|  | 145.903 |  |  |
| RS-11 | 29.407 | 145.910—145.950 | 29.410—29.450 |
|  | 29.453 | 21.210—21.250 | 29.410—29.450 |
|  | 145.907 | 21.210—21.250 | 145.910—145.950 |
|  | 145.953 |  |  |

**Table 5.24**  *continued*

| Satellite | Beacons | Uplinks | Downlinks |
|-----------|---------|---------|-----------|
| RS-12 | 29.406<br>29.454<br>145.912<br>145.959 | 145.910—145.950<br>21.210—21.250<br>21.210—21.250 | 29.410—29.450<br>29.410—29.450<br>145.910—145.950 |
| RS-13 | 29.458<br>29.504 | 145.960—146.000<br>21.260—21.300<br>21.260—21.300 | 29.460—29.504<br>29.460—29.504<br>145.960—146.000 |
| RS-14 | 145.822<br>145.922<br>145.838 | 435.020—435.100<br><br>435.040—435.120 | 145.850—145.930<br><br>145.860—145.940 |
| Oscar 10 | 145.810<br>145.987 | 435.025—435.175 | 145.830—145.980 |
| Oscar 11<br>(UoSat 2) | 145.825<br>435.025 | | |
| Oscar 13 | 145.813<br>145.975<br>2400.664 | 435.425—432.575<br>435.603—435.639 | 145.825—145.975<br>2400.711—2400.747 |
| Oscar 14<br>(UoSat 3) | 435.070 | 145.975 | 435.070 |
| Oscar 16<br>(PacSat) | 437.026<br>437.051<br>2401.143 | 145.900—145.960 | 437.051 |
| Oscar 17<br>(DOVE) | 145.825<br>2401.221 | | |
| Oscar 18<br>(WeberSat) | 437.102 | | |
| Oscar 19<br>(LUsat) | 437.126<br>437.154 | 145.840—145.900 | 437.154 |

**Table 5.24**  *continued*

| Satellite | Beacons | Uplinks | Downlinks |
|-----------|---------|---------|-----------|
| Oscar 20 (Fuji) | 435.797 435.910 | 145.900—146.000 | 435.800—435.900 |
| Oscar 21 (RS14) | 145.882 145.952 | 435.020—435.100 | 145.850—145.930 |
| Oscar 22 (UoSAT 5) | 435.120 | 145.900/145.975 | 435.120 |
| Oscar 23 (KitSat 1) | 435.175 | 145.850/145.900 | 435.175 |
| Oscar 25 (KitSat B) | | 145.870/145.980 | 435.175/436.500 |
| Oscar 26 (Itamsat) | | 145.875—145.950 | 435.867/435.822 |
| AMRAD (EyeSat 27) | | 145.850 | 436.800 |

Table 5.24 lists amateur satellites, together with allocated frequencies. With the exception of Oscar 10 and 13, all of the satellites are standard orbiting types. Oscar 10 and 13 operate in a highly elliptical orbit which means that they may remain in range for several hours. The RS series are Russian-built while some others have been made by the voluntary organisation, AMSAT.

The frequencies of most interest to scanner users are the downlink ones, but it should be noted that often some, if not all, of the satellites are in orbits that are out of UK range, and satellites are occasionally switched off for long periods, to allow for such things as battery charging from their solar panels.

### Weather satellites
Most people will be familiar with weather satellite pictures now commonly used during television weather forecasts. These pictures are transmitted from satellites in a coded fashion: circuits in the satellite

break the picture up into small segments which are then transmitted as a stream of audio tones. Upon reception at the ground station, these tones must be decoded and segments re-assembled back into a picture. Sophisticated receiving equipment is available for the job, but it is possible to use a home computer to get very acceptable results for a fraction of the price.

A number of UK companies can supply digitizers for PC, BBC, Atari and Amiga computers. However, it should be noted that although these signals are quite easy to receive, they are fairly wide band and computer pictures will only be possible with a scanner that has an intermediate frequency bandwidth of at least 30kHz in FM mode. For anyone with the technical knowledge it is not too difficult to change the IF filters on any scanner to achieve wider bandwidth.

## Table 5.25 Weather satellites

| Satellite | Frequency | Origin |
| --- | --- | --- |
| Meteor 3-3 | 137.85MHz | Russia |
| Meteor 3-4 | 137.30MHz | Russia |
| NOAA-9 | 137.62MHz | USA |
| NOAA-10 | 137.50MHz | USA |
| NOAA-11 | 137.62MHz | USA |
| NOAA-12 | 137.50MHz | USA |
| Meteosat 4 | 1691.000MHz | Geostationary Chan 2 |
| Meteosat 4 | 1694.500MHz | Geostationary Chan 1 |

Details of weather satellites are listed in Table 5.25, even though the average scanner user will not have facilities to convert them into pictures. Most scanner users will find the details useful if only to check that they can receive signals direct from space. Several weather satellites can be heard in the 137MHz band, but it should be noted that they are only switched on at certain times.

## Table 5.26 Miscellaneous satellites

| Satellite | Frequency | Details |
|-----------|-----------|---------|
| NASA Shuttles | 259.700 | AM voice |
|  | 270.000 | AM voice |
|  | 296.800 | AM voice |
| Mir (Russia) | 142.400 | FM voice |
|  | 143.625 | FM voice |
|  | 166.140 | Robot/beacon |
| Soyuz supply modules | 121.750 | FM voice |
| Navigation beacons | 149.000—150.050 Cicada | |
|  | 399.000—400.050 Transit | |

**Miscellaneous satellites**

A look at the frequency allocations in Tables 5.1 and 5.2 shows that several bands are allocated for space and satellite operation. Many of these bands have little, if any, activity and in recent years as technology has progressed, space communications have tended to move to higher frequencies — usually of several thousand Megahertz. Even so, there is occasionally voice traffic in some of the VHF bands and a list of typical users is given in Table 5.26. Do note, though, that they might not always carry transmissions. For instance two frequencies are shown for the NASA space shuttle but on any one flight this band might never be used. Keen space communications fans know that this side of the hobby often means much patience. If at first you hear nothing, try, try and try again.

In the two very narrow navigation satellite bands shown in Table 5.26 it will occasionally be possible to hear either the Russian 'CICADA' system or the USA's 'TRANSIT' service. In the UK reception of 'CICADA' signal transmissions is usually possible several times a day. They are AM signals sounding like fast Morse code.

## Military satcoms

Most military communications satellites are geostationary and are positioned around 35,000 Kilometres out from the equator. Their orbit is synchronized with the Earth's rotation so from the ground they always appear to be in the same position. Their relatively low power output and the distance means their signals are fairly weak by the time they reach us. Ideally a small dipole or ground plane aerial cut for about 270MHz will probably give better results than a discone (a masthead preamplifier does wonders but most casual listeners probably do not want to go to those lengths). If you want to make-up a small ground plane aerial then the active element should be about 260mm long. If you use a steerable log periodic then you should get quite good results.

Typical of the sort of satellites that can be heard are the American FleetSatcom series which provide global communications for the US navy. These satellites are transponders which means that their output is on a frequency related to the input frequency (which we are unlikely to hear anyway). Most use FM, although SSB does sometimes appear. Other modes include data, radioteletype and FAX. Four of these satellites are positioned around the globe at 25 degrees and 100 degrees West, and 75 degrees and 172 degrees East (all level with the equator). In Europe, Fleetsatcom West at 23 degrees longitude can be heard, and I have heard claims that, with a suitable aerial, it is also possible to hear the Indian Ocean (75 degrees East) satellite as well.

The FM used has wider deviation than you will find on normal commercial bands, typically it seems to be around 25kHz. For best reception you may need to switch your scanner to the WFM mode, unfortunately most scanners are not as sensitive in this mode.

### What will you hear?

The easiest transmissions to tune into are the FM voice channels. These often consist of messages being passed from ships or overseas bases back to the United States. There are also phone-patch transmissions between forces and their families on some channels. The digital/data transmissions do not appear to follow the usual commercial formats and one can assume that these are secure messages of strategic importance which have been encoded in some way. I have heard the voice channels being switched to FAX transmission and assume that these are normal group 3 FAX transmissions, although my own station is only equipped for radio style FAX which is not compatible and so I cannot be absolutely sure.

### Where to tune

Military satellite transmissions will be heard between 225 and 400MHz. Possibly the easiest voice channel to hear is Channel X-Ray on Fleetsatcom West on 261.675 MHz. This channel is used extensively for phone patches and is one channel which can often be received on nothing more than a telescopic aerial if you have a sensitive scanner.

Bands where you should find signals are listed in Table 5.27.

## Table 5.27 Military Satcoms

| User | Frequency |
| --- | --- |
| LeaSat (US Navy) | 243.850—243.900 |
| FleetSatcom (US Navy) | 243.960—244.100 |
| Marisat | 248.800—249.400 |
| LeaSat (US Air Force) | 249.350—249.850 |
| Fleetsatcom (US Navy) | 260.775—268.350 |

At the time of writing FM voice traffic was being logged on the following frequencies:
244.095, 249.550, 261.500, 261.650, 261.675, 261.950, 262.050, 262.100, 262.225, 262.300, 262.475, 263.625, 269.850 & 269.950 MHz.

# RT procedure 6

English is the most internationally accepted language in radio communications, yet many communicators appear to have a language all of their own. There is a good reason for some of the codes, abbreviations and expressions that are used on the air: so that misunderstandings can be avoided. The use of a set of common expressions means that even people who speak different languages can send and receive basic messages correctly. In some cases, however (CB being a good example), the expressions used are just part of the tradition which goes with the medium.

We shall first consider some things that are common to most operators.

## Phonetic alphabet

Sometimes, under difficult conditions, it may be impossible to tell what the user transmitting from another station is saying. Under such circumstances it is usual to spell out the message, coding the letters as words, using the 'phonetic alphabet':

| | |
|---|---|
| A Alpha | N November |
| B Bravo | O Oscar |
| C Charlie | P Papa |
| D Delta | Q Quebec |
| E Echo | R Roger |
| F Foxtrot | S Sierra |
| G Golf | T Tango |
| H Hotel | U Uniform |
| I India | V Victor |
| J Juliet | W Whisky |
| K Kilo | X X-ray |
| L Lima | Y Yankee |
| M Mike | Z Zulu |

These phonetics are widely used in callsigns. For instance, amateur station G7XYZ would be Golf Seven X-Ray Yankee Zulu. Similar use of phonetics will be heard in aircraft callsigns which are usually made up of a string of letters with the first or first two letters, denoting the country of registration.

Some expressions are common to most radio users:

*Roger* An almost universal expression meaning 'I understand or acknowledge receipt of your message'.

*Wilco* Not quite as common as *Roger*. It means I will comply with your instructions.

*Copy* A message or part of it. For instance, the expression 'I copy you' means I am able to understand you, I hear you.

*Mayday* The international call of distress. The word is repeated three times and means that an emergency situation has occurred. All stations on the frequency, except that calling *Mayday* and that providing assistance, must observe strict radio silence.

*Pan-Pan* A call indicating that assistance is required urgently but no one is in immediate danger.

*Affirmative* Means yes.

*Negative* Means no.

## Time

Even within the relatively close confines of Europe many countries may be in different time zones and so a standard time system has been adopted so that complex calculations can be avoided during radio communications. Coordinated Universal Time (UTC) is the same time as Greenwich Mean Time (GMT).

Occasionally, some radio operators will refer to UTC as 'Zulu', eg, '1500 hours Zulu' is 3 o'clock in the afternoon. British summer time (BST) is known as 'Alpha', that is, UTC + 1 hour. Virtually all radio traffic references to time are made using the 24 hour clock system.

## Amateurs

Amateurs form one of only two groups of radio users (the other is CB) who usually 'transmit blind': that is they put out calls for contact with anyone who happens to be on the same frequency or channel. Professional users, on the other hand, except in emergencies, only put out calls for specific stations. But amateurs, too, might well call up particular stations. And, even when transmitting blind, they may well specify that they only want contacts into a certain area. For instance, it is not unusual under 'lift' conditions to hear UK amateurs calling for contacts on the continent or even from a specific country. While most amateurs will happily chat to anyone who happens to be on the air many will, at times, only want to work long distances. One of the attractions of the hobby is being able, on occasions, to work not only far flung places but also small countries where there may only be a few amateurs. Such 'catches' are a little bit like a stamp collector finding a rare stamp.

Amateurs use expressions known as 'Q-codes' to abbreviate messages. Some typical Q-codes follow. Note that most can be either a statement or a question, eg, QRP can mean 'shall I reduce my power?' or 'reduce your power', depending on the context of use.

## International Q-codes

*QRM* Interference. This is 'man-made', such as noise from electrical equipment.

*QRN* Interference. Natural interference, such as static.

*QRP* Reducing transmitter power. The expression 'QRP station' means a transmitter that is always operated at very low power. Some amateurs specialise in this kind of operation.

*QRT* Stop sending/transmitting. A station saying "I am going QRT" usually means he is closing down.

*QRZ* Who is calling?

*QSB* Signals fading.

*QSK* Can I break in on your contact. Often a query from a station wanting to join in a 'net', that is, a group of amateurs passing conversation back and forth.

*QSL* Acknowledge receipt.

*QSO* Communicate or communication. For example 'I had a QSO with a French station'.

*QSY* Change frequency or channel. For example 'Let us QSY to 144.310MHz'.

*QTH* Location of station. Sometimes you may hear the expression 'QTH locator'. This is a grid system used by amateurs to work out the distances between each other.

There are many other Q-codes but they are rarely used by amateurs using speech for communications.

### Reporting codes

Amateurs, like other radio users, have a system of reporting on the signal that they receive. The other station will usually find this information useful as it can tell him what propagation conditions are like and if his equipment is performing correctly. Like some scanners, amateur radio transceivers usually have a signal strength meter to indicate received signal strength. The lower part of the scale is usually marked from 0 to 9, above this the scale is marked in decibels (dB). The internationally recognised method of reporting on signals is known as the 'RST code': R is readability, S is signal strength and T is tone. For speech communication the T is not used as it applies only to Morse code.

Amateurs will usually be heard to say something like 'you are four by seven'. That means readability 4, signal strength 7.

The code follows:

*Readability*
R1 Unreadable
R2 Barely readable
R3 Readable with considerable difficulty
R4 Readable with practically no difficulty
R5 Perfectly readable

*Signal strength*
S1 Faint, barely perceptible
S2 Very weak
S3 Weak
S4 Fair
S5 Fairly good
S6 Good
S7 Moderately strong
S8 Strong
S9 Extremely strong
S9 + Meter needle on the end of the scale

The last one is an unofficial code but often used and a corresponding measurement may be given in decibels, eg, 'You are 20dB over 9'.

**Call sign prefixes**
It is possible to identify the country from which a station is transmitting by the first few letters and/or numbers of the callsign. Table 6.1 lists typical countries whose stations may be heard in the UK on VHF and UHF under some lift conditions.

**Contest stations**
Occasionally you may hear contests in operation. Participating stations, operated by an individual or a group, are required to make as many

## Table 6.1 Amateur callsign prefixes, with associated countries

| Prefix | Country | Prefix | Country |
| --- | --- | --- | --- |
| C31 | Andorra | OE | Austria |
| CN | Morocco | OH | Finland |
| CT1,4 | Portugal | OHO | Aaland Island |
| CT2 | Azores | OJO | Market Reef |
| DA,DL | F.R. Germany | OK,OL | Czechoslovakia |
| DM,Y2-9 | D.R. Germany | ON | Belgium |
| EA | Spain | OY | Faroe Island |
| EA6 | Balearic Isles | OZ | Denmark |
| EA8 | Canary Isles | PA-PI | Netherlands |
| EA9 | Ceuta/Mellila | SK,SM | Sweden |
| EI,EJ | Eire | SV | Greece |
| EL | Liberia | SV9 | Crete |
| F | France | TA | Turkey |
| FC | Corsica | TF | Iceland |
| G | England | T9 | Bosnia |
| GD | Isle of Man | UA | Russia |
| GI | N. Ireland | UB5,UT5 | Ukraine |
| GJ | Jersey (CI) | UP2 | Lithuania |
| GM | Scotland | UQ2 | Latvia |
| GU | Guernsey (CI) | UR2 | Estonia |
| GW | Wales | YO | Rumania |
| HA,HG | Hungary | ZB2 | Gibraltar |
| HB | Switzerland | 3A | Monaco |
| HBO | Leichtenstein | 3V8 | Tunisia |
| HV | Vatican City | 4N | Serbia |
| I | Italy | 4U1 | United Nations |
| LA,LB | Norway | 7X | Algeria |
| LX | Luxembourg | 9A | San Marino |
| LZ | Bulgaria | 9H | Malta |

contacts as possible within a given space of time. The biggest such contest in the UK is the VHF National Field Day (NFD) organised by the Radio Society of Great Britain, which takes place every year on the first week-end in July between 3.00pm on the Saturday and 3.00pm on the Sunday. During the event the whole spectrum around 144.300MHz and 432.200MHz comes alive with thousands of transmitting stations. Unfortunately, most of the transmissions are SSB so will only be of interest to owners of more expensive scanners. However, for such owners this event usually provides an occasion to hear a lot of long distance stations. Lift conditions are normally good at this time of year and many continental stations beam their transmission towards the UK to take part in the contest.

### Special event stations
Occasionally you may hear 'special event stations' which are usually operated by a group of amateurs such as an amateur radio club. They are granted a special one-off callsign to celebrate special events such as a country fair. Callsigns are often granted to have some significance to the event. For instance, amateurs operating from the Totnes Agricultural Fair might use the callsign GB2TAF. The GB prefix is the normal one used for special event stations.

### Repeaters
Details of how repeaters work were outlined in Chapter 2. Repeaters in the 2 metre and 70 centimetre bands operate in FM mode and so can be received on any scanner that covers the bands. They are recognised as a regular transmission of Morse code containing the letters which identify which repeater they are. Amateurs often call blind on repeaters and you may well hear the expression 'This is G4HCL listening through EA'. That means that amateur station G4HCL has accessed the repeater with callsign GB3EA and is awaiting any replies.

## Marine

The international VHF marine band as we saw in Chapter 5 is channelized. The standard procedure at commencement of any transmission on the band is to first put out a call on channel 16: the calling and distress channel, requesting contact with a particular station. When that station replies, both then move to a 'working channel'.

This method of operation means that at any time there are hundreds of stations listening to channel 16, and so if any boat or ship needs help someone is bound to hear the call. A further advantage is that it enables shore stations to make general broadcasts to ships informing them of weather information, safety warnings and lists of ships (traffic lists) for whom there are telephone link calls. These transmissions are not made on channel 16 but the shore station tells ships which channel or channels to move to.

Vessels licensed for marine RT are given a callsign comprising letters, numbers or both, depending on where the ship is registered. Generally the official callsign is only used, however, when establishing link calls. For other contacts the vessel will only usually give the ship or boat's name.

A busy modern port needs radio communications to co-ordinate the movement and berthing of hundreds of trawlers, pleasure craft, ferries and cargo ships.

## Securité
Pronounced 'securitay' this word, repeated three times, precedes any broadcast transmission where there is reference to safety. Again, broadcasts telling ships that there is a securité message will be broadcast on channel 16, will give the channel to move to for the details.

Securité broadcasts usually concern 'navigational warnings'. Typically they might inform vessels that a certain beacon or lighthouse is out of action, or they might warn of floating obstructions such as cargo washed off a ship's deck or a capsized vessel.

Some shore stations have the task of making regular broadcasts in busy shipping areas where there may be a need to pass frequent safety messages. Typical is Cherbourg Radio (channel 11) which transmits safety information every half hour for the southern part of the English Channel — possibly the busiest shipping zone in the world.

## Weather
All coastal stations transmit regular weather forecasts and gale warnings. Again, forewarning of a weather forecast or gale warning will be made on channel 16 and the station will say which working channels will carry the forecast.

More localised forecasts are made by some ports, using the same procedure as the coastal station. Normally such forecasts are broadcast on the regular port operations channel.

## Port operations

So far we have looked largely at the kind of transmissions and broadcasts that are from coastal stations covering a wide area. However, the marine VHF band is also used for other kinds of contact, in particular port operations. Many ports are busy places and some have traffic handling facilities almost as sophisticated as airports.

Typical radio traffic concerns departure and arrival of ships, ferries and pleasure craft. Port controllers, for example, may have to hold some ships off-shore until other ships have left and made space for them. They may be contacted by yachts wanting mooring spaces in marinas. Other tasks involve liaison with bodies such as customs and immigration officers.

## Ship-to-ship

Several channels are set aside for ship-to-ship use. These are used for a variety of purposes: anything from the local yacht club marshalling a dinghy race to trawlermen discussing where the best catches are.

## Emergencies

Britain has probably the best marine emergency services in the world; its tradition as a seafaring nation is probably responsible for this. The waters around the British Isles are covered by lifeboat and coastguard stations, and back-up to these services comes from the RAF and Royal Navy. All services are on call to assist with emergencies at sea.

The first warning of an emergency concerning imminent danger to life will come with a 'Mayday' call. This is internationally recognised and will be made on channel 16. Normally, a coastal station or port will receive the call and put the emergency services into action. Where coastal stations are out of range, a ship may well respond to the Mayday. During this time all traffic, other than emergency traffic, is supposed to cease on channel 16.

No two emergencies are the same. In some instances it may just be a 'Pan Pan' or 'Securité' message from a small vessel lost in fog and worried about running onto rocks. In such cases coastal stations might be able to offer position fixes by taking bearings on the transmissions of the vessel in distress pinpointing the vessel's position.

At the other end of the scale, the emergency might be a ship sinking in a storm.

# Aviation

The world of aviation is the winner when we come to judge it in terms of the number of expressions and jargon. However, little of it is trivial. Aircraft crew cope with a variety of complex situations and may well be flying in and out of countries where air traffic controllers have little if any understanding of the English language.

Like the marine band the aircraft band is channelized, but the channels are referred to by their actual frequency and not by a channel number. The procedure for contacting a station is also very different. There is no common calling channel: a pilot wanting to call a ground station simply looks up the frequency and calls on it.

## Aircraft Callsigns

To the uninitiated, listening-in on the air bands can often be a frustrating experience not only because of the high level of jargon used by pilots and ground stations but also by the bewildering number of different callsigns that airlines and operators use.

Callsigns will in fact fall into one of two categories. The first is the prefix which denotes the country of origin, the second is a self-assigned name registered with the Telegraphic authorities in the country of registration. One of these options will be used by all civil aircraft. Military aircraft using civilian airways might also use a code name. Typical examples being "Reach" used by the United States Air Force and "Ascot" used by the British Royal Air Force Transport Group.

First the country prefix. Table 6.2 shows the letters and numbers associated with the registration system for any particular country, but do heed that it is common practice to only give the full callsign on the first contact with a ground station. From then on the last two letters or digits of the callsign are all that are used. These registration prefixes are normally used by light aircraft, those that are privately owned and the smaller commercial operators, although there are instances where major airlines will use these as well.

**Table 6.2 International Aircraft callsign and registration prefixes**

| Prefix | Country | Prefix | Country |
|--------|---------|--------|---------|
| A2- | Botswana | C2- | Nauru |
| A3- | Tonga | C3- | Andorra |
| A5- | Bhutan | C5- | Gambia |
| A6- | United Arab Emirates | C6- | Bahamas |
| A7- | Qatar | C9- | Mozambique |
| A9- | Bahrain | CC- | Chile |
| AP | Pakistan | CN- | Morocco |
| B- | China/Taiwan | CP- | Bolivia |
| C-F | Canada | CR- | Portugese Overseas Terr. |
| C-G | Canada | CS- | Portugal |

**Table 6.2**  *continued*

| Prefix | Country | Prefix | Country |
|---|---|---|---|
| CU- | Cuba | PZ- | Surinam |
| CX- | Uruguay | RDPL- | Laos |
| D- | Germany | RP- | Philippines |
| D2- | Angola | S2- | Bangladesh |
| D4- | Cape Verde Islands | S7- | Seychelles |
| D6- | Comores Is. | S9- | Sao Tome |
| DDR- | German D.R. (now deleted) | SE- | Sweden |
| DQ- | Fiji | SP- | Poland |
| EC- | Spain | ST- | Sudan |
| EI-/EJ- | Republic of Ireland | SU- | Egypt |
| EL- | Liberia | SX- | Greece |
| EP- | Iran | T2- | Tuvalu |
| ET- | Ethiopia | T3- | Kiribati |
| F- | France & French Terr. | T7- | San Marino |
| G- | Great Britain | TC- | Turkey |
| H4- | Solomon Islands | TF- | Iceland |
| HA- | Hungarian Peoples Rep. | TG- | Guatemala |
| HB- | Switzerland & Liechenstein | TI- | Costa Rica |
| HC- | Ecuador | TJ- | Cameroon |
| HH- | Haiti | TL- | Central African Rep |
| HI- | Dominican Republic | TN- | Rep of the Congo |
| HK- | Columbia | TR- | Gabon |
| HL- | South Korea | TS- | Tunisia |
| HP- | Panama | TT- | Chad |
| HR- | Honduras | TU- | Ivory Coast |
| HS- | Thailand | TY- | Benin |
| HZ- | Saudi Arabia | TZ- | Mali |
| I- | Italy | V2- | Antigua |
| J2- | Djibouti | V3- | Belize |
| J3- | Grenada | V8- | Brunei |
| J5- | Guinea Bissau | VH- | Australia |
| J6- | St Lucia | VN- | Vietnam |
| J7- | Dominica | VP-F | Falkland Islands |
| J8- | St Vincent | VP-LKA | St Kitts Nevis |
| OY- | Denmark | VP-LLZ | St Kitts Nevis |
| P- | North Korea | VP-LMA | Montserrat |
| P2- | Papua New Guinea | VP-LUZ | Montserrat |
| PH- | Netherlands | VP-LVA | Virgin Islands |
| PK- | Indonesia & W. Irian | VP-LZZ | Virgin Islands |
| PJ- | Netherlands Antilles | VQ-T | Turks & Caicos Isls. |
| PP-/PT- | Brazil | VR-B | Bermuda |

**Table 6.2**  *continued*

| Prefix | Country | Prefix | Country |
|--------|---------|--------|---------|
| VR-C | Cayman Islands | 5U- | Niger |
| VR-G | Gibraltar (currently not used. All aircraft registered in G.B.) | 5V- | Togo |
| | | 5W- | Polynesia (Western Samoa) |
| | | 5X- | Uganda |
| VR-H | Hong Kong | XC- | Mexico |
| VT- | India | XT- | Upper Volta |
| XA-/XB- | Mexico | XU- | Kampuchea |
| JA- | Japan | XY-/XZ- | Burma |
| JY- | Jordan | YA- | Afghanistan |
| LN- | Norway | YI- | Iraq |
| LQ-/LV | Argentina | YJ- | Vanuatu |
| LX- | Luxembourg | YK- | Syria |
| LZ- | Bulgaria | YN- | Nicaragua |
| MI- | Marshall Islands | YR- | Romania |
| N- | United States of America | YS- | El Salvador |
| OB- | Peru | YV- | Venezuela |
| OD- | Lebanon | Z- | Zimbabwe |
| OE- | Austria | 7P- | Lesotho |
| OH- | Finland | 7Q- | Malawi |
| OK- | Czechoslovakia | 7T- | Algeria |
| OO- | Belgium | 8P- | Barbados |
| ZA- | Albania | 8Q- | Maldives |
| ZK- | New Zealand | 8R- | Guyana |
| ZP- | Paraguay | 9G- | Ghana |
| ZS- | Republic of South Africa | 9H- | Malta |
| 3A- | Monaco | 9J- | Zambia |
| 3B- | Mauritius | 9K- | Kuwait |
| 3C- | Equatorial Guinea | 9L- | Sierra Leone |
| 3D- | Swaziland | 9M- | Malaysia |
| 3X- | Guinea | 9N- | Nepal |
| 4R- | Sri Lanka | 9Q- | Zaire |
| 4W- | Yemen Arab Republic | 9U- | Burundi |
| 4X- | Israel | 9V- | Singapore |
| 4YB- | Jordan/Iraq | 9XR- | Rwanda |
| 5A- | Libya | 9Y- | Trinidad & Tobago |
| 5B- | Cyprus | 5Y- | Kenya |
| 5H- | Tanzania | 6O- | Somalia |
| 5N- | Nigeria | 6V-/6W- | Senegal |
| 5R- | Madagascar (Malagasy Rep.) | 6Y- | Jamaica |
| 5T- | Mauritania | 7O- | Democratic Yemen |

## Callsigns

If the full call-sign consists of letters only then you can be almost certain that the call-sign being used is the standard country prefix followed by the aircraft registration. The vast majority of countries use two, three or four letter groups after the country prefix but there are a few exceptions and the notable ones are:

| | |
|---|---|
| United States of America | N followed by numbers or a mix of numbers and letters |
| Japan | JA followed by a 4 digit number |
| Venezuela | YV followed by a 3 digit number then suffixed with a single letter |
| China/Taiwan | B followed by a 3 or 4 digit number |
| Cuba | CU-T followed by a 4 digit number |
| Columbia | HK followed by a 4 digit number suffixed with X |
| Korea | HL followed by a 4 digit number |

All civilian aircraft have a registration. Generally, privately owned light aircraft or those operated as air-taxis will use their registration as their radio callsign.

Normal procedure for making contact with the ground station will be to give the full callsign. The controller will reply, perhaps, referring to the aircraft by the full callsign, in which case the pilot will again, when transmitting, use the full callsign. At some stage though, for the sake of brevity, the approach controller will just use the last two letters and from then on the pilot will do the same.

Larger aircraft, such as those used on regular passenger carrying routes, may use the same type of callsign, or a special callsign based on the airline's name and typically may also use the flight number for that service. Again the ground controller will probably, at some stage, abbreviate this and just use the number: from then on the aircrew will do the same.

Numbers preceded by the word 'Ascot' denote the callsign of a British military aircraft flying on a civilian route. The USAF equivalent is the prefix 'Mac'.

## Landing instructions

The first contact an aircraft has with an airfield is usually on the approach frequency. After transmitting on the frequency and identifying the aircraft, the pilot usually gives his aircraft position and altitude. The approach controller then transmits information relating to airfield barometric pressure (QFE), the wind direction and speed, the runway in use (runways are always identified by the compass heading needed to land on them), and details of other aircraft in the landing pattern or about to take off. Temperature and visibility in kilometres may be also given. If the weather is bad the RVR (runway visual range) may be referred to. The pilot needs to know the QFE (sometimes just called the 'fox echo') so that the aircraft's altimeter may be set so that it will read zero feet at runway level. Other information such as runway state (if affected by rain, ice or snow) may be transmitted, followed by instructions to remain at present altitude or start descending to circuit height (often about 1000 feet). Some of this information the pilot will repeat back.

As the aircraft gets closer to the airport there will come a stage where the approach controller instructs the pilot to change to the tower frequency. The pilot always repeats the frequency to be changed to: this is standard procedure when changing frequency at any point in a flight.

Now the pilot calls the tower and again will give his position and altitude. The aircraft may be making a straight-in approach, that is, arriving at the airfield in line with the runway or he may be 'joining the circuit'. The circuit is an imaginary path around the airfield in the form of a racetrack. It can be in a lefthand or righthand direction and, once joined, the pilot will report at various stages such as downwind leg, base leg and finals. Finals occur at a given distance from the runway and the pilot will always tell the controller when the aircraft is one mile out. Throughout this stage of the flight the pilot will be given various instructions and updated QFE, wind speed and direction information. At any stage of the approach the pilot may be told to divert course because the controller cannot yet fit him in with other traffic. The instruction may be to briefly orbit over a given position, or to fly out further to a given point and then re-join the landing pattern.

Once on the ground the pilot may be told to change frequency yet again (particularly at larger airfields), this time to speak to the ground handler. Here, instructions on which taxiways to use and where to park the aircraft will be given.

**Table 6.3 Airline call signs**

| Call sign | Operator | Country |
|-----------|----------|---------|
| Aceforce | NATO Command Europe | Mil |
| Ace Air | Air Cargo Express | USA |
| Actair | Air Charter and Travel | UK |
| Adria | Adria Airways | Yugoslavia |
| Aeradio | International Aeradio | UK |
| Aero | United States Army | US Mil |
| Aero Lloyd | Aero Lloyd | Germany |
| Aeroflot | Aeroflot | Russia |

**Table 6.3**  *continued*

| Call sign | Operator | Country |
|---|---|---|
| Aeromar | Com Aeromaritime d'Affretement | France |
| Aeromaritime | Aeromaritime | France |
| Aeromexico | Aeromexico | Mexico |
| Aeronaut | Cranfield Institute of Technology | UK Gov |
| Aeroperu | Aeroperu | Peru |
| Aeroswede | Syd Aero | Sweden |
| Afro | Affretair | Zimbabwe |
| Airafric | Air Afrique | Ivory Coast |
| Air America | Air America (C.I.A.) | USA |
| Air Atlantis | Air Atlantis | Portugal |
| Air Belgium | Air Belgium | Belgium |
| Air BVI | Air BVI | UK |
| Air Canada | Air Canada | Canada |
| Aircal | Air Caledonie | France |
| Air Falcon | Europe Falcon Service | France |
| Air Ferry | British Air Ferries | UK |
| Air Force One | US President | US Mil |
| Air Force Two | US Vice-President | US Mil |
| Air France | Air France | France |
| Air Freighter | Aeron International | USA |
| Air Hong Kong | Air Hong Kong | Hong Kong |
| Air India | Air India | India |
| Air Lanka | Air Lanka | Sri Lanka |
| Air London | Air London | UK |
| Air Mauritius | Air Mauritius | Mauritius |
| Airmil | Spanish Air Force | Spain |
| Air Portugal | Air Portugal | Portugal |
| Air Rwanda | Air Rwanda | Rwanda |
| Air Services | Austrian Air Services | Austria |
| Air Tara | Air Tara | Ireland |
| Airtax | Birmingham Aviation | UK |
| Air Zaire | Air Zaire | Zaire |
| Air Zimbabwe | Air Zimbabwe | Zimbabwe |
| Airafric | Air Afrique | Ivory Coast |
| Airbiz | Maersk Commuter | Denmark |
| Airbridge | Air Bridge Carriers | UK |
| Aircargo | Intavia | UK |
| Airgo | Airgo | UK |
| Airmove | Skywork | UK |
| Airnav | Air Navigation and Trading | UK |

**Table 6.3**   *continued*

| Call sign | Operator | Country |
|---|---|---|
| Alisarda | Alisarda | Italy |
| Alitali | Alitalia | Italy |
| All Nippon | All Nippon | Japan |
| American | American Airlines | USA |
| Amtran | American Trans-Air | USA |
| Anglo | Anglo Cargo | UK |
| Argentine | Aerolineas Argentinas | Argentina |
| Armyair | Army Air Corps | UK Mil |
| Ascot | RAF 1 Group Air Transport | UK Mil |
| Aspro | Intereuropean Airways | UK |
| Atlantic | Air Atlantique | UK |
| Augusta | Augusta Airways | Australia |
| Austrian | Austrian Airlines | Austria |
| Aviaco | Aviaco | Spain |
| Avianca | Avianca | Colombia |
| Ayline | Aurigny Air Services | UK |
| | | |
| Backer | British Charter | UK |
| Bafair | Belgian Air Force | Belgium |
| Bafjet | British Air Ferries Business Jets | UK |
| Bahrain One | The Amiri Flight | Bahrain |
| Bailair | Balair | Switzerland |
| Balkan | Balkan Bulgarian Airlines | Bulgaria |
| Batman | Ratioflug | Germany |
| Bangladesh | Bangladesh Biman | Bangladesh |
| Beaupair | Aviation Beauport | UK |
| Beeline | Biggin Hill Executive | UK |
| Birmex | Birmingham European | UK |
| Biztravel | Business Air Travel | UK |
| Beatours | British Airtours | UK |
| Blackbox | Bedford Royal Aircraft Estab. | UK Gov |
| Blackburn | British Aerospace (Scampton) | UK |
| Bluebird | Finnaviation | Finland |
| Bodensee | Delta Air | Germany |
| Botswana | Air Botswana | Botswana |
| Braethens | Braethens SAFE | Norway |
| Bristol | British Aerospace (Bristol) | UK |
| Bristow | Bristow Helicopters | UK |
| Britannia | Britannia Airways | UK |
| Britanny | Brit Air | France |

**Table 6.3**  *continued*

| Call sign | Operator | Country |
| --- | --- | --- |
| British Island | British Island Airways | UK |
| Brunei | Royal Brunei Airlines | Brunei |
| Busy Bee | Busy Bee | Norway |
| | | |
| Caledonian | British Caledonian Airways | UK |
| Camair | Cameroon Airlines | Cameroon |
| Canada | Worldways Canadian | Canada |
| Canadian | Canadian Airlines | Canada |
| Canforce | Canadian Air Force | Canada |
| Cargo | Safair Freighters | Rep. S. Africa |
| Cargolux | Cargolux | Luxembourg |
| Cathay | Cathay Pacific Airways | Hong Kong |
| Cayman | Cayman Airways | Cayman Islands |
| Cedar Jet | Middle East Airlines | Lebanon |
| Chad | Chad Air Services | Chad |
| Channex | Channel Express | UK |
| China | C.A.A.C. | China |
| City | N.L.M. City Hopper | Holland |
| Clansman | Airwork Limited | UK |
| Conair | Conair | Denmark |
| Condor | Condor Flugdienst | Germany |
| Contactair | Contactair | Germany |
| Continental | Continental Airlines | USA |
| Corsair | Corse Air | France |
| Crossair | Crossair | Switzerland |
| Cubana | Cubana | Cuba |
| Cyprus | Cyprus Airways | Cyprus |
| | | |
| Dantax | Aalborg Airtaxi | Belgium |
| Databird | Air Nigeria | Nigeria |
| Dash | Air Atlantic | UK |
| Delta | Delta Air Lines | USA |
| Deltair | Delta Air Transport | Belgium |
| DLT | D.L.T. | Germany |
| Dominair | Aerolineas Dominicanes | Dominican Rep. |
| Dragon | Welsh Airways | UK |
| Dynamite | Dynamic Air | Holland |
| | | |
| Egyptair | Egyptair | Egypt |
| El Al | El Al | Israel |

**Table 6.3**  *continued*

| Call sign | Operator | Country |
|-----------|----------|---------|
| Elite | Air 3000 | Canada |
| Emery | Emery Worldwide | USA |
| Emirates | Emirate Airlines | U. A. E, |
| Espania | CTA Espania | Spain |
| Ethiopian | Ethiopian Airlines | Ethiopia |
| Euralair | Euralair | France |
| Euroair | Euroair Transport | UK |
| Eurotrans | European Air Transport | Belgium |
| Evergreen | Evergreen International | USA |
| Excalibur | Air Exel | UK |
| Executive | Extra Executive Transport | Germany |
| Express | Federal Express | USA |
| | | |
| Falcon Jet | Falcon Jet Centre | UK |
| Ferranti | Ferranti Ltd | UK |
| Finnair | Finnair | Finland |
| Flamingo | Nurnberger Flugdienst | Germany |
| Food | Food Brokers Limited | UK |
| Fordair | Ford Motor Company | UK |
| Foyl | Air Foyle | UK |
| Fred Olsen | Fred Olsen Air Transport | Norway |
| | | |
| Gatwick Air | Gatwick Air Taxis | UK |
| Gauntlet | Boscombe Down (MOD) | UK Mil |
| German Cargo | German Cargo | Germany |
| Germania | Germania | Germany |
| Ghana | Ghana Airways | Ghana |
| Gibair | GB Airways Limited | UK |
| Golf November | Air Gabon | Gabon |
| Granite | Business Air | UK |
| Greenlandair | Gronlandsfly | Denmark |
| Gulf Air | Gulf Air | Oman |
| Guyair | Guyana Airways | Guyana |
| | | |
| Hapag-Lloyd | Hapag-Lloyd | Germany |
| Hatair | Hatfield Executive Aviation | UK |
| Hawker | British Aerospace (Dunsfold) | UK |
| Hunting | Hunting Surveys | UK |
| | | |
| Iberian | Iberia | Spain |

**Table 6.3**   *continued*

| Call sign | Operator | Country |
|---|---|---|
| Iceair | Icelandair | Iceland |
| Indonesian | Garuda Indonesian Airways | Indonesia |
| Interflug | Interflug | Germany |
| Iranair | Iran Air | Iran |
| Iraqi | Iraqi Airways | Iraq |
| Janus | Janus Airways | UK |
| Japanair | Japan Air Lines | Japan |
| Jetset | Air 2000 | UK |
| Joker | Germania | Germany |
| Jordanian | Royal Jordanian Airline | Jordan |
| K.L.M | K.L.M. | Holland |
| Karair | Kar-Air | Finland |
| Kenya | Kenya Airlines | Kenya |
| Kestrel | Airtours | UK |
| Kilo Mike | Air Malta | Malta |
| Kilroe | Air Kilro | UK |
| Kittyhawk | Queen's Flights | UK Mil |
| Koreanair | Korean Air | Korea |
| Kuwaiti | Kuwait Airways | Kuwait |
| Leopard | Queen's Flights | UK Mil |
| Libair | Libyan Arab Airlines | Libya |
| Lion | British International Helicopters | UK |
| Lovo | Lovaux Limited | UK |
| Lufthansa | Lufthansa | Germany |
| Luxair | Luxair | Luxembourg |
| Macline | McAlpine Aviation Limited | UK |
| Madair | Air Madagascar | Madagascar |
| Maerskair | Maersk Air | Denmark |
| Malawi | Air Malawi | Malawi |
| Malaysian | Malaysian Airlines System | Malaya |
| Malev | Malev | Hungary |
| Mamair | Marine and Aviation Management | UK |
| Mann | Alan Mann Helicopters | UK |
| Marocair | Royal Air Maroc | Morocco |
| Martinair | Martinair | Holland |
| Mediterranean | Mediterranean Express | UK |

**Table 6.3**  *continued*

| Call sign | Operator | Country |
|---|---|---|
| Merlin | Rolls Royce Military | UK |
| Metman | Meteorological Research Flight | UK Gov |
| Metro | Bohnstedt Petersen Aviation | Denmark |
| Midas | Milford Docks Air Services | UK |
| Midland | British Midland Airways | UK |
| Midwing | Airborne of Sweden | Sweden |
| Mike Romeo | Air Mauritania | Mauritania |
| Minair | C.A.A. Flying Unit | UK Gov |
| Minerve | Minerve | France |
| Monarch | Monarch Airlines | UK |
| Nationair | Nation Air | Canada |
| National | Airmore Aviation | UK |
| Navy | Royal Navy | UK Mil |
| Neatax | Northern Executive Aviation | UK |
| Netherlands | Royal Netherlands Air Force | Holland |
| Netherlines | Netherlines | Holland |
| New Zealand | Air New Zealand | New Zealand |
| Newpin | British Aerospace (Hawarden) | UK |
| Nigerian | Nigerian Airways | Nigeria |
| Nightflight | Night Flight | UK |
| Norseman | Norsk Air | Norway |
| Northair | Northern Air Taxis | UK |
| Northwest | Northwest Orient | USA |
| November Lima | Air Liberia | Liberia |
| November Papa | Heavylift Cargo Airlines | UK |
| Nugget | Farnborough Royal Aircraft Estab. | UK Gov |
| Olympic | Olympic Airways | Greece |
| Orange | Air Holland | Holland |
| Orion | Orion Airways | UK |
| Overnight | Russow Aviation | Germany |
| Palmair | Palmair | UK |
| Pakistan | Pakistan International | Pakistan |
| Para | Army Parachute Centre | UK Mil |
| Paraguaya | Lineas Aereas Paraguayas (LAP) | Paraguay |
| Partnair | Partnair | Norway |
| Pearl | Oriental Pearl Airways | UK |
| Philair | Philips Aviation Services | Holland |

**Table 6.3**  *continued*

| Call sign | Operator | Country |
| --- | --- | --- |
| Philippine | Philippine Airlines | Philippines |
| Plum | PLM Helicopters | UK |
| Police | Police Aviation Services | UK |
| Pollot | Polski Linie Lotnicze (LOT) | Poland |
| Port | Skyworld Airlines | USA |
| Puma | Phoenix Aviation | UK |
| | | |
| Quantas | Quantas | Australia |
| Quebec Tango | Aer Turas | Rep. Ireland |
| | | |
| Racal | Racal Avionics | UK |
| Rafair | Royal Air Force | UK Mil |
| Rainbow | Queen's Flights | UK Mil |
| Reach | USAF Air Mobility Command | US Mil |
| Regal | Crown Air | Canada |
| Rescue | R.A.F. rescue | UK Mil |
| Richair | Rich International | USA |
| Rogav | Rogers Aviation | UK |
| Rushton | Flight Refuelling Limited | UK |
| | | |
| Sabena | Sabena | Belgium |
| Sam | U.S.A.F. Special Air Mission | US Mil |
| Saudia | Saudia | Saudi Arabia |
| Scandanavian | Scandanavian Airlines System | Sweden |
| Scanwings | Maimo Aviation | Sweden |
| Seychelles | Air Seychelles | Seychelles |
| Shamrock | Air Lingus | Ireland |
| Short | Short Brothers | UK |
| Sierra India | Arab Wings | Jordan |
| Singapore | Singapore Airlines | Singapore |
| Sky Express | Salair | Sweden |
| Somalair | Somali Airlines | Somalia |
| Southern Air | Southern Air Transport | USA |
| Spantax | Spantax | Spain |
| Special | Metropolitan Police Air Unit | UK |
| Speedbird | British Airways | UK |
| Speedfox | Jetair Aps | Denmark |
| Speedpack | International Parcel Express | USA |
| Springbok | South African Airways | Rep. S. Africa |
| Starjet | Novair | UK |

**Table 6.3**  *continued*

| Call sign | Operator | Country |
| --- | --- | --- |
| Stellair | Stellair | France |
| Sterling | Sterling Airways | Denmark |
| Sudanair | Sudan Airways | Sudan |
| Surinam | Surinam Airways | Surinam |
| Swedair | Swedair | Sweden |
| Swedeline | Linjeflyg | Sweden |
| Swedic | Swedish Air Force | Sweden |
| Swissair | Swissair | Switzerland |
| Syrianair | Syrian Arab Airlines | Syria |
| Tarnish | British Aerospace (Warton) | UK |
| Tarom | Tarom | Romania |
| Teastar | Trans European | UK |
| Tee Air | Tower Air | UK |
| Tennant | British Aerospace (Prestwick) | UK |
| Tester | Empire Test Pilots School | UK Mil |
| Thai Inter | Thai International Airlines | Thailand |
| Tibbet | British Aerospace (Hatfield) | UK |
| Tiger | Flying Tiger Line | USA |
| Tradewinds | Tradewinds Airways | UK |
| Trans Arabian | Trans Arabian Air Transport | Sudan |
| Trans Europe | Trans Europe Air Charter | UK |
| Trans-Med | Trans Mediterranean Airways | Lebanon |
| Transway | TEA Basle | Switzerland |
| Transworld | Trans World Airlines | USA |
| Tunair | Tunis-Air | Tunisia |
| Turkair | Turk Hava Yollari (THY) | Turkey |
| Tyrolean | Tyrolean Airways | Austria |
| Uganda | Uganda Airlines | Uganda |
| Uni-Air | Uni-Air | France |
| Unicorn | Queen's Flights | UK Mil |
| UTA | U.T.A. | France |
| Varig | Varig | Brazil |
| Vectis | Pilatus Britten-Norman | UK |
| Viasa | Viasa | Venezuala |
| Victor Kilo | Airbus Industrie | France |
| Victor Yankee | Air Belgium | Belgium |
| Viking | Scanair | Sweden |

**Table 6.3**  *continued*

| Call sign | Operator | Country |
|-----------|----------|---------|
| Virgin | Virgin Atlantic | UK |
| Wardair | Wardair | Canada |
| Watchdog | Ministry of Ag. Fisheries & Food | UK Gov |
| West Indian | British West Indian Airways | Trinidad |
| White Star | Star Air | Denmark |
| Wigwam | C.S.E. Aviation | UK |
| Woodair | Woodgate Air Services | UK |
| World | World Airways | USA |
| Worldways | Worldways Canada | Canada |
| Yemeni | Yemen Airways | Yemen PDR |
| Zambia | Zambia Airways | Zambia |
| Zap | Titan Airways | UK |

*Suffixes*

Occasionally a suffix will be added to the group of numbers following the above call sign to denote a special characteristic of the flight. These are usually as follows although it should be noted that British Airways operate a different system.

*A* Added where a flight has been doubled up so that two aircraft are using the same prefix and numerals (for example one aircraft will be suffixed A and the other B).

*F* Aircraft carrying freight only.

*P* Aircraft positioning to another location with no passengers on board.

*Q* Aircraft details have been changed to a standard flight plan (for example the regular aircraft has been substituted with another type).

*T* Training flight.

*X* Allocated by controllers to avoid confusion when two aircraft have identical numbers even though their prefixes may differ.

*Heavy* tells controllers that the aircraft is a wide-bodied type.

Private aircraft and those operated by smaller operators such as air taxis may well use just their registration. In Britain this will consist of the prefix 'G' followed by up to four letters. On establishing first contact with a controller the pilot will give his call sign in full. For instance G-ABCD would be "Golf-Alpha Bravo Charlie Delta". However, the controller may well abbreviate this to "Golf-Charlie Delta" or even just "Charlie Delta".

## SRA and PAR radar let–down

Occasionally, in bad visibility, a pilot may need to be 'talked-down'. SRA (surveillance radar approach) may be used to give the pilot precise instructions to reach the end of the runway. Normally, the airfield has a special frequency for this and once the pilot has established contact with the controller there is a point when the controller tells the pilot not to acknowledge further instructions. From then on, the controller gives the pilot a running commentary on the aircraft's position in relation to an imaginary line drawn outwards from the runway, known as the 'centre-line'. Compass headings may be given to the pilot, to steer the aircraft, in order to get on to the centre-line. Other information given tells the pilot how far the aircraft is from the runway and what height it should be at. At a point about half a mile from the runway, the controller announces that the approach is complete. If the pilot cannot see the runway at this stage the approach must be abandoned for another, or the aircraft is diverted to another airfield. Failing to touch-down results in a 'go-around' (formerly an 'overshoot').

PAR (precision radar approach) is similar, but also tells the pilot altitude and whether or not the aircraft is on the 'glide slope'.

### Startup

The procedure at the start of a flight varies from airfield to airfield. On smaller airfields the pilot may start the aircraft and then ask for take-off instructions. The ground controller transmits details of which runway is in use, QFE and wind, then instructs the pilot to start taxiing to a holding point just before the end of the runway. Once the runway is clear, the controller allows the aircraft to take off and relays other instructions such as which height to climb to and when the aircraft can start turning on course.

At bigger airfields, particularly those in busy flight areas, the procedure may be far more complicated and will depend to some extent on whether the flight is VFR (visual flight rules) or IFR (instrument flight rules). The first, VFR, is where an aircraft flies solely by dead reckoning. In other words, the pilot navigates by using a compass and a map, looking out of the aircraft windows for landmarks. The second, IFR, is where the pilot uses radionavigation and instruments to cover the route. Most commercial flights are IFR and such flights are always along designated airways routes. Prior to a flight the pilot files a flight plan with Air Traffic Control which is telexed to controllers on the aircraft's route, who are then aware of the type of aircraft, altitude requested and destination.

At commencement of the flight the pilot informs the tower that all is ready. At this stage the controller may well only say the aircraft is clear to start up and, perhaps, will give the temperature. Once the pilot informs the controller the aircraft is ready for take-off, taxiing

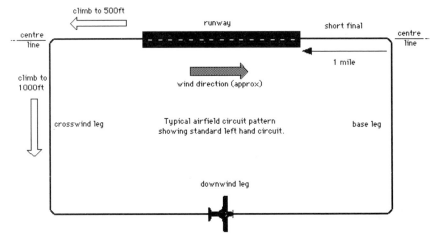

Typical airfield circuit pattern showing standard left hand circuit.

instructions, the QFE, the runway in use and the wind details are all given. At this stage, or shortly after, clearance is given to the pilot detailing destination, the airways to use and altitudes. In the UK airways are identified by colours (red, blue, green, white, amber) with a number. After the actual take-off, the aircraft may be handed over to another controller, such as approach, before the pilot is finally told to contact 'airways' or 'information' services.

### Airways

Busy air routes, such as those over Europe, are divided up into countries and regions which have central control points for all the air routes in the sectors. Although VFR flights at low altitudes can, by and large, choose the course they fly, this is not the case at higher altitudes in the airways. Now we are in the realm of 'controlled airspace' and pilots *must* fly along a certain course at a certain height. The airways are marked at regular points, and where they cross, by beacons on the ground. These are used for navigation purposes and also form what are known as 'compulsory reporting points': as the aircraft passes over a beacon the pilot must report to the sector controller, giving the name of the beacon, flight level (at higher altitudes the height is abbreviated, eg, 10,000 feet becomes 'flight level one-zero-zero'), and 'forward estimate' time for the next reporting point. These points are referred to by the name of the place where the beacon is sited.

Towards the end of the journey the pilot may be given a fairly complex set of instructions. Landing at major airports like London Heathrow may, at busy times, involve joining the 'stack': an imaginary spiral staircase in the sky. The aircraft joins at the top and flies a racetrack

shaped circuit, slowly dropping to different flight levels until, at the
bottom, it is routed to the airfield.

### Flight information

Everything above 25,000 feet is 'controlled airspace' (in some regions
airspace below that altitude is controlled, too). Pilots can obtain details
of traffic movements in the region from the UIR (upper-flight information region) service. Below that level, information is provided by
the FIR (flight information region) service. Note that both the UIR
and FIR are *advisory* services: they provide information for pilots but
do not control the movement of aircraft.

A further advisory service is available for small aircraft on VFR flights:
LARS (lower airspace radar service). The facility is provided by the
various MATZ (military aerodrome traffic zones) up and down the
country. Again, they do not control flights but merely offer information
regarding other aircraft in the area.

### Company frequencies

Most airlines use 'company frequencies'. Any one frequency, however,
may be used by several airline operators to contact company ground
stations. An example of the use of company frequencies could be when
an aircraft wishes to contact the operations department of the company
base at the destination airfield, in order to give the estimated time of
arrival or request special services such as wheelchairs for invalid
passengers. Other messages may concern servicing required on the
aircraft: instruments may need adjusting, or there may be minor
technical problems that engineers will need to correct before the
aircraft takes-off again.

## Glossary

The following list of abbreviations and expressions are regularly used
during typical transmissions between ground and air.

*Abort* Abandon (ie, abandon take-off).
*AFIS* Airfield flight information service.
*AIREP* Report for position and weather in flight.
*Airway* Defined flight path.
*amsl* Above mean sea level.
*APU* Auxiliary power unit (backup when engines are off).
*ASDA* Runway accelerated stop distance.
*ASI* Air speed indicator.
*ATA* Actual time of arrival.
*ATC* Air traffic control.

*ATIS* Automatic terminal information service.
*Avgas* Aviation grade petrol.
*Avionics* Aircraft electronics.
*Backtrack* Taxi back down the runway.
*Beacon* Station transmitting continuous navigation signal.
*CAT* Clear air turbulence.
*CBs* Cumulo nimbus (thunder clouds).
*Conflicting* Conflicting traffic, etc, possible collision course.
*Decimal* Decimal point as in frequency, eg, 128.65MHz.
*Cav-OK* Ceiling and visibility are good.
*DF* Direction finding by radio.
*DME* Distance measuring equipment.
*Drift* Lateral movement off desired track.
*ETA* Estimated time of arrival.
*FIR* Flight information region.
*Flameout* Total power loss on jet or turbo prop engine.
*Gear* Undercarriage.
*Glidepath* Line of descent on landing.
*GMC* Ground movement controller.
*GMT* Greenwich Mean Time.
*Go around* Overshoot runway and re-join circuit.
*GPU* Ground power unit.
*Greens* Landing gear down and locked indicators.
*Homer* Homing beacon.
*IAS* Indicated air speed.
*IFR* Instrument flight rules.
*ILS* Instrument landing system.
*IMC* Instrument meteorological conditions.
*JET A1* Jet and turbo-prop fuel (kerosene).
*Knots* Nautical miles per hour.
*LARS* Lower airspace radar service.
*Localiser* Glidepath beacon.
*Mach* Speed in relation to the speed of sound.
*MATZ* Military aerodrome traffic zone.
*METAR* Meterological report (not a forecast).
*Navaid* Navigational aid.
*NavCom* Combined communication and navigation radio.
*Navex* Navigation exercise (training flight).
*NDB* Non-directional beacon.
*NOTAM* Notice to airmen.
*Okta* An eighth. Used to denote cloud density.
*Ops* Operations.
*Orbit* Fly in a circle.
*Overshoot* No longer used, see 'go around'.
*Pax* Passengers (eg, 64 pax on board).

*PAR* Precision approach radar.
*PPO* Prior permission only (restricted airfields).
*QDM* Magnetic heading.
*QFE* Barometric pressure at aerodrome.
*QNH* Barometric pressure at sea level.
*Roll-out* Stopping distance after touchdown.
*RSR* Route surveillance radar.
*RVR* Runway visual range.
*SAR* Search and rescue.
*SELCAL* Selective calling system (activates radio by code).
*SID* Standard instrument departure.
*SIG* Significant.
*SitRep* Situation report.
*Squawk* Switch transponder on.
*Squawk ident* Select 'identification' mode on transponder.
*SRE* Surveillance radar element.
*STOL* Short take-off and landing.
*Stratus* Low misty cloud (often obscures runway approach).
*TAI* True air speed indicator.
*TACAN* Tactical air navigator.
*TAF* Terminal area forecast.
*TAR* Terminal area radar.
*TAS* True air speed.
*TMA* Terminal control area.
*Traffic* Aircraft in flight.
*UIR* Upper flight information region.
*US* Unserviceable.
*UTC* Universal time constant (GMT).
*VASI* Runway lights angled to give a visual glide slope.
*VFR* Visual flight rules.
*VMC* Visual meteorological conditions.
*VOLMET* Continuous weather forecast.
*VOR* VHF omni-direction range beacon.
*VSI* Vertical speed indicator (rate of climb).
*VTOL* Vertical take-off and landing.
*WX* Weather.

## NASA shuttles

Three UHF frequencies (see Chapter 5) have been used by the NASA shuttles over the years but it should be noted that on some missions, the communications have been restricted to frequencies which are outside the range of ordinary scanners. However, UHF communications are heard on some flights, particularly those involving spacewalks (EVA—

Extra Vehicular Activity).

It must be stressed that shuttle communications are unlikely to be heard on a scanner which is simply being used with an ordinary discone aerial. A Helix aerial (proper helix—not the rubber duck type) or crossed dipoles designed for the frequency and a masthead pre-amplifier are advisable for best results.

The following abbreviations are ones commonly used during the lift-off phase (frequently re-broadcast via the media) and during some stages of the flight.

*AFSCN* Air Force Satellite Control Network.
*ALT* Approach for Landing Test programme.
*AMU* Astronaut manouvering unit.
*APS* Alternate Payload Specialist.
*APU* Auxiliary Power Unit.
*ASE* Airborne Support Equipment.
*ATE* Automatic Test Equipment.
*ATO* Abort to Orbit.
*BFC* Backup Flight Control.
*CAPCOM* Capsule Communicator.
*CCAFS* Cape Canaveral Air Force Station.
*CCMS* Checkout, Control and Monitor Sub-systems.
*CDR* Commander.
*CDMS* Command and Data Management Systems Officer.
*CDS* Central Data Systems.
*CIC* Crew Interface Coordinator.
*CIE* Communications Interface Equipment.
*CTS* Call to Stations.
*DCC* Data Computation Complex.
*DCS* Display Control System.
*DIG* Digital Image Generation.
*DFI* Development Flight Instrumentation.
*DFRF* Dryden Flight Research Facility.
*DMC* Data Management Coordinator.
*DOD* Department of Defence.
*DPS* Data Processing System.
*EAFB* Edwards Air Force Base.
*ECLSS* Environmental Control and Life Support System.
*EMU* Extra Vehicular Mobility Unit.
*ESMC* Eastern Space and Missile center.
*ET* External Tank.
*EVA* Extra Vehicular Activity.
*FAO* Flight Activities Officer.
*F/C* Flight Controller.
*FD* Flight Director.

*FDO* Flight Dynamics Officer.
*FOD* Flight Operations Directorate.
*FOE* Flight Operations Engineer.
*FOSO* Flight Operations Scheduling Officer.
*FR* Firing Room.
*FRC* Flight Control Room.
*FRCS* Forward Reaction Control System.
*FRF* Flight Readiness Firing.
*FRR* Flight Readiness Review.
*GAS* Getaway Special.
*GC* Ground Control.
*GDO* Guidance Officer.
*GLS* Ground Launch Sequencer.
*GN* Ground Network.
*GNC* Guidance, Navigation and Control Systems Engineer.
*GPC* General Purpose Computer.
*GSE* Ground Support Equipment.
*GSDC* Goddard Space Flight Center.
*IG* Inertial Guidance.
*ILS* Instrument Landing System.
*IMF* In-Flight Maintenance.
*INCO* Instrumentation and Communications Officer.
*IUS* Inertial Upper Stage.
*IVA* Intra Vehicular Activity.
*JSC* Johnson Space Center.
*KSC* Kennedy Space Center.
*LC* Launch Complex.
*LCC* Launch Control Center.
*LCS* Launch Control System.
*LOX* Liquid Oxygen.
*LPS* Launch Processing System.
*MCC* Mission Control Center.
*MD* Mission Director.
*ME* Main Engine.
*MECO* Main Engine Cut-Off.
*MET* Mission Elapsed Time.
*MLS* Microwave Landing System.
*MOD* Mission Operations Directorate.
*MOP* Mission Operations Plan.
*MPS* Main Propulsion System.
*MS* Mission Specialist.
*MSCI* Mission Scientist.
*MSFC* Marshall Space Flight Center.
*NASCOM* Nasa Communications Network.
*NOCC* Network Operations Control Center.

*NSRS* NASA Safety Reporting System.
*OAA* Orbiter Access Arm.
*OC* Operations Coordinator.
*OFI* Operational Flight Instrumentation.
*OMS* Orbiter Manouvering System.
*PDRS* Payload Deployment and Retrieval System.
*PLT* Pilot
*POD* Payload Operations Director.
*PS* Payload Specialist.
*RMS* Remote Manipulator System.
*RTLS* Return to Launch Site.
*SIP* Standard Interface Panel.
*SLF* Shuttle Landing Facility.
*SN* Space Network.
*SPOC* Shuttle Portable On-board Computer.
*SRB* Solid Rocket Booster.
*SRM* Solid Rocket Motor.
*SSC* Stennis Space Center.
*SSCP* Small Self-Contained Payload.
*SSP* Standard Switch Panel.
*SSME* Space Shuttle Main Engines.
*TACAN* Tactical Air Navigation.
*TAL* Trans-Atlantic Abort Landing.
*TDRS* Tracking Data and Relay Satellite.
*WSMV* Western Space and Missile Center.

# Scanner and accessories review 7

A look at the equipment available in Britain.

This chapter looks at the equipment which is on offer from British dealers and if you own the original *Scanners 1* book you will see that the range has considerably changed, with some new names such as Yupiteru, Alinco and Kenwood.

In order to keep the review to manageable proportions I have deleted many of the early scanners which were included in earlier editions because they were still widely available on the second-hand market. Instead, and in response to comments from readers, I have included some general notes on what to look for when buying used equipment, together with additional information from Chris Lorek.

The comments which accompany some models are our own and are based either on measured technical results, on personal experience with the scanner, or general impressions gained from friends and trade sources. Although we have both owned and used many scanners (and according to our wives, far too many) the comments should not be interpreted as a recommendation for any particular model.

## Buying guide

If you have read the book so far you should have a fairly good idea by now which features you want on a scanner, and should be able to choose one from the information given in this chapter. However let us recap on a few points.

Scanner buyers broadly fall into one of three categories: those whose interest lies in just one band (usually airband or marine enthusiasts), those whose interest covers a limited range of two or more bands and finally those enthusiasts who want to be able to tune most, if not all, of the VHF/UHF range.

### Airband scanners

Although the majority of scanners cover the civil airband, many of them offer performance which is something of a compromise. Airband transmissions are AM mode and the ideal circuitry for AM differs to that for FM. Although the majority of dual or multimode scanners offer adequate performance on airband, they rarely achieve the same level of performance as dedicated airband scanners such as the Sony, WIN or Signal models where the RF, IF and AGC circuits are optimised for the band and mode.

### Banded scanners

These are scanners which offer coverage of selected bands in the VHF and UHF ranges. Their coverage is normally of those bands which are of most interest to scanner enthusiasts but you should be aware that some sets are aimed at the US market and others at the European market and both types are on sale in Britain. The difference between the two is usually in the lower frequency ranges, typically the US versions cover 29-54MHz, whilst European versions cover 65-88MHz (PMR and emergency service 'LOW' bands) instead.

Typically, banded scanners will cover the above mentioned bands together with the 118-174MHz and 406-512MHz. These cover the majority of air, marine and land mobile bands but one point to watch is that most banded scanners do not allow you to switch between AM and FM. Instead, where airband is included, the scanner automatically switches to AM only when tuned to the airband. For some scanner buyers in Britain this can be a distinct disadvantage as AM is still quite widely used by some services in other bands. Notable exceptions to this are the Black Jaguar and some AOR and ICOM models, where the mode is programmed into memory along with the frequency. The Black Jaguar is also unusual in that it offers segmented coverage of the military airband between 200-280 and 360-520MHz.

### Wideband scanners

These are the most versatile of scanners and AOR were the first to venture into the field with their classic AR2001 which covered 25-550MHz with no gaps and offered programmable selection of AM and narrow or wide FM on any frequency. Subsequently the AR2002, Regency and Realistic models have followed with tuning as high as 1300MHz and the only band omitted in some cases being 500-800MHz which is the television broadcast band. Yaesu (giving SSB as well as the usual AM/FM) and Kenwood have models that scan up to just over 900MHz and in the case of the Kenwood you even get Long, Medium and Short wave coverage as well. The ultimate machines in this class are the ICOM R-7100, IC-R9000, and AOR AR3000A with multimode and coverage up to 2000MHz

## Where to buy

The most important advice is to buy from a dealer who will have proper facilities to repair any equipment he sells you. Statistically, if your new scanner is going to break down in the first few years of use it will do so in the first few weeks you own it, and there can be nothing more infuriating than waiting for weeks or even months for it to be repaired. If you buy a scanner from a dealer who specialises in this kind of equipment (most amateur radio equipment shops do have facilities) then repair should be fairly fast. On the other hand if you buy from the high street shop that sells a few TVs, radios and household appliances they are unlikely to have the kind of sophisticated equipment nor the experience to repair or re-align sophisticated VHF/UHF equipment. Never mind what the salesman says, it is a specialised area of servicing.

With a specialised dealer you will also get proper advice on choosing a scanner. Salesmen who work in the majority of amateur radio type shops are usually enthusiasts and know their products well. On the other hand I could fill a book with some of the fantastic claims and howlers I have heard pour from the mouths of shop assistants selling scanners in Hi-Fi/TV shops.

## Buying used equipment

Used equipment is often advertised in the small advertisement sections of the many magazines devoted to amateur radio and hobbyist electronics. When buying a used scanner the first thing to check is the frequency coverage and, if it is important to your choice of listening, whether or not the mode is selectable on all bands. For instance, the Bearcat 220 and its many variants regularly appear these days and although they have fair performance they do not allow AM reception on any frequencies other than airband.

When checking a scanner prior to purchase take a careful look at its general appearance. In the days when I used to service such equipment it became obvious that the majority of scanners appearing on the service bench looked as if they'd been ill-treated. Dented or cracked cases, holes drilled in the cases and loose or broken controls. Also watch out for case screws which have chewed-up heads — a sure sign that someone has been at the innards. Beware of any scanner that looks as if it has been modified or tinkered with. If you can arrange to try the scanner for a day or two (offer a deposit if you have to) and see if it is possible to have a look inside the casing (watch how you treat the case screws though). Check for any signs of repairs or modifications and pay particular attention to tuning coil slugs. Any wax seals over them should be completely untouched and closely inspect any exposed ones to make sure that there are no minute chips around the adjustment slots nor that the slugs themselves are cracked. Note that alignment of some scanners can be a costly affair and unless you own some very sophisticated test equipment you will not be able to do it yourself.

I may seem a little cynical in my above comments but experience in the trade has shown that very many people just do not seem to be able to resist the temptation of having a 'tweak'. The worst offenders are often those people with a little knowledge of radio circuitry and so be doubly cautious if the seller seems to be well versed in technology.

Obviously you should ask for a demonstration of the scanner and do not be afraid to ask if the owner has had any problems with it or had it repaired.

### Prices
I have avoided listing prices in this edition as currency fluctuations on world currency markets can lead to quite dramatic price swings. A glance at a current issue of a magazine aimed at the amateur radio or electronic hobbyist market will usually reveal dealer advertisements carrying up to date prices. The small ads' in the same magazines will usually give a good guide to second-hand prices as well.

The technical performance figures, where given below, are *real* measurements of a typical and representative sample of the scanner model in each case. All the results are from measurements made in exactly the same way, and are independent of any manufacturer's 'claims' or 'specifications', which due to the different methods of each manufacturer's specifications can often give a meaningless comparison!

For the technically-minded, the results given here are measured as:
*Sensitivity;* Input signal level in $\mu$V pd giving 12dB SINAD.
*Adjacent channel selectivity;* Increase in level of interfering signal, modulated with 400Hz at 1.5kHz deviation, above 12dB SINAD reference level to cause 6dB degradation in 12dB on-channel signal.
*Blocking;* As adjacent channel selectivity.
*Intermodulation Rejection;* Increase over 12dB SINAD level of two interfering signals giving identical 12dB SINAD 3rd order intermodulation product (i.e., the unwanted on-channel signal produced from two off-channel signals).
All measurements, except sensitivity where stated, were taken on 145MHz NFM to ensure uniformity (apart from airband only sets where 125MHz AM was used).

## Alinco DJ-X1D

Type:      Handheld
Coverage:  500kHz—1300MHz continuous
Models:    AM, FM, Wide FM

Sensitivity:              20MHz 0.37$\mu$V AM, 0.20$\mu$V FM
                          145MHz 0.16$\mu$V AM, 0.13$\mu$V FM
                          435MHz 0.18$\mu$V AM, 0.12$\mu$V FM
                          934MHz 0.20$\mu$V FM
Adjacent Channel:  12.5kHz 18.9dB
                          25kHz 32.4dB
Blocking:          100kHz 40.9dB
                          1MHz 80.6dB
                          10MHz 87.1dB
Intermodulation:   25/50kHz 24.0dB
                          50/100kHz 27.9dB

An extremely wideband scanner, it fits a lot of frequency coverage into a small size. Some 'European' versions of this model come supplied with coverage of the amateur bands only, all other frequency ranges being locked out unless you tap in the right numbers (which the UK distributors supply on an information sheet with the set), so beware if you're buying from abroad. The 'D' suffix of the DJ-X1D is supposed to mean it's an improved version of the DJ-X1, better suited to handling strong signals. It does give good performance from 'out of band' signals, but connect an outside aerial and you'll most likely have a *lot* of problems from signals up to a few channels away from the one you're tuned to. This causes an awful lot of hassle when you're trying to search across a band, the squelch just opens up all over the place. The UK distributors offer a crystal filter modification for this, which is well worth having. I can't see why the manufacturers omitted this just to save a pound or two in price.

**AOR AR-1500EX**

Type:       Handheld
Coverage:   500MHz—1300MHz continuous
Modes:      AM, FM, SSB with built-in BFO
Channels:   1000

Sensitivity:              20MHz 0.18μV 0.12μV FM
                          145MHz 0.22μV AM 0.13μV FM
                          435MHz 0.45μV AM 0.38μV FM
                          934MHz 0.57μV FM
Adjacent Channel:  12.5kHz 34.0dB
                          25kHz 53.5dB
Blocking:              100kHz 48.0dB
                          1MHz 75.0dB
                          10MHz 97.0dB
Intermodulation:    25/50kHz 45.0dB
                          50/100kHz 48.0dB

This handheld scanner sells at only a little more than AOR's similar,
but AM/FM only, AR-2000 scanner, yet it gains a lot from its switchable BFO (Beat Frequency Oscillator). This lets you use the set to far
greater advantage on HF, for example, allowing reception of HF
Airband (used when craft are above the oceans, out of VHF range),
utility stations, and radio amateurs. AOR (UK) agree with me that the
scanner can't be classed as a purpose-designed SSB receiver, but it's
certainly OK for 'occasional' listening around on this mode. The
wideband coverage offered on VHF and UHF doesn't let you miss a
thing, and you might even be able to tune into 2m, 70cm and 23cm
SSB stations during contests which very few other scanners at this
price will let you do.

**AOR AR-2000**
Type:         Handheld
Coverage:  500kHz—1300MHz continuous
Modes:      AM, FM, Wide FM
Channels:   1000

This set is essentially identical to the AR-1500 but without the BFO facility. It's still a current model at the time of writing, but with the AR-1500 being just a few pounds more look out for this set as a 'good buy', especially secondhand, for wideband AM/FM listening.

## AOR AR-2002

Type:       Base/mobile
Coverage:   25—550MHz, 800—1300MHz
Modes:      AM, FM, Wide FM
Channels:   20

This set is 'just about' current, and looks broadly similar in styling to the superb but quite different AR-3000A. The AR-2002 is reputed to give good performances on-air, as well as being easy to use. A very wideband coverage will let you listen to plenty of things, but you only have 20 memories available to store all those interesting frequencies in. It does, however, have an RS-232 remote control connector, which allows you to use the power of your PC for this. If you're after something to use at home and don't mind the limited built-in memories, look out for one of these in years to come, you could get a good bargain.

## AOR AR-2800

Type:       Base/mobile
Coverage:   500kHz—600MHz, 800MHz—1300MHz
Modes:      AM, FM, Wide FM, SSB
Channels:   1000

Sensitivity:              20MHz 0.57$\mu$V AM
                          145MHz 0.31$\mu$V AM, 0.20$\mu$V FM
                          435MHz 0.28$\mu$V FM
                          934MHz 0.29$\mu$V FM
Adjacent Channel:         12.5kHz 33.0dB
                          25kHz 45.8dB
Blocking:                 100kHz 56.5dB
                          1MHz 75.5dB
                          10MHz 97.0dB

It's a 'plasticky' radio, rather unlike AOR's offerings of the AR-2002 and AR-3000A, but it packs in a lot of frequency coverage at a reasonable price. Like the AR-1500 handheld, this one also has a switchable BFO so you can tune into SSB signals on HF and VHF/UHF bands. A nice 'extra' touch is a vertical bargraph made up of LEDs to give a relative display of the received signal level. The very

wideband coverage, with just a 'gap' in between (which is used for TV broadcasting in the UK) should let you tune into lots of signals, the sensible number of 1000 channels being more than enough to suit most user's needs in terms of frequency storage. Watch out though, it isn't a purpose-made HF SSB receiver, it'll 'curl up' if you put a well-sited outdoor aerial on it. Fortunately, you can switch in an internal attenuator to reduce the effects of this – I needed this in permanently whenever I tried the receiver on HF. For searching around on VHF/UHV, either AM or FM, an 'AF scan' toggle switch is hidden at the back of the case.

**AOR AR-3000A**

| | |
|---|---|
| Type: | Base/mobile |
| Coverage: | 100kHz—2036MHz |
| Modes: | AM, FM, Wide FM, CW, LSB, SSB |
| Channels: | 400 |

Sensitivity:

20MHz $0.12\mu$V SSB $0.34\mu$V AM $0.16\mu$V FM
145MHz $0.17\mu$V SSB $0.48\mu$V AM $0.24\mu$V FM
435MHz $0.18\mu$V SSB $0.51\mu$V AM $0.25\mu$V FM
934MHz $0.26\mu$V FM

```
Adjacent Channel:  12.5kHz 42.0dB
                   25kHz 52.5dB
Blocking:          100kHz 67.0dB
                   1MHz 79.0dB
                   10MHz 94.5dB
Intermodulation:   25/50kHz 41.5dB
                   50/100kHz 41.0dB
```

If you think of what you'd like in a mobile or base scanner and then make a 'wish list', this one's probably got the lot. With coverage up to 2036MHz, you could even have a go at tuning in some of the geostationary communications satellites, and at the other end of the spectrum, short wave broadcast, utility, amateur, and HF airband and marine signals. Add a PC running AOR's 'AcePac 3A' software with its spectrum scope, automatic logging, and so on, and you have a very, very powerful listening station. It's little wonder the UK government are reputed to have bought a load of these for themselves. It isn't cheap, but it's worth every penny.

*My comments:* This is the one scanner I'd love to have in my radio station.
*Peter's comments:* Grovel in front of your bank manager!

## Bearcat BC-890XLT

Type:       Base
Coverage:   29—54, 108—512MHz, 806—1300MHz
Modes:      AM, FM
Channels:   200

Sensitivity:            29MHz 0.32$\mu$V FM
                        145MHz 0.34$\mu$V FM
                        435MHz 0.55$\mu$V FM
                        934MHz 0.27$\mu$V FM
Adjacent Channel:   12.5kHz 4.8dBdB
                        25kHz 56.4dB
Blocking:           100kHz 68.3dB
                        1MHz 79.3dB
                        10MHz 86.3dB

A large sized base scanner from Bearcat, offering quite an impressive looking desktop set. It's packed with handy operating 'niceties', such as an automatic store facility and quick access for scanning your favourite banks of frequencies, which are arranged as 20 banks of 10 channels each. 'Turbo Scan' gives a super-fast scan rate of around 100 channels per second, meaning you shouldn't miss very much. The frequency steps can usefully be programmed to either 5kHz, 12.5kHz, or 25kHz. So you're not 'stuck' with 5kHz steps on VHF like of lot a scanners designed for the US market, as this one is.

### Bearcat BC-2500XLT

Type:      Handheld
Coverage:  25—550, 760—1300MHz
Modes:     AM, FM, Wide FM
Channels:  400

Bearcat, after having almost dominated the handheld scanner market in the 'early days' with their excellent range of scanners, seemed to go a little quiet. However, this handheld looks set to provide a welcome 'comeback' for the company. This one's a 'full-feature' model from Bearcat, with 400 channels arranged into 20 banks, and an 'automatic store' to help fill these for you with locally active frequencies. 'Turbo scan' mode lets you hunt around at almost 100 channels per second, and for manual tuning a rotary knob is fitted. The set automatically switches between AM and FM depending on the sub-band selected (AM for Civil and Military airband plus 25—29MHz, FM otherwise), which could either be useful or limiting, depending on your needs.

**Black Jaguar MkIV**

| | |
|---|---|
| Type: | Handheld |
| Coverage: | 28—30MHz, 60—88MHz, 115—178MHz, 210—260MHz, 410—520MHz |
| Modes: | AM, FM |
| Channels: | 16 |

*Peter's comments:* Very wideband coverage and programmable AM/FM have made this a popular scanner. Rather bulky and heavy but owners swear by this set's performance, and coverage of some of the military UHF airband is unusual.

## Fairmate HP-2000
Type:      Handheld
Coverage:  100kHz—1300MHz
Modes:     AM, FM, Wide FM
Channels:  1000

Looking remarkably similar to the AR-2000, it also has many of the same facilities, although the lower tuning range has been extended to 100kHz. It was introduced to the UK some time ago, and continues to sell well.

## Icom IC-R1

Type:        Handheld
Coverage:    100kHz—1300MHz
Modes:       AM, FM, Wide FM
Channels:    100

Sensitivity:              30MHz 0.34μV AM 0.32μV FM
                          145MHz 0.31μV AM 0.25μV FM
                          435MHz 0.42μV AM 0.27μV FM
                          934MHz 0.38μV FM
Adjacent Channel: 12.5kHz 21.8dB
                          25kHz 33.0dB
Blocking:                 100kHz 31.0dB
                          1MHz 67.5dB
                          10MHz 79.5dB
Intermodulation:   50/100kHz 24.0dB

The tiny wideband handheld that made the other manufacturers turn green with envy. This small package, which fits nicely in the palm of your hand, squeezes in a very wideband coverage. The set has a number of nice features, like switchable steps of 0.5, 5, 8, 9, 10, 12.5, 20, 25 and 50kHz for tuning increments – the 9kHz steps for example are superb for stepping through each station on medium wave. Another potentially useful mode is 'Auto-Memory Write Scan' where you can set the receiver searching across a band, and it will automatically store the first 19 channels where it finds a signal. Unfortunately, the set suffers from the manufacturer's attempts to try to squeeze an awful lot in and then make it at a given price. I found the set was almost useless in busy radio areas, and the 'Auto' scan quickly filled up all 19 channels with just one strong station, which caused the squelch to raise on plenty of channels either side of the 'real' one. Again, a simple crystal filter modification improves this no end. Raycom Ltd., for example, provide a modification service.

### Icom IC-R100

Type:              Base/mobile
Coverage:          100kHz—1800MHz
Modes:             AM, FM, Wide FM
Channels:          100

Sensitivity:               30MHz 1.12$\mu$V AM 0.51uV FM
                           145MHz 0.39uV AM 0.18$\mu$V FM
                           435MHz 0.58$\mu$V AM 0.27$\mu$V FM
                           934MHz 0.23$\mu$V FM
Adjacent Channel:          12.5kHz 42.3dB
                           25kHz 62.3dB
Blocking:                  100kHz 75.5dB
                           1MHz 91.5dB
                           10MHz > 105dB
Intermodulation:           50/100kHz 55.0dB

A high quality receiver in a car-radio sized case. I was very tempted to use it as one when I tested it, but thought it was far too good for this. For weather satellite enthusiasts and Mir space station listeners, a handy feature of this receiver, besides its switchable VHF preamp to boost weak signals, is a switchable AFC (Automatic Frequency Control) to keep track of 'Doppler Shift'. The 1800MHz upper frequency coverage invites 'interesting' reception of the various things that go on up there, like signals from geostationary satellites as well as 1700MHz land-based digital telecommunication systems.

**Icom ICR-7100**
Type:       Base
Coverage:   25MHz—2000MHz
Modes:      AM, FM, Wide FM, LSB, USB
Channels:   900

This receiver, like its predecessor the ICR-7000, has been the choice of 'serious' VHF/UHF listeners for some time, including many professional users. Its SSB reception capability lets you listen to plenty of 'extra' activity, and the 2000MHz upper limit tuning (although the specifications are only guaranteed up to 1300MHz) again puts it in the realms of the 'serious listening' category. Remote computer control using Icom's CI-V system is built in, the software's up to you though.

## Icom ICR-9000

Type:       Base
Coverage:   100kHz—2000MHz
Modes:      AM, FM, Wide FM, SSB, CW, FSK
Channels:   1000

One for the 'serious listener' and a set certainly also aimed at the professional user. It's a full-blooded base station VHF/UHF communications receiver more than a 'scanner', and the 75mm Cathode Ray Tube display is used to good effect as a narrowband 'monitor' to show you what's going on up to 100kHz either side of your tuned frequency. Icom's CI-V remote control system is available, with professional software (at a professional price) available for use with a PC.

*Peter's comments:* The scanner owes its origins to the IC-R7000 which broke new ground by taking scanning out of the realms of 'technology' and into the professional/commercial market. Bearing in mind the far higher cost compared with the IC-R7000, specifications such as sensitivity do not seem to have been improved. There appears no way of individually locking out the memory channels and the so-called spectrum analyzer would be of limited use because of the small bandwidth available.

## Kenwood RZ-1

Type:          Base/mobile
Coverage:   500kHz—905MHz
Modes:       AM, FM, Wide FM
Channels:   100 (HRT May 88)

Sensitivity:                20MHz 1.70µV AM
                               145MHz 5.01µV AM 0.28µV FM
                               435MHz 1.09µV FM
Adjacent Channel:   12.5kHz 34.5dB
                               25kHz 40.5dB
Intermodulation:     50/100kHz 64.0dB

This set has the unique ability to store a large seven digit alpha-numerical 'tag' of the station name or usage for each frequency you program in, which can scan or tune through in the same way as you can with the numbered memory channels – quite useful as a 'memory jogger'. For communications listening, it's a bit on the 'deaf' side on AM, but the wideband coverage including HF could make it a 'different' sort of car radio to have, although to listen to FM stereo you'll need an external stereo amplifier.

*Peter's comments:* Very wide coverage from LW upwards but the lack of SSB will limit its usefulness on the HF band. A major complaint from owners is that you cannot squelch in AM mode and even the importers admit they are not quite sure what to make of the RZ-1. Perhaps this is the ultimate car radio (which is what Kenwood intended it to be) for the owner of a Ferrari, Porsche or similar machine who likes something to fiddle with whilst parked on the M25.

## Netset PRO-44

Type:          Handheld
Coverage:   68—88, 108—137, 137—174, 380—512MHz (AM)
Modes:       FM, AM on Airband
Channels:   50

| Sensitivity: | 145MHz 0.44μV |
| | 435MHz 0.70μV |
| Adjacent Channel: | 12.5kHz 11.4dB |
| | 25kHz 69.3dB |
| Blocking: | 100kHz 61.4dB |
| | 1MHz 85.7dB |
| | 10MHz 86.5dB |
| Intermodulation: | 25/50kHz 56.3dB |
| | 50/100kHz 56.9dB |

It's cheap, it's remarkably similar to the earlier but more expensive Realistic PRO-43 sold by the same chain of retailers, and like its predecessor it's also available in the high street. It isn't designed specifically for UK use – on VHF you're stuck with 5kHz steps and no AM apart from on the airband section, and on UHF you'll hear signals on the 'image' frequency (i.e., not the one you're tuned to) twice as strong as the one you want to listen to. Again, it's cheap, it's easily available, and that's what'll sell it.

## Netset PRO-46

| | |
|---|---|
| Type: | Handheld |
| Coverage: | 68—88, 108—137, 137—174, 406—512, 806—956MHz |
| Modes: | FM, AM on Airband |
| Channels: | 100 |

| | |
|---|---|
| Sensitivity: | 145MHz 0.26µV |
| | 435MHz 0.24µV |
| | 934MHz 0.48µV |
| Adjacent Channel: | 12.5kHz 13.3dB |
| | 25kHz 64.4dB |
| Blocking: | 100kHz 63.2dB |
| | 1MHz 78.6dB |
| | 10MHz 88.9dB |
| Intermodulation: | 25/50kHz 60.3dB |
| | 50/100kHz 59.1dB |

This one's rather similar in terms of coverage to its 'smaller brother' the Netset PRO-44, but adds coverage of 806-956MHz, with small 'missing segments' corresponding to the cellular frequency bands used in the US (but not in the UK). This is a 'dead giveaway' of its intended market, and again you're stuck with 5kHz steps on VHF and no AM apart from the Airband range. The poor image rejection here is in the 900MHz region, where it receives 'image' signals slightly stronger than the wanted signal. However, it's readily available in the high street and it's reasonably priced.

**Netset PRO-2032**
Type:      Base/mobile
Coverage:  68—88, 108—137, 137—174, 380—512, 806—960MHz
Modes:     FM, AM on Airband
Channels:  200

Another 'high street' scanner, this one's sure to be a popular choice in the UK due to its wide availability. A fast scanning rate of 25 memories per second, or 50 frequencies per second in 'search' mode, should mean you don't miss much while the set's looking around for signals. 5kHz steps on VHF together with AM only on Airband is a limitation, although the 'value for money' aspect makes up for this.

**Nevada MS-1000**
Type:      Base/Mobile
Coverage:  500MHz—600MHz, 800—1300MHz
Modes:     AM, FM, Wide FM
Channels:  1000

Having similar features to some of the Yupiteru base/mobile scanners, this one's an 'OEM' model from the UK firm of Nevada. The wideband coverage should make sure you've plenty to listen to, and the UK source may be an advantage in terms of 'backup'.

## Realistic PRO-39

Type:       Handheld
Coverage:   68—88, 108—137, 137—174, 806—956MHz
Modes:      FM, AM on Airband
Channels:   200

A 10 channel 'monitor bank', which you can use as a 'scratch pad' when scanning, helps you fill the set's memory channels adding to the 200 channels. This one's reasonably popular due to its wide availability, although the lack of switchable AM/FM can cause limitations.

## Realistic PRO-41

Type:       Handheld
Coverage:   68—88, 137—174, 406—512MHz
Modes:      FM
Channels:   10

Having just 10 channels which you manually program, this is a low-cost scanner that's available at an economic price. It doesn't have a 'search' facility, so you need to know which frequencies you want to listen to before you can listen to anything at all. But this type of scanner (under the Bearcat BC-50 title plus one or two others) has been quite popular amongst users such as Marine Band listeners who wanted to 'keep an ear open' on just a few channels. I use one of these daily just to scan around my locally-used 2m and 70cm repeater channels.

**Realistic PRO-43**

Type:       Handheld
Coverage:   68—88, 118—174, 220—512, 806—1000MHz
Modes:      AM, FM
Channels:   200

Sensitivity:              145MHz 0.26μV AM 0.13μV FM
                          435MHz 0.83μV AM 0.43μV FM
                          934MHz 0.55μV AM 0.28μV FM
Adjacent Channel:  12.5kHz 7.0dB
                          25kHz 33.3dB
Blocking:          100kHz 44.5dB
                          1MHz 71.2dB
                          10MHz 94.0dB
Intermodulation:   50/100kHz 49.7dB

Marketed as a 'high performance' scanner, this was the first handheld model from Realistic to have switchable AM and FM across its frequency coverage range. No longer do you have to 'put up' with AM on Airband only from high-street handheld scanners. A fast scanning facility together with 10 'monitor' memories in addition to the 'normal' memory channels make it quite powerful in use. The set looks smart, it's easy to use, and as well as being quite sensitive on VHF (to pick up weak signals) I found it had reasonable built-in protection against out-of-band signals which many scanners fall down on badly.

**Realistic PRO-2006**

| | |
|---|---|
| Type: | Base/mobile |
| Coverage: | 25—520, 760—1300MHz |
| Modes: | AM, FM, Wide FM |
| Channels: | 400 |

| | |
|---|---|
| Sensitivity: | 29MHz 0.22$\mu$V FM |
| | 145MHz 1.08$\mu$V FM |
| | 435MHz 0.39$\mu$V FM |
| | 934MHz 0.48$\mu$V FM |
| Adjacent Channel: | 12.5kHz 27.5dB |
| | 25kHz 50.3dB |
| Blocking: | 100kHz 69dB |
| | 1MHz 88dB |
| | 10MHz 94dB |
| Intermodulation: | 50/100kHz 66.5dB |

From the number of these being 'snapped up' by scanner purchasers when it first came out, this set looks like it's one of the most popular base scanners on the UK market. Switchable AM and FM across its coverage range gives it that bit more 'usefulness' in the UK, and unlike earlier Realistic models you can choose step sizes of 5kHz, 12.5kHz, or 50kHz. Although it's not one of the cheapest sets, my sample worked well on the air, and the wide frequency coverage I'm sure is likely to make the set a hot rival to other 'up market' scanners available from specialist dealers.

**Shinwa SR-001**

| | |
|---|---|
| Type: | Base/mobile |
| Coverage: | 25—1000MHz |
| Modes: | AM, FM, Wide FM |
| Channels: | 200 |

Sensitivity:           25MHz 5.20µV AM 2.51µV FM
                       145MHz 0.68µV AM 0.36µV FM
                       435MHz 1.07µV AM 0.43µV FM
                       934MHz 4.32uV AM 2.15µV FM
Adjacent Channel:  12.5kHz 26.0dB
                       25kHz 53.0dB
Blocking:              100kHz 76.5dB
                       1MHz 88.5dB
                       10MHz 96.5dB
Intermodulation:   25/50kHz 50.5dB
                       50/100kHz 68.8dB

This one looks like it was designed to be a hot contender for the 'alternative car radio' market, although the manufacturer's choice of including a TV/Video style remote control with the radio is rather puzzling. Despite its features, this set doesn't quite seem to have 'caught on'. I do see them advertised from time to time, although my sample had a couple of problems, such as noise being received around 28MHz from the internal microprocessor, and being on the deaf side at the upper UHF range. Maybe this is why they're not too popular? Otherwise, it worked quite well.

**Signal R535**
Type:       Base/mobile/transportable
Coverage:  108—143, 220—380MHz
Modes:      AM
Channels:  60

*Peter's comments:* A specialised airband receiver with options available to enable it to be used while being carried around. A fairly tedious type of programming is involved but the set is highly spoken of by airband enthusiasts.

**Sony Air-7**
Type:        Handheld
Coverage:  100kHz—2.2MHz, 76—136MHz
Modes:      AM, FM, Wide FM
Channels:  30

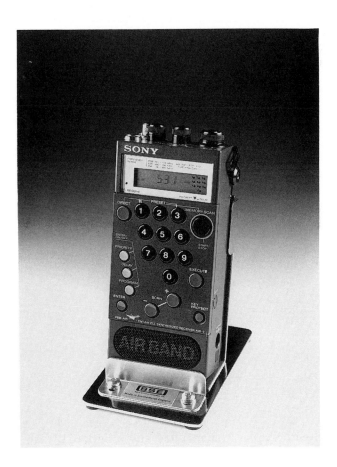

*Peter's comments:* Bulky, heavy, limited coverage and expensive. However, airband fans say it performs superbly and I'm told the AGC (very important with AM) is excellent.

**Sony PRO-80**
Type:      Handheld
Coverage:  150MHz—108MHz, 115—223MHz
Modes:     AM, FM, SSB
Channels:  40

*Peter's comments:* Similar in shape, size, and weight to the Air-7 and also expensive. Although the PRO-80 performs well, is built to Sony's usual high standard, and includes LW, MW, and full HF coverage, it does not include UHF. The VHF coverage is provided by a plug-in adaptor which seems a bit of a scruffy afterthought on the part of the designer.

**Standard AX-700**

Type:        Base/mobile
Coverage:   50—905MHz
Modes:       AM, FM, Wide FM
Channels:   100

Sensitivity:                145MHz 0.39$\mu$V AM 0.18$\mu$V FM
                            435MHz 0.26$\mu$V AM 0.25$\mu$V FM
                            905MHz 0.54$\mu$V AM 0.36$\mu$V FM
Adjacent Channel:  12.5kHz 31.0dB
                            25kHz 65.3dB
Blocking:                 100kHz 73.0dB
                            1MHz 78.0dB
                            10MHz >100dB
Intermodulation:    50/100kHz 58.5dB

If you fancy keeping an eye on what's going on above and below the channel you're tuned to, as well as listening to what you've tapped in on the keypad, this one's for you. It has a panoramic display in the form of a LCD bargraph, showing signal levels across a frequency range of 1MHz, 250kHz, or 100kHz. Some users might find the 905MHz upper frequency limiting – as far as I'm aware no-one's marketed the set in the UK with this extended higher.

**WIN 108**

Type:        Handheld
Coverage:   108—143MHz
Modes:       AM
Channels:   20

*Peter's comments:* A scanner that has received mixed reactions. Some owners speak highly of it but some magazine reviews have been critical with claims that the keyboard is flimsy and difficult to operate and sensitivity could be better on a set designed solely for AM mode.

### Yaesu FRG-9600

| | |
|---|---|
| Type: | Base/mobile |
| Coverage: | 60—950MHz |
| Modes: | AM, FM, Wide FM, SSB |
| Channels: | 100 (HRT Jul 87) |

It's been around for ages, and it still keeps going strong. It received a very useful 'boost' in the form of an internal HF converter from Raycom, extending the coverage down to 500kHz, and many of these sets are to be found on the secondhand market with this fitted.

*Peter's comments:* Well built but it has a strange feature that after about ten seconds it resumes scanning even if the station it stopped on is still transmitting. Various computer interfaces are available.

### Yupiteru VT-125

| | |
|---|---|
| Type: | Handheld |
| Coverage: | 108—142MHz |
| Modes: | AM |
| Channels: | 30 |

| Sensitivity: | 118MHz 0.35μV |
|---|---|
| | 125MHz 0.34μV |
| | 136MHz 0.34μV |

Adjacent Channel:  25kHz 60.8dB
                   50kHz 66.3dB
Blocking:          100kHz 70.0dB
                   1MHz 89.0dB
                   10MHz 84.5dB
Intermodulation:   25/50kHz 50.5dB
                   50/100kHz 50.0dB

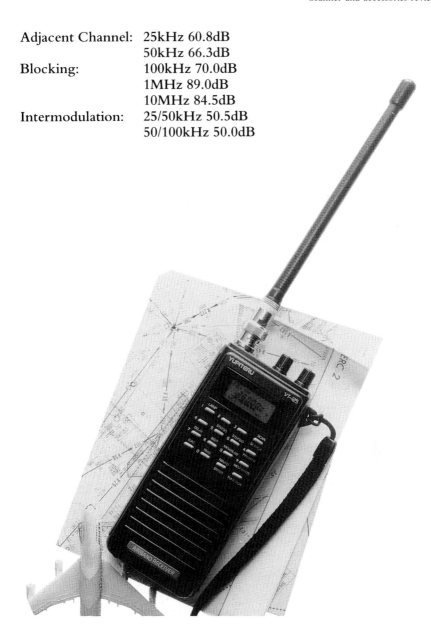

This appears to be a 'cut down' version, dedicated for Civil Airband listening, of Yupiteru's other 'do everything' handheld scanners. It's very light and easy to carry around, and doesn't cost the earth. Watch out for the narrow filtering, as this could distort some of the (deliberately) offset signals from land based Airband transmittors. The available 30 memory channels could be limiting for active airband enthusiasts.

## Yupiteru VT-150
Type:      Handheld
Coverage:  142MHz—170MHz
Modes:     FM
Channels:  100

The dedicated 'Marine Band' cousin to the Airband VT-125 handheld
scanner. Again it looks very much like a 'cut down' version of
Yupiteru's 'do everything' handheld scanners, but again without the
higher price tag. A possible choice for the user interested primarily in
Marine Band monitoring, although the 30 channels could be a bit
limiting.

## Yupiteru VT-225
Type:      Handheld
Coverage:  108—142.1, 149.5—160, 222—391MHz
Modes:     AM, FM
Channels:  100

| | |
|---|---|
| Sensitivity: | 130MHz 0.29$\mu$V AM |
| | 155MHz 0.16$\mu$V FM |
| | 250MHz 0.32$\mu$V |
| Adjacent Channel: | 12.5kHz 48.3dB |
| | 25kHz 52.0dB |
| | 50kHz 56.3dB |
| Blocking: | 100kHz 63.5dB |
| | 1MHz 91.0dB |
| | 10MHz 94.5dB |
| Intermodulation: | 25/50kHz 53.0dB |
| | 50/100kHz 62.5dB |

This set from the Yupiteru collection looks like it's meant for Airband (Civil and Military) and Marine Band enthusiasts, a bit of a 'mixture' in fact. They obviously feel there's a 'niche' market for such a set, and I believe they could well find it amongst users wanting a lightweight scanner to carry to air shows and the like.

### Yupiteru MVT-3100

Type:       Handheld
Coverage:   143—162.025, 347.7125—452, 830—960MHz
Modes:      FM
Channels:   100

| Sensitivity: | 145MHz 0.21µV FM |
| | 435MHz 0.18µV FM |
| | 934MHz 0.35µV FM |
| Adjacent Channel: | 12.5kHz 37.6dB |
| | 25kHz 45.7dB |
| Blocking: | 100kHz 62.8dB |
| | 1MHz 77.4dB |
| | 10MHz 69.3dB |
| Intermodulation: | 25/50kHz 61.7dB |
| | 50/100kHz 59.5dB |

This one's another 'niche market' set from Yupiteru, although quite what 'niche', I'm not too sure. It's 'hard programmed' with 10kHz steps over 143—155MHz and 430—440MHz, this includes the 2m and 70cm amateur bands, which instantly cuts out half of all the 25kHz channels used. However, I found it to be a very good performer on 156MHz Marine Band when I used it on the water, and the set very rapidly steps through programmed memory channels 30 at a time. A further useful feature is that it has up to 100 'pass' frequencies, which you can automatically program to skip with the set in 'search' mode.

**Yupiteru MVT-7000**
Type:       Handheld
Coverage:   1—1300MHz continuous
Modes:      AM, FM, Wide FM
Channels:   200

Sensitivity:              29MHz 0.18µV FM
                          145MHz 0.24µV FM
                          435MHz 0.24µV FM
                          934MHz 0.25µV FM
Adjacent Channel:  12.5kHz 17.0dB
                          25kHz 47.0dB
Blocking:            100kHz 61.0dB
                          1MHz 84.0dB
                          10MHz 89.0dB
Intermodulation:    50/100kHz 52.0dB

The tuning range of this set actually covers down to 100kHz with reduced sensitivity, so as well as being a 'listen to everything on VHF/UHF' you can also tune into Medium Wave and HF broadcast stations for that bit of 'alternative' listening. This one's a competitor in terms of frequency coverage to the IC-R1 and DJ-X1, and although it doesn't have the small size of its competition, it doesn't have the poor performance of the others in terms of strong signal handling either. You pays your money and takes your choice.

**Yupiteru MVT-7100**
Type:       Handheld
Coverage:   1—1300MHz continuous
Modes:      AM, FM, Wide FM, LSB, USB
Channels:   1000

Sensitivity:              20MHz 0.16µV SSB 0.22µV AM 0.13µV FM
                          145MHz 0.18µV SSB 0.25µV AM 0.16µV FM

435MHz 0.26μV SSB 0.35μV AM 0.16μV FM
934MHz 0.33μV SSB 0.37μV AM 0.21μV FM

|  | |
|---|---|
| Adjacent Channel: | 12.5kHz 34.1dB |
| | 25kHz 48.4dB |
| Blocking: | 100kHz 55.5dB |
| | 1MHz 85.5dB |
| | 10MHz 93.8dB |
| Intermodulation: | 25/50kHz 65.3dB |
| | 50/100kHz 65.3dB |

The very wide frequency coverage, together with 'real' SSB reception
and the ability to tune (and store frequencies) on SSB in 50Hz steps,
has made this a very sought-after set amongst scanner devotees. I've
used one on many occasions, and I've always been sad to give it back,
it just looks like I'll have to buy one of these when I've saved up. About
the only thing I don't like about it is the telescopic whip, which will
surely break in use, but at least this lets you adjust its length to 'peak'
on the part of the set's very wide frequency range you're listening to
at any given time.

### Yupiteru MVT-8000

Type:        Base/mobile
Coverage:  8—1300MHz continuous
Modes:      AM, FM, Wide FM
Channels:   200

Essentially a 'base/mobile' version of the Yupiteru MVT-7000, adding a switchable attenuator to help with strong signals from external aerials. It offers a wide frequency coverage in a very small case, which should fit quite neatly in your car as well as presenting a smart 'low profile' on a desktop.

## Aerials

I do not propose here to go into a long review of all the aerials available such as dipoles, whips, discones, etc as they are available from a wide range of sources. Instead, what are presented here are a few of the more unusual aerials which may be of interest to scanner users.

*Product:* Radac
*Manufacturer:* Revco (available from Garex).
*Description:* This is what is known as a 'Nest of dipoles' type of aerial. It is quite an old idea which has been re-vamped to meet the needs of scanner users. In theory it provides reception on six bands which are determined by the length of each of the individual dipole sections. The manufacturers say that for those six bands, aerial gain will be better than a discone. Elements can be anywhere in the range 25—500MHz.
*Peter's Comments:* I have had several arguments with scanner buffs over the virtues of the Radac when compared with a discone. I have never been a discone lover and believe that manufacturers make some quite outrageous claims for the performance of these devices (claiming 20 to 1300MHz coverage for instance). My own experience with the Radac, which has been purely subjective, is that on the selected bands performance is better than a discone. If the bands are evenly spread across the spectrum then even at midway between bands performance is usable, albeit a compromise. I've owned several discones and found all of them to have performance that falls off rapidly above 200MHz. I suspect that although the theoretical VSWR of such devices remains relatively constant across the range some other factor, possibly radiation angle, does not. I personally prefer the nest of dipoles but will concede that the scanner owner who wants to constantly hunt all VHF/UHF frequencies may be better off with a discone.

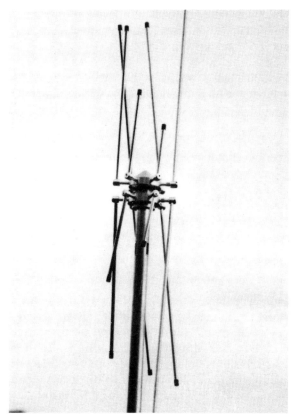

Radac aerial

The Create CLP-5130-1 50-1300MHz Log-Periodic. Shown here mounted for horizontal polarization.

*Product:* Create CLP5130-2.

*Type:* Log periodic.

*Description:* A 20 element Log periodic aerial with coverage from 105MHz to 1300MHz. The gain is quoted as 11—13dB with a front to back ratio of 15dB. The aerial has a width of 1.4 metres and is 1.4 metres long. VSWR across the range is quoted as 2:1 and terminations are via an N-socket. Available from South Midlands Communications Ltd.

*Product:* Create CLP5130-1.

*Type:* Log periodic.

*Description:* A wider band version of the above aerial covering 50—1300MHz. A 24 element unit which is 3 metres wide and 2 metres long, otherwise the specifications are similar. Available from South Midlands Communications Ltd.

*Product:* Diamond D707.

*Type:* Multiband pole.

*Description:* The aerial consists of a slim pole 95cms long which contains a broadband 20dB gain signal pre-amplifier. However, no details are given of the type of elements employed nor the performance across the range which is quoted as 2—1500MHz. The aerial is supplied with a small power unit which sends voltage for the pre-amplifier up the coaxial feeder cable and some provision is made in the interface to vary the gain of the system. Available from Waters and Stanton.

*Product:* Diamond D505.

*Type:* Multiband mobile aerial.

*Description:* Essentially a mobile version of the above aerial with the same specficiations. The unit consists of a mobile mounting whip with two loading coils and built-in pre-amplifier. The antenna is 80cms long. Available from Waters and Stanton.

### Sandpiper

Sandpiper manufacture an extremely wide range of aerials and it would be impossible to provide a complete list of their products. However, I would mention a few of their products which are of particular interest to scanner owners. First, they manufacture log periodics, discones and nests of dipoles (several versions of each covering different frequency ranges) as well as several versions of a multi-band mobile aerial which can also be used as a base for anyone who cannot mount a discone.

They can also supply high gain colinears for air and marine bands and the same bands are covered by a range of helical aerials for handsets. Because Sandpiper manufacture these products on a sort of modular basis they can supply helicals for instance, for any band with any type of plug (including right angle connections). Their range stretches to yagis and dipoles for virtually any frequency and again, because of the method of manufacture involved, costs are virtually the same as for an off-the-shelf product.

Should you want to build your own aerial then Sandpiper can also supply both aluminium and fibreglass tubing as well as connector blocks and all the usual fittings. Again the range is so vast it is impossible to cover it here and you should contact them (address at the back of the book) and get a copy of their lists.

### Nevada
Nevada can supply a range of plug-in aerials for portable handhelds. These include UHF and Airband helicals and telescopics terminated in BNC, TNC or N-type plugs. Nevada also supply the Weltz/Royale discone under their own brand name, model WB1300.

### Tuneable Aerial Filter
Many of the scanners I've detailed here have an enormous frequency coverage in a very small package. But unfortunately selectivity and strong signal handling characteristics have sometimes been sacrificed to save space and cost, which means that unwanted signal breakthrough can be a big problem.

Attaching a microscopic handheld to a rooftop aerial is often a good recipe for disappointment. One remedy from strong local signals but in a different band is to use a notch filter, which is a high-Q tuned circuit plugged in line with the aerial and can be adjusted to attenuate an unwanted signal. One type, covering the 85—175MHz range is marketed by Garex Electronics. It simply fits in line with the aerial feeder, and lets you tune unwanted signals out. Provided the interference is spaced more than 10MHz away, there's little difference in the signal you want to hear.

### Mobile Scanner Aerials
If you're using your handheld scanner on the move, then a suitable aerial fitted to the outside of the car can make a tremendous difference. 'Putting up' with the set-top aerial is OK as a temporary measure, but you won't get the best from your scanner. Purpose-designed mobile scanners will, of course, always need some form of external aerial.

Very often, a simple quarter wave whip, cut for the centre frequency of the band you're mainly interested in (such as Civil Airband), can make a reasonable 'all-round' aerial for mobile scanner use. See Chapter 4 for details of lengths needed.

Wideband aerials are a different matter though. A number of multiband aerials are available from amateur radio and scanner dealers, including wideband amplified types. A handy tip is that a 'dual band' whip for the 2m and 70cm amateur bands makes a good all-round VHF/UHF mobile scanner aerial.

If you'd prefer not to drill holes or clip aerial mounting brackets to your car gutter or boot lip, then a glass-mounted wideband aerial could be useful. A 'glassmount' aerial sticks onto one of the windows of your car, usually the rear windscreen, using the glass as a 'dielectric' between the inner and outer fittings. Waters and Stanton Electronics distribute what could be an ideal aerial, which is designed for wideband scanner receive-only use over 30—1200MHz. This is the Pro-Am TGSBNC, and it comes with everything you need apart right down to the BNC plug at the end of the length of coax. The aerial element itself can be unscrewed from its base for carwashes or security against other damage when not in use. If you're fitting one of these, make sure you get the position 'right first time' (check the travel of windscreen wipers) as it's very difficult, if not impossible, to change once it's stuck! A re-mounting kit is, however, available should you change cars.

Pro-Am TGS BNC wideband scanner aerial.

## Aerial Amplifiers

A number of wideband aerial preamps are available, from firms such as Solid State Electronics and Garex, Garex, for example, produce the GA-4M GAsFET amplifier covering 20—1000MHz, and also produce a low cost VHF Airband preamplifier which is designed to cover 118—137MHz with strong out-of-band signals attenuated. SSE supply the 'Jim' series of preamplifiers which can be switched to either wideband or narrow, plus other accessories such as handheld base and mobile mounts and chargers.

The Jim M-75 aerial amplifier.

## Indoor Scanner Aerials

If you're 'stuck' with using an indoor aerial, then try at least to get this near to a window, you'll usually notice a big improvement. One type of 'portable' scanner aerial I use is available from Garex, which I just hang from my bedroom curtain rail for 'out of shack' listening. It's a lightweight arrangement using ribbon cable elements and comes fitted with 4m of coax and a BNC plug.

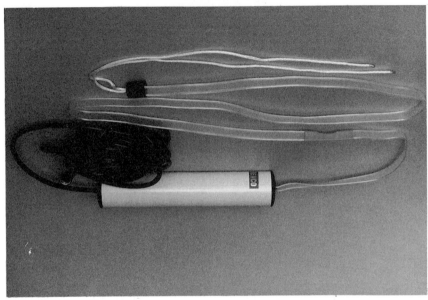

Garex portable aerial.

# UK Scanner and 8
# accessory manufacturers,
# importers, distributors
# and dealers

This list is restricted to those firms offering full mail order facilities. To locate retailers in your own area try the yellow pages of the telephone directory under headings such as 'Communications', 'Amateur Radio', 'C.B. Radio', etc.

AIR SUPPLY
83B High Street
Yeadon
Leeds LS19 7TA
Tel: 0532 509581
Scanners, Aero charts, aerials

ALAN HOOKER ELECTRONICS
42 Nether Hall Road
Doncaster DN1 2PZ
Tel: 0302 325690
Scanners, aerials and fax/data decoders

AMATEUR RADIO COMMUNICATIONS LIMITED
38 Bridge Street
Earlestown
Newton-le-Willows
Merseyside WA12 9BA
Tel: 0925 229881
Scanners, internal and external HF adaptors, aerials, books

AOR (UK) LTD.
Adam Bede High Tech Centre
Derby Road
Wirksworth
Derbyshire DE4 4BG
Tel: 0629 825926
UK distributors of AOR scanners, aerials, and PC control software for
AOR scanners


A.R.E COMMUNICATIONS LIMITED
6 Royal Parade
Hangar Lane
Ealing
London W5A 1ET
Tel: 081 997 4476
Scanners, books, preamps, aerials


ARGUS SPECIALIST PUBLICATIONS LTD.
Argus House
Boundary Way
Hemel Hempstead
Herts HP2 7ST
Tel: 0442 66551
Publishers of specialist books and magazines on scanners, amateur
radio, and electronics. The magazine *Ham Radio Today* incorporates
a 'Scanners' section every month, featuring several pages of scanner
articles and advertisements


ASK ELECTRONICS
248 Tottenham Court Road
London W1P 9AD
Tel: 071 637 0353
HF receivers, scanners, accessories


THE AVIATION HOBBY CENTRE
1st Floor
Main Terminal
Birmingham Intl Airport
W. Midlands B26 3QJ
Tel: 021 742 0424
Scanners, aerials and books

BREDHURST ELECTRONICS LIMITED
High Street
Handcross
West Sussex RH17 6BW
Tel: 0444 400786
Scanners, base and mobile aerials and books


CIRKIT DISTRIBUTION LIMITED
Park Lane
Broxbourne
Herts EN10 7NQ
Tel: 0992 444111
Scanners, books, RF plugs, sockets and components


DATONG ELECTRONICS LIMITED
Clayton Wood Close
West Park
Leeds LS16 6QE
Tel: 0532 744822
HF adaptors, direction finding equipment, active HF aerials


DEWSBURY ELECTRONICS
176 Lower High Street
Stourbridge
West Midlands DY8 2TG
Tel: 0384 390063
Scanners, aerials


ELLIOTT ELECTRONICS
26/28 Braunstone Gate
Leicester
Tel: 0533 553293
Scanners, aerials, preamps, books


FLIGHTDECK
192 Wilmslow Road
Heald Green, Cheadle
Cheshire SK8 3BH
Tel: 061 499 9350
Scanners, aero charts and books, aerials

FLYING SHOP
Biggin Hill Airport
Westersham
Kent TN16 3BN
Tel: 0959 576370
Airband guides and scanners


GAREX ELECTRONICS
Station Yard
South Brent
South Devon TQ10 9AL
Tel: 0364 72770
Scanners, aerials, books, computer control systems, converters, weather satellite systems, preamps. Manufacturers of Revco aerials


HAYDON COMMUNICATIONS
132 High Street
Edgware
Middlesex HA8 7EL
Tel: 081 951 5782
Scanners and accessories


ICOM (UK) LIMITED
Sea Street
Herne Bay
Kent CT6 8LD
Tel: 0227 363859
Scanners, aerials. Branches in Birmingham and London


ICS ELECTRONICS LIMITED
Unit V, Rudford Industrial Estate, Ford,
Arundel
West Sussex BN18 0BD
Tel: 0903 731101
Fax and multi-mode data decoders


INTERPRODUCTS
8 Abbot Street
Perth PH2 0EB
Scotland
Tel: 0738 44199
Wide range of books and frequency lists

## JAVIATION
Carlton Works
Carlton Street
Bradford
West Yorkshire BD7 1DA
Tel: 0274 732146
Scanners, aerials, aviation charts, frequency lists, preamps,
airband crystals

## LEE ELECTRONICS
400 Edgeware Road
London W2
Tel: 071 723 5521
UK distributors of 'Standard' scanners and amateur radio equipment,
plus aerials and accessories

## LINK ELECTRONICS
216 Lincoln Road
Peterborough PE1 2NE
Tel: 0733 345731
Scanners, aerials, suppliers of *Netset* and *Realistic* products

## LINKS COMMUNICATIONS
Crossways Centre
Braye Rd
Vale
Guernsey C.I.
Tel: 0481 48360
Scanners and aerials (VAT free export)

## LOWE ELECTRONICS LIMITED
Chesterfield Road
Matlock
Derbyshire DE4 5LE
Tel: 0629 580800
Scanners, HF receivers, HF and VHF/UHF aerials

## MAPLIN ELECTRONIC SUPPLIES LIMITED
P.O. Box 3
Rayleigh
Essex SS6 8LR
Tel: 0702 552911
Wide range of plugs, connectors, power supplies, Ni-Cads,
books, etc.

MARTIN LYNCH
140-142 Northfield Avenue
Ealing
London W13 9SB
Tel: 081 566 1120
Scanners, aerials, books


NEVADA COMMUNICATIONS
189 London Road
North End
Portsmouth PO2 9AE
Tel: 0705 662145
Scanners (agents for Uniden Bearcat, Jim, and Black Jaguar),
books, aerials, preamps


PW PUBLISHING LIMITED
Enefco House
The Quay
Poole
Dorset BH15 1PP
Tel: 0202 678558
Large range of books


QUANTEK ELECTRONICS
3 Houdley Road
Birmingham B31 2HL
Scanners, aerials


RADCOM ELECTRONICS
Midleton Enterprise Park
Midleton
Co. Cork
Tel: 021 632725, 021 613241
Scanners, aerials, preamps


RADIO AMATEUR SUPPLIES (NOTTINGHAM)
3 Farndon Green
Woollaton Park
Nottingham NH8 1DU
Tel: 0602 280267
Scanners, aerials

## RADIO SHACK LIMITED
188 Broadhurst Gardens
London NW6 3AY
Tel: 081 624 7174
Scanners, aerials, fax decoders and books

## RAYCOM LIMITED
P.O. Box 73
Alcester
Warwickshire
B49 5SB
Tel: 0789 400600
Modifications to scanners for improved performance

## REG WARD & COMPANY LIMITED
1 Western Parade
West Street
Axminster
Devon EX13 5NY
Tel: 0297 34918
Scanners, aerials

## SANDPIPER COMMUNICATIONS
Pentwyn House
Penyard
Llwydcoed
Aberdare
Mid Glamorgan CF44 0TU
Tel: 0685 870425
Aerial manufacturers

## SEAWARD ELECTRONICS
Kings Hill Industrial Estate
Bude
Cornwall
Tel: 0288 55998
Scanners, aerials and accessories

## SISKIN ELECTRONICS
Southampton Road
Hythe
Southampton SO4 6WQ
Tel: 0703 849962
Data and weather satellite decoders

## SOLID STATE ELECTRONICS
6 The Orchard
Bassett Green Village
Southampton SO2 3NA
Tel: 0703 769598
Manufacturers of preamps, and accessories for handheld scanners such as chargers, desk stands, and mobile mounts


## SOUTH ESSEX COMMUNICATIONS LTD
191 Francis Road
Leyton
London E10 6NQ
Tel: 081 558 0854, 081 556 1415
Dressler aerials, masthead preamps


## SOUTH MIDLANDS COMMUNICATIONS LIMITED
SM House
School Close
Chandlers Ford Industrial Estate
Eastleigh
Hampshire SO5 3BY
Tel: 0703 255111
(branches in Leeds, Chesterfield, Birmingham and Axminster).
Scanners, aerials, converters and frequency guides


## SRP TRADING
Unit 20
Nash Works
Forge Lane
Belbroughton
Stourbridge
Worcs DY9 9TD
Tel: 0562 730672
Suppliers of scanners, books, and their 'unique' type of discone aerial


## STEPHENS JAMES LIMITED
47 Warrington Road
Leigh
Lancashire WN7 3AE
Tel: 0942 676790
Scanners, aerials and fitting kits

TANDY
INTERTAN UK LIMITED
Tandy Centre
Leamore Lane
West Midlands WS2 7PS
Sole suppliers of Realistic scanners. Tandy shops are located throughout
Britain, check your area telephone directory for the nearest branch.

TIMESTEP COMMUNICATIONS
PO Box 2001
Newmarket CB8 8QA
Receivers, aerials, and PC based systems for weather satellite
reception

TMP COMMUNICATIONS
Unit 27
Pinfold Industrial Estate
Pinfold Lane
Buckley
Clwyd
Tel: 0244 549563
Scanners, aerials, and Amiga software for remote control of base
scanners

UPPINGTON LIMITED
12-14 Pennywell Road
Bristol
BS5 0TJ
Tel: 0272 557732
Scanners and aerials

WATERS & STANTON ELECTRONICS
22 Main Road
Hockley
Essex SS5 4QS
Tel: 0702 206835, 204965
Scanners, preamps, converters, books (list publishers), aerials
including glass-mount mobile type

## Organisations

**MARINE, LAND MOBILE, ETC, GOVERNMENT
REGULATORY BODY**

**RADIOCOMMUNICATIONS AGENCY**
Waterloo Bridge House,
Waterloo Road, London SE1 8UA
Tel: 071 215 2150

**REMOTE IMAGING GROUP**
(International Group for Weather Satellite and Fax Reception)
P.O. Box 142
Rickmansworth
Hertfordshire
WD3 4RQ

# Scanners 2  9

*Scanners 2* is the perfect match to the book you are reading now. *Scanners 2* in an international edition, that goes into the subject of the more advanced scanner user and also covers VHF/UHF monitor receivers.

Here are some of the subjects that are covered:

*Modifications:* Simultaneous AM/FM for the SX-200 and Bearcat 220FB.

*Common faults:* SX-200 (various improvements), Bearcat 220 (power supply), AOR 2001 (off frequency), etc.

*DIY accessories:* Active antenna, SX-200 front panel S-Meter, B.F.O., broadband and narrow band masthead amplifiers, power supplies, auto NiCad charger, 12V to 6V or 9V adaptor for portables and automatic recording switch.

*Project:* Build a 10 channel crystal controlled pocket or mobile scanner. Easy to build VHF/FM design that uses parts available from regular component suppliers.

*Computer control:* A detailed look at the advantages of using a personal computer to control a scanner (AOR 2002, ICOM, SX-400, etc.)

*DXing:* Using your scanner for long distance reception. How to recognise the signs that a lift is on, where to tune and hear stations from as far away as the USA under the right conditions. List of VHF broadcast stations, beacons, repeaters, etc.

*Spectrum:* Full international spectrum allocations for all three ITU regions from 26—1300MHz.

*Callsigns:* Full list of International, Air and Marine Callsigns and registrations.

*Airports:* Spot frequencies of the world's major airports.

# 10 H.F. Bandplans

For the first time I have included a simple bandplan of the High Frequency part of the spectrum (also known as short wave) because many scanners now cover these frequencies. The list only gives a broad idea of what is allocated where. Should you want to know more about specific allocations then I would suggest you read my book *Short Wave Communications* (published by P.W. Publishing Ltd) which is available from bookshops and specialist scanner dealers.

**Table 10.1**

| Region 1 From—To | Region 2 From—To | Region 3 From—To |
|---|---|---|
| | 1605—1625 | |
| 1606.5—1625 | | 1606.5—1800 |
| | BROADCASTING | |
| MARITIME MOBILE | FIXED | |
| FIXED | | MOBILE |
| LAND MOBILE | | RADIOLOCATION |
| | | RADIONAVIGATION |
| 1625—1635 | 1625—1705 | |
| RADIOLOCATION | BROADCASTING | |
| | FIXED | |
| | MOBILE | |
| 1635—1800 | | |
| MARITIME MOBILE | | |
| FIXED | | |
| LAND MOBILE | | |
| | 1705 -1800 | |
| | FIXED | |
| | MOBILE | |

**Table 10.1**  *Continued*

| Region 1<br>From—To | Region 2<br>From—To | Region 3<br>From—To |
|---|---|---|
| | RADIOLOCATION<br>AERONAVIGATION | |
| 1800—1810<br>RADIOLOCATION | 1800—1850<br>AMATEUR | 1800—2000<br>AMATEUR<br>FIXED<br>MOBILE (not aero) |
| 1810—1850 | RADIONAVIGATION | |
| | | Radiolocation |
| AMATEUR | | |
| 1850—2000<br>FIXED<br>MOBILE (not aero) | 1850—2000<br>AMATEUR<br>FIXED<br>MOBILE (not aero)<br>RADIOLOCATION<br>RADIONAVIGATION | |
| 2000—2025<br>FIXED<br>MOBILE (not aero) | 2000—2065<br>FIXED<br>MOBILE | 2000—2065<br>FIXED<br>MOBILE |
| 2025—2045<br>FIXED<br>MOBILE (not aero)<br>Meteorological Aids | | |
| 2045—2160<br>MARITIME MOBILE<br>FIXED<br>LAND MOBILE | 2065—2107<br><br>MARITIME MOBILE | 2065—2107<br><br>MARITIME MOBILE |
| 2160—2170 | 2107- 2170<br>FIXED<br>MOBILE | 2107- 2170<br>FIXED<br>MOBILE |
| RADIOLOCATION<br>2170—2173.5<br>MARITIME MOBILE | 2170—2173.5<br>MARITIME MOBILE | 2170—2173.5<br>MARITIME MOBILE |
| 2173.5—2190.5<br>MOBILE (distress) | 2173.5—2190.5<br>MOBILE (distress) | 2173.5—2190.5<br>MOBILE (distress) |
| 2190.5-2194<br>MARITIME MOBILE | 2190.5-2194<br>MARITIME MOBILE | 2190.5-2194<br>MARITIME MOBILE |
| 2194—2300<br>FIXED<br>MOBILE (not aero) | 2194—2300<br>FIXED<br>MOBILE | 2194—2300<br>FIXED<br>MOBILE |
| 2300—2498<br>FIXED | 2300—2495<br>FIXED | 2300—2495 |

**Table 10.1**  *continued*

| Region 1<br>From—To | Region 2<br>From—To | Region 3<br>From—To |
|---|---|---|
| MOBILE (not aero)<br>BROADCASTING | MOBILE<br>BROADCASTING | |
| 2498—2502 | 2495—2502 | 2495—2502 |
| STANDARD<br> FREQUENCY &<br> TIME SIG (2500 kHz)<br>space research<br>2502—2625 | STANDARD<br> FREQUENCY &<br> TIME SIG (2500 kHz)<br>space research<br>2502—2505 | STANDARD<br> FREQUENCY &<br> TIME SIG (2500 kHz)<br>space research<br>2502—2505 |
| FIXED<br><br>MOBILE (not aero)<br><br>2625—2650<br><br>MARITIME MOBILE<br>MARITIME<br>RADIONAVIGATION<br>2650—2850<br>FIXED<br>MOBILE (not aero) | STANDARD<br> FREQUENCY &<br> TIME SIG (2500 kHz)<br>2505—2850<br>FIXED<br>MOBILE | STANDARD<br> FREQUENCY &<br> TIME SIG (2500 kHz)<br>2505—2850<br>FIXED<br>MOBILE |
| 2850—3155 | 2850—3155 | 2850—3155 |
| AERONAUTICAL<br> MOBILE<br>3155—3200<br>FIXED<br>MOBILE (not aero)<br>3200—3230<br>FIXED<br>MOBILE (not aero)<br>BROADCASTING<br>3230—3400<br>FIXED<br>MOBILE (not aero)<br>BROADCASTING<br>3400—3500 | AERONAUTICAL<br> MOBILE<br>3155—3200<br>FIXED<br>MOBILE (not aero)<br>3200—3230<br>FIXED<br>MOBILE (not aero)<br>BROADCASTING<br>3230—3400<br>FIXED<br>MOBILE (not aero)<br>BROADCASTING<br>3400—3500 | AERONAUTICAL<br> MOBILE<br>3155—3200<br>FIXED<br>MOBILE (not aero)<br>3200—3230<br>FIXED<br>MOBILE (not aero)<br>BROADCASTING<br>3230—3400<br>FIXED<br>MOBILE (not aero)<br>BROADCASTING<br>3400—3500 |

**Table 10.1**   *continued*

| Region 1<br>From—To | Region 2<br>From—To | Region 3<br>From—To |
|---|---|---|
| AERONAUTICAL<br>  MOBILE<br>3500-3800<br>AMATEUR<br>FIXED<br>MOBILE (not aero) | AERONAUTICAL<br>  MOBILE<br>3500—3750<br>AMATEUR<br><br>MOBILE<br>3750—4000<br>AMATEUR | AERONAUTICAL<br>  MOBILE<br>3500—3900<br>AMATEUR<br>FIXED |
| 3800—3900 | FIXED<br>MOBILE (not aero) | |
| FIXED<br>MOBILE (not aero)<br>LAND MOBILE<br>3900—3950<br>AERONAUTICAL<br>  MOBILE | 3900—3950 | AERONAUTICAL<br>  MOBILE<br>BROADCASTING |
| 3950—4000<br>FIXED<br>BROADCASTING | 3950—4000 | FIXED<br>BROADCASTING |
| 4000—4063<br>FIXED<br>MARITIME MOBILE | 4000—4063<br>FIXED<br>MARITIME MOBILE | 4000—4063<br>FIXED<br>MARITIME MOBILE |
| 4063—4438<br>MARITIME MOBILE | 4063—4438<br>MARITIME MOBILE | 4063—4438<br>MARITIME MOBILE |
| 4438- 4650<br>FIXED<br>MOBILE (not aero) | 4438- 4650<br>FIXED<br>MOBILE (not aero) | 4438- 4650<br>FIXED<br>MOBILE (not aero) |
| 4650—4750 | 4650—4750 | 4650—4750 |
| AERONAUTICAL<br>  MOBILE<br>4750—4850<br>FIXED<br>AERONAUTICAL<br>  MOBILE<br>LAND MOBILE<br>BROADCASTING | AERONAUTICAL<br>  MOBILE<br>4750—4850<br>FIXED<br>MOBILE (not aero)<br><br>BROADCASTING | AERONAUTICAL<br>  MOBILE<br>4750—4850<br>FIXED<br>BROADCASTING<br><br>Land Mobile |
| 4850—4995<br>FIXED<br>LAND MOBILE<br>BROADCASTING<br>4995- 5005 | 4850—4995<br>FIXED<br>LAND MOBILE<br>BROADCASTING<br>4995- 5005 | 4850—4995<br>FIXED<br>LAND MOBILE<br>BROADCASTING<br>4995- 5005 |

**Table 10.1**  *continued*

| Region 1<br>From—To | Region 2<br>From—To | Region 3<br>From—To |
|---|---|---|
| STANDARD<br>FREQUENCY<br>TIME SIG (5000 kHz) | STANDARD<br>FREQUENCY<br>TIME SIG (5000 kHz) | STANDARD<br>FREQUENCY<br>TIME SIG (5000 kHz) |
| 5005—5060 | 5005—5060 | 5005—5060 |
| FIXED | FIXED | FIXED |
| BROADCASTING | BROADCASTING | BROADCASTING |
| 5060—5250 | 5060—5250 | 5060—5250 |
| FIXED | FIXED | FIXED |
| Mobile (not aero) | Mobile (not aero) | Mobile (not aero) |
| 5250—5450 | 5250—5450 | 5250—5450 |
| FIXED | FIXED | FIXED |
| MOBILE (not aero) | MOBILE (not aero) | MOBILE (not aero) |
| 5450—5480 | 5450—5480 | 5450—5480 |
| FIXED | AERONAUTICAL<br>MOBILE | FIXED |
| AERONAUTICAL<br>MOBILE<br>LAND MOBILE | | AERONAUTICAL<br>MOBILE<br>LAND MOBILE |
| 5480—5730 | 5480—5730 | 5480—5730 |
| AERONAUTICAL<br>MOBILE | AERONAUTICAL<br>MOBILE | AERONAUTICAL<br>MOBILE |
| 5730—5950 | 5730—5950 | 5730—5950 |
| FIXED | FIXED | FIXED |
| LAND MOBILE | MOBILE (not aero) | Mobile (not aero) |
| 5950—6200 | 5950—6200 | 5950—6200 |
| BROADCASTING | BROADCASTING | BROADCASTING |
| 6200—6525 | 6200—6525 | 6200—6525 |
| MARITIME MOBILE | MARITIME MOBILE | MARITIME MOBILE |
| 6525—6765 | 6525—6765 | 6525—6765 |
| AERONAUTICAL<br>MOBILE | AERONAUTICAL<br>MOBILE | AERONAUTICAL<br>MOBILE |
| 6765—7000 | 6765—7000 | 6765—7000 |
| FIXED | FIXED | FIXED |
| Land Mobile | Land Mobile | Land Mobile |
| 7000—7100 | 7000—7100 | 7000—7100 |
| AMATEUR<br>AMATEUR-SATELLITE | AMATEUR<br>AMATEUR-SATELLITE | AMATEUR<br>AMATEUR-SATELLITE |
| 7100—7300 | 7100—7300 | 7100—7300 |
| BROADCASTING | AMATEUR | BROADCASTING |
| Above 7300 kHz<br>allocations for all three<br>regions are identical. | | |

**Table 10.1**  *continued*

| From | To | Allocation |
|------|------|------------|
| 7300 | 8100 | FIXED and Land Mobile |
| 8100 | 8195 | FIXED and MARITIME MOBILE |
| 8195 | 8815 | MARITIME MOBILE |
| 8815 | 9040 | AERONAUTICAL MOBILE |
| 9040 | 9500 | FIXED |
| 9500 | 9900 | BROADCASTING |
| 9900 | 9995 | FIXED |
| 9995 | 10005 | STANDARD FREQUENCY & TIME SIG (10000 kHz) |
| 10005 | 10100 | AERONAUTICAL MOBILE |
| 10100 | 10150 | FIXED and Amateur |
| 10150 | 11175 | FIXED and Mobile (not aero) |
| 11175 | 11400 | AERONAUTICAL MOBILE |
| 11400 | 11650 | FIXED |
| 11650 | 12050 | BROADCASTING |
| 12050 | 12230 | FIXED |
| 12230 | 13200 | MARITIME MOBILE |
| 13200 | 13360 | AERONAUTICAL MOBILE |
| 13360 | 13410 | FIXED and RADIO ASTRONOMY |
| 13410 | 13600 | FIXED<br>Mobile (not aero) |
| 13600 | 13800 | BROADCASTING |
| 13800 | 14000 | FIXED<br>Mobile (not aero) |
| 14000 | 14250 | AMATEUR<br>AMATEUR-SATELLITE |
| 14250 | 14350 | AMATEUR |
| 14350 | 14990 | FIXED<br>Mobile (not aero) |
| 14990 | 15010 | STANDARD FREQUENCY & TIME SIG (15000 kHz) |
| 15010 | 15100 | AERONAUTICAL MOBILE |
| 15100 | 15600 | BROADCASTING |
| 15600 | 16360 | FIXED |
| 16360 | 17410 | MARITIME MOBILE |
| 17410 | 17550 | FIXED |
| 17550 | 17900 | BROADCASTING |
| 17900 | 18030 | AERONAUTICAL MOBILE |
| 18030 | 18068 | FIXED and Space Research |

**Table 10.1**   *continued*

| From | To | Allocation |
|------|-----|-----------|
| 18068 | 18168 | AMATEUR AND AMATEUR-SATELLITE |
| 18168 | 18780 | FIXED |
| 18780 | 18900 | MARITIME MOBILE |
| 18900 | 19680 | FIXED |
| 19680 | 19800 | MARITIME MOBILE |
| 19800 | 19990 | FIXED |
| 19990 | 20010 | STANDARD FREQUENCY & TIME SIG (20000 kHz) Space Research |
| 20010 | 21000 | FIXED and Mobile |
| 21000 | 21450 | AMATEUR and AMATEUR-SATELLITE |
| 21450 | 21850 | BROADCASTING |
| 21850 | 21870 | FIXED |
| 21870 | 21924 | AERONAUTICAL FIXED |
| 21924 | 22000 | AERONAUTICAL MOBILE (R) |
| 22000 | 22855 | MARITIME MOBILE |
| 22855 | 23000 | FIXED |
| 23000 | 23200 | FIXED and Mobile (not aero) |
| 23200 | 23350 | AERONAUTICAL FIXED and MOBILE |
| 23350 | 24000 | FIXED and MOBILE (not aero) |
| 24000 | 24890 | FIXED and LAND MOBILE |
| 24890 | 24990 | AMATEUR and AMATEUR-SATELLITE |
| 24990 | 25010 | STANDARD FREQUENCY & TIME SIG (25000 kHz) Space Research |
| 25010 | 25070 | FIXED and MOBILE (not aero) |
| 25070 | 25210 | MARITIME MOBILE |
| 25210 | 25550 | FIXED and MOBILE (not aero) |
| 25550 | 25670 | RADIO ASTRONOMY |
| 25670 | 26100 | BROADCASTING |
| 26100 | 26175 | MARITIME MOBILE |
| 26175 | 27500 | FIXED and MOBILE (not aero) |
| 27500 | 28000 | METEOROLOGICAL AIDS, FIXED and MOBILE (CB) |
| 28000 | 29700 | AMATEUR and AMATEUR-SATELLITE |
| 29700 | 30005 | FIXED and MOBILE |
| 30005 | 30010 | SPACE OPERATION (satellite identification) FIXED, MOBILE and SPACE RESEARCH |
| 30010 | 37500 | FIXED and MOBILE |

# Index

# Notes

# Notes

# Notes

# Notes

# Notes

# Notes

# Notes

# Hobby magazines

## with International appeal

**Electronics Today International** is Britain's leading magazine for the electronics enthusiast and is renowned for its ability to keep pace with the leading edge of technology. Look no further for quality constructional projects, tutorials and general features covering current affairs in science and technology

**Ham Radio Today** caters for both the experienced user and newcomer to amateur radio. WIth informative features, the latest news and practical projects, this magazine covers all aspects of this growing field. Ham Radio Today is an invaluable compliment for any licensed radio amateur worldwide.